"What an engaging and illuminating book Jim Belcher has written. He carries us on an intellectual, biographical and geographical journey with his spiritual and theological heroes. You will not be surprised to find that his heroes are yours also. But this absorbing and honest book gives that rarest of gifts: a new, poignant way of thinking about familiar history. In the process, his pilgrimage enhances our own."

Michael Cromartie, vice president, Ethics and Public Policy Center, Washington, DC

"The first chapter was my favorite—until I read the second. The second chapter was my favorite—until I read the third. Chapter by chapter, Jim takes you and your family on a practical theology pilgrimage through Europe that will expand your vision for Christ-centered living. You'll be thinking about it and talking about it long after you finish the final page."

Kara Powell, executive director, Fuller Youth Institute, Fuller Theological Seminary, author of *Sticky Faith*

"'Come and see' is always and everywhere the invitation to the truest learning, and Jim Belcher is a remarkably gifted teacher, drawing young and old, believer and skeptic, into his own pilgrimage. Allowing us the unusual grace of seeing over his shoulder and through his heart as he leads his family into the stories of the people and places that have shaped his own soul, Belcher asks the honest questions about life and the world that we all ask, and answer. I want everyone I know and love to read *In Search of Deep Faith,* learning from Dr. Belcher about the things that matter most. A *Pilgrim's Progress* for the twenty-first century."

Steven Garber, The Washington Institute, author of *The Fabric of Faithfulness*

"This book had me at hello. The more I read, however, the more I was drawn into Belcher's earnest pursuit of the holy and found my own faith being deepened. Belcher is a master weaver of memoir, history, art, literature and theology—strands not easily brought together in one place. Upon the last page, I am reminded of Thomas Merton's words, '*Sit finis libri, non finis quaerendi*'— 'Let this be the end of the book but by no means the end of the searching.' Powerful and moving, *In Search of Deep Faith* offers a pilgrimage through the pages not to be missed."

Carolyn Weber, author of *Surprised by Oxford* and *Holy Is the Day*

"Winston Churchill famously said, 'The farther backward you can look, the farther forward you are likely to see.' My friend Jim Belcher points the way forward by taking us on a compelling journey back through time and place in search for the ways in which the Christian faith has impacted the world, transformed people and shaped cultures. The fruit of Jim's year-long pilgrimage throughout Europe, *In Search of Deep Faith* is a personal, probing and provocative adventure into the robust realism of the Christian faith. Highly recommended."

Tullian Tchividjian, senior pastor of Coral Ridge Presbyterian Church and author of *One Way Love*

"Jim Belcher's intimate portrayal of his family's year-long journey through Europe reminds us that it is in life's pain, suffering and trials that we discover beauty, and its Creator."

Daniel A. Siedell, author of *God in the Gallery*

"A generation that desires to be 'radical' needs to be reminded that the word actually means 'rooted.' Jim Belcher's beautifully written family adventure through Europe provides an accessible, and touchingly personal, introduction to our Christian roots and church history. He reminds us that if we think we've seen farther, it's only because we stand on the shoulders of giants."

Skye Jethani, author of *With* and *Futureville*

"Equal parts pilgrimage memoir, parenting book, theological reflection and biography collection, *In Search of Deep Faith* takes you on a particularly fascinating journey. That combination might sound strange, but it totally works, allowing us to view historical authors, theologians, artists and dissidents through the eyes of the author and his family, and to reflect on theological anchor points as if we were traveling with them."

Mark Oestreicher, partner, The Youth Cartel

IN SEARCH

OF

DEEP FAITH

A Pilgrimage into the Beauty, Goodness
and Heart of Christianity

JIM BELCHER

IVP Books

An imprint of InterVarsity Press
Downers Grove, Illinois

InterVarsity Press
P.O. Box 1400, Downers Grove, IL 60515-1426
World Wide Web: www.ivpress.com
Email: email@ivpress.com

InterVarsity Press® is the book-publishing division of InterVarsity Christian Fellowship/USA®, a movement of students and faculty active on campus at hundreds of universities, colleges and schools of nursing in the United States of America, and a member movement of the International Fellowship of Evangelical Students. For information about local and regional activities, write Public Relations Dept., InterVarsity Christian Fellowship/USA, 6400 Schroeder Rd., P.O. Box 7895, Madison, WI 53707-7895, or visit the IVCF website at www.intervarsity.org.

Scripture quotations, unless otherwise noted, are from The Holy Bible, English Standard Version, copyright © 2001 by Crossway Bibles, a division of Good News Publishers. Used by permission. All rights reserved.

While all stories in this book are true, some names and identifying information in this book have been changed to protect the privacy of the individuals involved.

Design: Cindy Kiple
Interior design: Beth Hagenberg
Cover image: St. Paul's Cathedral from Canon Alley, English Photographer. Private Collection / © Look and Learn / Peter Jackson Collection / The Bridgeman Art Library
Other permissions may be found in the back of the book.

ISBN 978-0-8308-3774-8 (print)
ISBN 978-0-8308-9576-2 (digital)

Printed in the United States of America ∞

Library of Congress Cataloging-in-Publication Data
A catalog record for this book is available from the Library of Congress.

P	19	18	17	16	15	14	13	12	11	10	9	8	7	6	5	4	3	2	1
Y	29	28	27	26	25	24	23	22	21	20	19	18	17	16	15	14	13			

We came by the friendly light of a full moon to the little inn which we had left that morning before daybreak. Then, while the servants were busy preparing our supper, I spent my time in a secluded part of the house, hurriedly and extemporaneously writing all this down, fearing that if I were to put off the talk, my mood would change on leaving this place, and I would lose interest in writing to you.

Petrarch, *"The Ascent of Mount Ventoux,"* 26 April 1336

*Thus says the L*ORD*:*
"Stand by the roads, and look,
      and ask for the ancient paths,
where the good way is; and walk in it,
      and find rest for your souls."

Jeremiah 6:16

CONTENTS

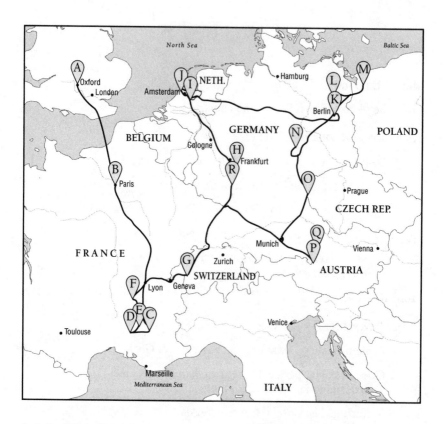

A. Oxford, United Kingdom
B. Paris, France
C. Lourmarin, France
D. Arles, France
E. Saint-Rémy-de-Provence, France
F. Le Chambon-sur-Lignon, France
G. Huemoz, Ollon, Switzerland
H. Frankfurt, Germany
I. Eck en Wiel, The Netherlands

J. Haarlem, The Netherlands
K. Berlin, Germany
L. Ravensbrück, Germany
M. Szczecin, Poland
N. Buchenwald, Weimar, Germany
O. Flossenbürg, Germany
P. Berchtesgaden, Germany
Q. Salzburg, Austria
R. Heidelberg, Germany

A NEED DEEP WITHIN
THE HUMAN HEART

I pulled off the road into a parking lot. The violent, early April wind shook our RV, rattling the windows and the door. Our shiny, white twenty-seven-foot camper with the words "vacation rental" plastered on the side stood out conspicuously among the sea of economy cars and old buildings. As people walked by they stopped to gaze at us, undoubtedly wondering what this large camper was doing in this city so far from any vacation spot.

The GPS said we were two blocks from our destination. We were thirty kilometers inside the Polish border, in the city of Stettin, the capital city of West Pomeranian, Poland, population five hundred thousand.

I shuttered the RV, like a child who thinks covering his eyes will make him invisible.

"I will be right back," I said. "I just want to go check it out."

I locked the RV, leaving my wife and four young children inside. I walked past once-grand houses that were now in disrepair, the toll of fifty years of Communism. Graffiti defaced a wall. Paint peeled and chipped off houses. People coming home from work walked fast, bracing themselves against the cold wind. For the first time in eight months in England and Western Europe, I felt unsafe. As the late afternoon sun fell behind buildings, a cold depression descended on me.

After some searching, I located my target, the Dietrich Bonhoeffer Study Center, the only house on the street that had been restored to its former glory. I climbed the steep steps to the front door, located on the second floor. My heart sank. It was closed. I walked around the sprawling estate looking for another entrance. No luck.

What were we going to do now? I was ready to give up, frustrated and impatient. Why had I risked coming this far without a confirmed appointment, something I *never* did on our travels? I had tried for months to connect with the center via email, with no success. My guess is that they didn't speak English. When the thirty-year director of the Bonhoeffer Home in Berlin told me a day earlier that he had never once been to the study center I should have taken that as a warning. But I had not. Now I felt dumb.

Walking back to the RV, I reminded myself that this visit was not completely unwise. It was my best chance to find someone who knew the location of the illegal underground seminary that Bonhoeffer led during World War II. According to historical accounts, it was located just five kilometers away, in the town of Finkenwalde. I told myself again that to be able to see the spot where Dietrich had managed, against all odds, to train young men for the ministry not in the state church but in the newly formed Confessing Church, whose pastors refused to take the loyalty oath to Hitler, was important for our pilgrimage. Every day they risked their lives. Every day they stood against the Nazi machine, witnessing to another reality, an alternative truth and a transformed community. I had hoped to show my family this spot and tell them about Bonhoeffer's book *Life Together*, the blueprint for this radical community, the book that changed my life.

I quickly rehearsed the past eight months in my mind, trying to stay optimistic. England, France, Holland, Switzerland, Germany and now Poland—all these places we had visited, the people we had met, the historical heroes we had encountered were worth the effort;

our pilgrimage into deep faith had already borne fruit in our lives and I knew that to keep going would bring more surprises and lessons of God's grace. This was no time to give up, especially with three more challenging months of travel left.

Back at the RV, my family was safely ensconced inside. "Dad, where have you been?" my girls asked me as I climbed back into the cab. "This place is a little creepy. Can we get out of here?" they said.

I plugged the Polish name for Finkenwalde into my GPS. It located the town. Hope rekindled. But the reading said it was three hundred kilometers away. Clearly not the town we wanted. I looked at the paper map of Poland but didn't find Finkenwalde. I hated to give up, but I didn't want to put my family in any more danger. No one knew where we were. We didn't speak a word of Polish or German. Everything we had taken on the trip—our laptops, our money, our clothes—was in the vehicle. We could easily be robbed. And what if we got a flat tire or the RV broke down? The RV rental agreement did not include Poland in its insurance coverage. Why had I forgotten that until we were already in Poland? I decided not to tell Michelle. We had enough to worry about.

A gang of teenagers walked by, shouting to one another, startling my kids. I realized we still needed to get back to Berlin, three hours away, and check into a new campsite before it closed for the night. Free camping on the side of a road in Berlin was not something I wanted to try. I had heard horror stories about others who had tried this and had gotten robbed. I turned the key, starting the powerful motor.

"Should we keep looking?" I asked Michelle, as I looked over to her.

"I will support whatever decision you make," she said.

Paralyzed with indecision, I recalled something my daughter Meghan had asked many times over the past eight months: "Daddy, can you tell me again why we had to come on this trip?"

Nine months earlier. Mid-August 2010, on a cool summer day, having arrived in Oxford two weeks earlier, we were standing in the Bodleian, the main research library of the University of Oxford and the oldest in Britain. On the ground floor of the library sits the Divinity School room, built in the 1480s. Designed in the perpendicular Gothic style, with lierne vaulting and bosses and immense windows, it is an extraordinary achievement. C. S. Lewis once called it "the most beautiful room in Oxford."

"Dad, that is where Harry's hospital bed was in the movie," Jonathan said. My son was referring to Harry Potter's accident during a quidditch match that landed him in the infirmary. As I looked out the large, paneled window toward St. Mary's spire in the distance, I thought to myself, *As infirmaries go, this would not be a bad place to recuperate. I am ready for some convalescence.*

I had come to Oxford and this year abroad in part to rest. After a decade of starting and leading a new church, having four children, writing my first book and fixing up an old house, I was exhausted. I wasn't burned out or washed out or struggling with my faith. I wasn't bitter or angry or trying to run away. I wasn't at a crisis point or lost or in need of direction. Any of those would have made a good story. But I was simply worn out, depleted, like Bilbo in the *Lord of the Rings*: "I feel all thin, sort of *stretched* . . . like butter that has been scraped over too much bread." I needed time away, to rest and to contemplate.

A year before we arrived, Michelle and I had begun talking about a two-month sabbatical, common for pastors to take every seven years and something I had never taken in seventeen years of ministry. But I did not think two months was enough, and I worried about returning after my time away still tired and unable to do a good job at the church. It wouldn't be fair to them. We began talking about a furlough, a year-long break, which missionaries take every five years to recuperate, regain perspective and recharge before going back to the field. To me that sounded like the prescription for what ailed me.

"But how in the world can we do that?" Michelle asked, looking incredulous. "The church can't give you that."

Of course she was right. This got me thinking about my future at the church. I had gone to Newport Beach, California, to plant a church. After ten years, I realized, my job was done. We had accomplished what we had set out to do. The church was established, healthy, and not dependent on my personality or my leadership. It would thrive without me. My gifts are in starting, not maintaining, and I began to think that this might be a good time to resign and move into the next stage of my life. So I made a bold decision.

In April of 2010 I stepped out of the ministry at Redeemer Church. The church and the elders graciously accepted my decision. Four months later, after long days of sorting, discarding, packing and loading all our possessions and furniture into a storage unit, renting out our house, and shutting down our life in the States, we were here in Oxford, the city of "dreaming spires."

My goal was to recuperate—to experience some deep rest for the first time in a decade and a half. But I was not interested in just physical and emotional rest. I might have done that under a palm tree in Hawaii. It certainly would have been warmer. What I really needed was spiritual rest. I needed to take stock of my life, rediscover where I came from and where I may be going. I wanted to take a year to walk in the steps of my heroes, read their books again and marinate in their lives—go deeper into their stories and learn from them all over again. It was going to be like a pilgrimage, a time to spiritually and experientially connect with the places and people that had most influenced me. And, most importantly, to reconnect with God.

John Inge, in his *A Christian Theology of Place*, says that a pilgrimage is characterized by three things: a rediscovery of our roots, an understanding that life is a journey and a new focus on our true destination. Roots, journey, destination. "Pilgrimage," he says, "speaks to a need deep within the human heart." As J. G. Davies adds, "Pilgrims are stimulated to hope and to seek for the transcendent promised at the end of their journey." As Jeremiah wrote long ago, "Stand by the roads, and look, and ask for the ancient paths, where the good way is; and walk in it, and find rest for your souls" (Jeremiah 6:16).

That is what I needed—rest for my soul. I needed to be reminded of who I am, of where I come from, that life is a journey and that my hope is built on knowing my destination. Through men like Thomas Cranmer, C. S. Lewis, William Wilberforce and Dietrich Bonhoeffer, and women like Davy Vanauken, Magda Trocmé, Corrie and Betsie ten Boom, and Maria von Trapp and the places they lived simply and acted heroically, I wanted to experience in my soul deep faith again.

But this pilgrimage was not just for me; it was also for my family. Michelle needed it too. She desired some time away from the bubble that was pastoral ministry, where every decision or action was open to scrutiny, where private life was difficult to maintain and where the pressure of the ministry never ends. She needed time away to recharge as well, to find rest for her soul, to rediscover deep faith.

But no less important, the pilgrimage was for my four children, Jordan, Jonathan, Lindsay and Meghan. We worried about their faith—would they grow strong in their trust of God or would they fall away? Recent studies of young people, even those who grew up

From left to right: Lindsay, Michelle, Meghan, Jim, Jonathan, Jordan

in the faith, were not comforting. On this pilgrimage we wanted to introduce them to the historic people who had most influenced us, the ones most responsible for our understanding of deep faith. We hoped that experiencing these stories would shape their imaginations differently than the stories in our culture.

Now was the time. With my boys, Jordan and Jonathan, at that crucial preteen age, we felt that if we did not take this trip now, in a few years it might be too late; they would be too busy and involved with friends, school and sports to pull them away. And once I accepted my next call, whether another pastorate or seminary teaching, we would not have this chance for an extended time away for another ten years, if ever. We knew we needed to seize the moment, take the plunge, leave our home and friends behind, and embark on this adventure, this pilgrimage. We knew it was risky to leave a secure job in the midst of a recession, but we realized it was now or never. So we stepped out in faith.

This book is about the pilgrimage my family took to England and Europe from August 2010 to June 2011. When we set out for Oxford, Michelle and I knew some of the lessons we wanted to teach our children, and we had in mind a number of historical characters and places we wanted to study and experience. But we had only the vaguest idea of which ones we would choose and what order we would follow. Like my favorite travel writer, Robert D. Kaplan, we wondered "how to recapture the sense of endless possibilities before the accumulation of deeds to justify: when one was unaccountable to time because there was always time to make up for a mistake." At that moment, all we knew was that the journey would begin in Oxford. We had plans to travel to Europe, but we did not know if I would go alone or take the family along. Where and when we would go would have to unfold as part of the pilgrimage. But this was part of the adventure, enjoying the serendipity of travel, learning to depend on God, and being open to new and profound experiences.

There is nothing like it, which is why people have been going on pilgrimages for thousands of years.

Before I begin to recount our adventure, I want to invite you along on this pilgrimage, to allow my family and I to be your tour guides. You may never go on a pilgrimage like we did, but you are already on one in your own life, right where you live. As you experience our pilgrimage, it is my prayer that it deepens and gives new perspective to your own pilgrimage. You may be young or old, you may be weary or content, you may have faith or you may not—but wherever you are on the pilgrimage of faith I hope this book stirs something in you. If you are in search of a deeper faith, I pray that you will find it in these pages. If you are a parent looking to love and shape your children, I pray that you will be inspired by our travels and the lessons we learned. If you are a skeptic giving Christianity a second look, I pray that you will be startled by what you experience as you come along with us. And for everyone who takes the time to follow us on this pilgrimage, I pray that you are deeply changed, as we were, by taking this trip in search of deep faith. And now it is time for me to write this all down "before my mood would change," as Petrarch said so long ago.

Part One

REDISCOVERING
OUR ROOTS

Cranmer –

Balliol College –
  cobblestone cross inlaid
St Michael's @ the North Gate –
    where Bocardo prison was
University Church of St Mary
       the Virgin – Cranmer's Pillar
  St Mary's Tower

CS Lewis
    Magdalen Chapel
    Eagle & Child Pub
    Addison's Walk
    The Kilns – his home
Harry Potter
    Great Hall of Christ Church
       Dining room

one

OXFORD

*The City of Spires, Pilgrims
and Martyrs*

Oxford, a medieval city sitting on a floodplain between two rivers, the Isis and Cherwell, has been at the center of Britain's academic and religious life for a millennium. Its beginnings shrouded in mystery and myth, the city has been inhabited for three to four thousand years. With tree-lined streets, grand medieval buildings, bells pealing, and the bustle of college students and dons heading off to class, Oxford, "that sweet City with her dreaming spires," has inspired generations as its beauty and charm stir thoughts of the poetic and the divine. For many, Oxford is the soul of the nation, England at its best. In 1586 William Camden wrote, "Our most noble Athens, the seat of English Muses, the prop and pillar, nay the sun, the eye, the very soul of the nation." Oxford seemed like the perfect place for us to revive our souls and to start our pilgrimage.

We arrived at our new house on a cool, drizzly, early August morning. We had rented a three-bedroom home in Summertown, north Oxford, a section of the city filled with lush oak trees and large, detached Edwardian homes originally built to house professors with families after it was no longer mandatory for dons to remain single. Our home, a worn-out, two-story house with a large, overgrown English garden that wrapped from the front to the back of the house, had two large rooms on the ground floor with plenty of space and light. One of the rooms would double as a dining room and a home-school room. My wife, Michelle, herself a former teacher, planned to instruct our four children, Jordan (age 11), Jonathan (9), Lindsay (6) and Meghan (4). We had shipped over boxes of books and curriculum for their studies.

Our plan was to spend August settling in. We spent the first three weeks buying furniture, outfitting our kitchen (the house was unfurnished), opening a bank account, ordering Wi-Fi and buying six used bikes. Our savvy friends Bill and Kye Prevette, career missionaries who lived a few streets from us and who had set up home in numerous countries over the years, saved us weeks of futility, steering us in the right direction time and time again. Christian Hofreiter, whose study desk was next to mine at Wycliffe, helped us track down free furniture. Their kindness was, as Patrick Leigh Fermor said on his travels through Europe eighty years ago, a "marvelous instance of a kindness and hospitality that was to occur again and again on these travels."

Knowing the first month would be grueling, we didn't plan too many learning trips or much homeschooling. But soon we got anxious to find some focus, to begin reminding ourselves why we were there and what we hoped to accomplish as a family. We needed some form to our freedom, some direction to our drifting. But it kept raining. So we remained put.

After three straight weeks of cold rain, the sun finally came out. The air was crisp, clean smelling, as if it were already autumn. Dressed in layers, we mounted our bikes and headed for the center of Oxford. Having finally set up the house, I wanted to begin our pilgrimage with something easy, some low-lying fruit: the Oxford Martyrs. Trials, dungeons, burnings at the stake—all good topics to capture the attention of kids and get them excited about history and the importance of faith.

I wanted to investigate the Oxford Martyrs as well. One of the martyrs, Thomas Cranmer, was one of my great heroes of the faith. Along with being the one most responsible for the sweeping religious changes in England in the sixteenth century and writing the *Book of Common Prayer*, one of the most influential books ever written in England, he has had a profound impact on my spiritual life. Back in college I had discovered an eighty-year-old copy of the *Book of Common Prayer* in a secondhand bookstore and began using it for my devotional time each morning. I loved its reverence and sublime language. Over the years I have collected more versions of the book,

From left to right: Jonathan, Jordan, Michelle, Lindsay, Meghan

using the prayer services and collects to guide my time in prayer. When I started Redeemer Church, I inserted many of Cranmer's prayers into our services. One of my favorite lines comes from the Prayer for Humble Access and had shaped my congregation and me week after week: "We do not presume to come to this thy Table, O merciful Lord, trusting in our own righteousness, but in thy manifold and great mercies." His prayers had given my faith a new beauty and a more profound articulation than I was ever capable of on my own. They became my prayers, and his words became my sustenance on the pilgrimage of life.

Standing with our bikes on the corner of Banbury Road, the buses roared by us, smoke bellowing out their tailpipes. We headed across the street, determined to find a safer way to the center of Oxford. Riding past brick schoolhouses, finely manicured parks, Gothic churches and small alleyways, we had never experienced such a feast for the eyes; it was as if we had been transported to a different age. Halfway into our journey, we stopped to admire the well-preserved one-time residence of J. R. R. Tolkien, the Oxford don and famous author. As huge fans of *The Lord of the Rings*, my boys were thrilled to discover his house. I pointed out the room that Tolkien might have used when he wrote *The Hobbit*.

After winding our way around the back of Wycliffe Hall, the Anglican training college of Oxford University where I was a temporary scholar in residence, past the University Parks and down Parks Road, we arrived in what had been the center of medieval Oxford. Our focus was to learn about Cranmer, his two friends and their last days. I wanted my kids to understand the importance of faith and how to become people of courage and conviction. I didn't know it at the time, but walking the path of the martyrs would do more than that—it would spark my thinking on what pilgrimage was about and why seeing life through this metaphor had real consequences for human flourishing. It would also show me why this trip was so important for my family, and particularly for my children, to prepare them for adulthood and living their faith on their own.

Time had run out. On October 16, 1555, the authorities took Nicholas Ridley and Hugh Latimer to a ditch near Balliol College, just outside the city walls, to be burned at the stake. Thomas Cranmer, the archbishop, remained in the Bocardo, just blocks away. A crowd including the vice chancellor, the mayor and other important dignitaries had gathered to watch the execution. Armed soldiers were out in force, the authorities fearing trouble.

As they stood back to back at the stake, Ridley attempted to comfort Latimer, who was much older and suffering from bad health. Loud enough for some spectators to hear, he said, "Be of good heart, brother, for God will either assuage the fury of the flame or else strengthen us to abide it." Confident and defiant to the end, Ridley then bellowed to the crowd: "So long as the breath is in my body, I will never deny my Lord Christ and his truth. God's will be done in me."

It had all begun when Henry VIII had established Protestantism as the official religion of England, severing ties with Rome. When Henry died, his son, Edward, took the throne. Immediately, he over-turned the law for mandatory clerical celibacy, reformed the Mass and mandated that worship services be conducted in English, not Latin. These reforms transformed the religious and political land-scape of England. But the changes would not last. In 1553, at the age of fifteen, Edward became ill and died. Before his death he attempted, unsuccessfully, to block his illegitimate half-sister Mary from the throne. In order to keep a Catholic off the throne, Archbishop Thomas Cranmer took part in the political plot. It failed, and he re-gretted his participation in it immediately, knowing it was not the way of the Bible.

When Mary came to power she immediately set about to crush the Reformation and reestablish Roman Catholicism. In four short years she would martyr over three hundred Protestants, while many others died in prison or fled into exile, earning her the nickname Bloody Mary. She hoped to wipe out Protestantism from the top, and her biggest target was Cranmer, the archbishop of Canterbury and the brains behind the English Reformation.

In 1553, Mary arrested and imprisoned Cranmer, along with influ-ential leaders Latimer and Ridley, in the Tower of London. Quickly, Cranmer admitted treason; he repented and asked for mercy. This put Mary in a quandary. Cranmer was the most prominent leader of the English Reformation, a movement that wanted religious freedom for all. She did not want to release him; she wanted him dead. Yet she did not feel she could execute a repentant archbishop without stirring up violent unrest. It was too risky, especially so soon into her reign. So Mary came up with another plan. If she could find him guilty of a

more serious crime—theological heresy—then that would not only
make him unqualified to be the supreme leader of the Church of
England, but it would also be punishable by burning. But to accomplish this she needed to transfer the three prisoners to Oxford, a city
that was loyal to the monarchy.

Imprisoned in different cells in the Bocardo Prison, located over
the North Gate of the town wall, the three prisoners were brought on
Saturday, April 14, 1554, to St. Mary the Virgin Church, also known
as the University Church, for a formal disputation. They were quickly
found guilty. Six days later, Friday, April 20, Cranmer, Ridley and
Latimer were brought before the commissioners at St. Mary's to hear
the verdict of the disputation. The commissioners found them guilty

The north gate of the City Oxford, with the tower of St. Michael's
church just inside the city. The Bocardo prison was above the gate. It
was demolished in 1771.

of heresy and gave them the opportunity to recant. One at a time, they each refused. The commissioners then informed them that as heretics they were no longer members of the Church.

They were taken back to the Bocardo. Mary now had what she wanted—the ability to spread the news that Cranmer, Ridley and Latimer where heretics who would be executed. The Reformation had officially been embarrassed and discredited.

For seventeen months the three Reformers languished in prison because the time was not right for executing them. Queen Mary did not yet have the political support to burn them as heretics, and until she was able to consolidate her power and reestablish the Catholic Church in England, she thought it too risky to execute them, particularly Cranmer, the reigning archbishop.

Finally, in the autumn of 1554, Mary had sufficiently reunited the country with Rome and could legally try the three men, giving her the political cover she sought. It was a show trial from the start, the outcome already predetermined. The commission representing Mary tried Cranmer first; it took two days, Ridley and Latimer only one day each. The commission was not authorized to condemn and excommunicate Cranmer. Only the pope could do this. So the court documents were sent to Rome for a verdict. The decision could take months, so back to the Bocardo he went. Ridley and Latimer's cases were more straightforward; after all, they were not the archbishop. On October 1, they were excommunicated. The date for the execution was set. They were given another chance to recant, but they refused, sealing their fate.

On October 16, as they waited for the fire to be set, they prepared themselves by prayer. Ridley's brother-in-law interrupted their praying to give each of them a bag of gunpowder to tie around their necks. This, he told them, would shorten their sufferings. They took the bags gladly, as a sign of God's mercy.

The executioner stepped forward to light the fire. This time it was Latimer's turn to embolden Ridley. He said, in words that have become immortal, "Be of good comfort, Master Ridley, and play the man. We shall this day light such a candle, by God's grace, in England, as I trust shall never be put out." The fire was lit. The kindling caught quickly, engulfing the stake in black smoke. Bishop Latimer, old and frail, was overcome with smoke inhalation and died instantly. Ridley, however, was not so fortunate. What happened next shocked the crowds, as well as an important bystander watching from a nearby tower.

BROAD STREET, OXFORD

After parking our bikes near Blackwell's bookstore, walking west down Broad Street, we arrived at Balliol College, founded in 1263, one of Oxford's oldest colleges. With my back to the college, I pointed toward the street. "Who can find the spot of the martyrs' execution?" I asked my kids.

Lindsay found the site first, giving a little hop of excitement. "Here it is, Dad."

The others ran over to it. The marker was a series of cobblestones, arranged in a cross inlaid in the street. There is also a plaque on the wall of the front of the Balliol College, right near the main entrance, to memorialize the location. Standing there, we watched people walk right over the cross, unaware of what took place there or its significance.

Dodging the pedestrian and bicycle traffic (this end of Broad Street is off limits to cars), I quickly tried to think of a way to summarize what happened here. Was this the time to talk about religious violence, so common even in our day? While I knew the story of Cranmer and his friends could teach us much about faith and courage, I have never thought the historic church was right for settling disagreements by killing their opponents. Both sides did it to each other—the Catholics to the Protestants and the Protestants to the Catholics—but it was never right. Yet in spite of the wrongness, their actions did demonstrate one thing: they took religious faith seriously and knew that it had important consequences for life and society. They were right about that.

I decided to begin with what they knew: that Cranmer had written a number of the prayers we said in our worship services at Redeemer.

"Oh, that guy," said Jordan, our oldest. "I remember those prayers. I love those."

I then gave them a quick summary of the Reformation and the issues fought over. I did not go into great detail; that would have been lost on Lindsay and Meghan. But I tried to impress on them the importance of faith, that what we believe has dramatic implications for our life now and in eternity, and that this kind of faith is worth dying for. At least these men thought so. And they died right there, I said, pointing to the cobblestone cross.

I asked them if they would be willing to be burned at the stake for their beliefs. They didn't answer.

"Or would you recant," I asked them, "and say you don't really believe in order to save your life?" They laughed nervously.

I pushed a little harder, with a little more enthusiasm. It was on-the-go teaching. You may never have to face that dilemma, I told them, but what if someday someone asks you if you are a Christian? Will you deny it? How strong are your convictions, your roots? Can you defend your faith? Is your passion for the faith strong enough to offset the temptations of the world? Or will you just keep quiet about what you believe and go with the flow of those around you?

Again, they didn't say anything. They just looked down at the ground.

That moment made concrete something Michelle and I had struggled with for years. How do we get our kids to take faith seriously? To see that it has life-and-death implications? To understand that if their faith is not strong they will betray it when they get older?

As we lingered around the cross, I felt the anxiety of raising kids in the faith. I have a friend who used to be a pastor and who has five kids. Three of them have spent time in prison, one has fathered a child out of wedlock and two others are struggling to find their way. My friend is torn up inside; he feels like a failure. He tells me not to worry; I won't make the same mistakes. But I am not so sure. Every time I turned around it seemed I was talking to a pastor or leader in the church who had had wayward children. Was it the culture? Was it the unique pressure of growing up a pastor's kid? Was it just adolescent sin? Probably it was all three. So how could we raise kids who wouldn't walk away from the faith when they left home?

Some of my anxiety at that moment came from a book I had just read: *Soul Searching* by Christian Smith and Melinda Denton. It was a book based on their monumental study, the National Study on Youth and Religion (NSYR), which found most high-schoolers, even if they grew up in a religious home, were unable to meaningfully articulate their faith. The danger was that when they got to college and faced all the temptations of university life, both morally and intellectually, they would abandon the faith because it did not mean much to them and, in fact, got in the way of their happiness and success.

According to Smith and Denton, for the Christian kids, the culprit is what they call *Moralistic Therapeutic Deism* (MTD), the belief that God wants people to be good and nice, that "the central goal of life is to be happy and to feel good about oneself," that "God does not need to be particularly involved in our lives except when he is needed to resolve a problem" and that "good people go to heaven when they die." MTD is different than historic Christianity. For the kids who subscribe to MTD, religion is no more than a hobby that gets abandoned in college. Certainly it is not something worth dying over. It is more like eating vegetables: good for you but not always necessary. So they set it aside. In fact, they put it in what Tim Clydesdale calls the "identity lock box." Once inside that box, they never take it out again in college.

Standing near the place of the martyrs, bikes rattling by us, these findings worried me. Were we giving them more than MTD? Would our children know and experience deep faith? Or would they put it into an "identity lock box" when they went off to college?

And what about my faith? Was it strong enough to resist what the culture says is true, good and beautiful and instead cling to the story of the gospel, with its own grand vision of reality, truth and goodness? At that moment, I was not sure I could be a martyr for the faith like Cranmer, Ridley and Latimer.

So what needed to be done? Kenda Creasy Dean, who conducted many of the interviews for the NSYR, writes in her book *Almost Christian* that children need to develop a "consequential faith"—a faith that matters. That is what I wanted for my kids, and for myself as well. That was why we were at the cross; we were there to begin developing a consequential faith. If pilgrimage is about finding our roots, as Inge writes, Broad Street was a good place to start.

Before leaving I considered finishing the story of Ridley and Latimer's execution, but then I thought otherwise. I did not want to give Lindsay and Meghan nightmares.

Latimer had died quickly. Ridley, however, suffered terribly in the last minutes. The wood and hay on his side had been packed too tightly, and with not enough air getting into it only the lower half caught fire, causing his legs to burn off; his upper body was untouched. He screamed in agony. "For God's sake let the fire come to me! I cannot burn! Lord have mercy on me!" Finally, someone loosened the logs, letting the fire breathe; the flame shot high into the air. The fire quickly reached the bag of gunpowder, mercifully ending Ridley's life.

Unbeknown to Ridley and Latimer, their dear friend Cranmer had witnessed the burning. Barred from saying his last farewell to his friends, Cranmer was forced by the authorities to watch the burnings from the tower of the North Gate. He had never seen or attended a burning, and certainly he did not expect to witness one so badly mismanaged. The screams of his friend Ridley penetrated to his core.

Cranmer was petrified of dying by burning. At one point, Ridley, before he was executed, had smuggled a letter to Cranmer's cell in the Bocardo stating the case for them all in blunt words: "Turn or Burn." For Cranmer, he needed to find a way *not* to turn and *not* to burn. As mortified as he was to burn at the stake, he was even more anxious over the thought that he could deny his beliefs and turn his back on Christ.

In solitary confinement, cold and lonely, he soon began to waiver;

he was being worn away psychologically, emotionally and physically, like a child on the playground being bullied incessantly. Would he turn so as not to burn? Could he hang on? Would his beliefs and convictions sustain him against constant psychological abuse?

By January 1556, Rome's decision had reached Oxford: Heretic. Excommunication. Cranmer was devastated at the news. Now, with his friends gone, his wife and children in exile, and his execution imminent, he made a fatal, psychological mistake: he befriended his jailer, his captor. That decision would have dramatic and historical ramifications.

A PRISON DOOR

From Broad Street we walked west to the intersection of St. Giles and George Street. Just south of the intersection, St. Giles becomes Cornmarket, about the place that the old north wall once stood. Shortly inside the ancient boundaries of the wall, we reached St. Michael's at the North Gate, a thirteenth-century parish church. The church tower, of Saxon origin, is older, dating from 1050, the oldest structure in Oxford. Attached to the tower, atop where the gate into the city once stood, is where the Bocardo prison perched.

We walked through the welcome center and into the back of the church. Immediately we saw the entrance to the tower. We started climbing, pausing midway up on a landing. Propped up against a wall is an old medieval door, worn but in remarkably good shape. With her usual enthusiasm for living history, Michelle excitedly pointed to the sign that said this was the actual prison door that held Cranmer and, for a time, Ridley and Latimer. It is the only surviving piece of the Bocardo prison, destroyed centuries before.

Doors always make me think of pilgrims. They can be a symbol for coming home, finding a haven or discovering a sanctuary. But they also can symbolize going out to begin the journey or quest. As Bilbo once said to Frodo, "It's a dangerous business . . . going out your door. You step into the Road, and if you don't keep your feet, there is no knowing where you might be swept off to."

Pilgrimage is about roots, as we have seen, but it is also about the journey. Inge says that a "pilgrimage is symbolic of that larger journey of the Christian life." We are all on a journey whether we admit it or not. For the Christian, the journey is not always pleasant or safe, and often includes suffering. The reality of suffering in the Christian life runs counter to the mentality of Moralistic Therapeutic Deism, which has as its goal crafting a life of comfort, ease and success. In that view, suffering signifies a lack of faith or, worse, a hidden, unconfessed sin. It is never seen as a normal part of the journey or the result of a life lived dedicated to the kingdom.

So often our children are taught that faith is about being nice and fair to all. These are good virtues. The problem is that Christianity is more than being nice or kind. It is more than personal success and happiness. It contains, Kenda Creasy Dean says, a creed, a community and a hope. It can be articulated, defended and may call us to die for it. As Dean says, "For Christians, faith means cleaving to the person, the God-man, of Jesus Christ, joining a pilgrim journey with other lovers and following him into the world. Christian formation invites young people into this motley band of pilgrims" and prepares them to be sent out in mission to worship God in their vocations and turning this "capsized world" right-side up. If parents and the church communicate to our kids that the heart of Christianity is only being nice, fair, happy and successful, they will have no resources, no tools, no map in which to navigate the journey of life, particularly when suffering comes—and it most certainly will come.

We did not want our children ill prepared for the journey of life. We took them to the tower and talked to them about the Bocardo because we wanted them to see that suffering and persecution are real and that if their faith is to survive the challenge of suffering, they would need to know how to live wisely and with understanding. They would need to understand how truth, beauty and goodness, the realities of God's good creation and his Word would guide them into deep faith. They needed the tools and experience to articulate their faith in difficult times, to navigate the world, to serve the kingdom and push back on the places where the culture did not honor God, and to experience divine communion. In short, they needed a road map for the journey. But finding maps and the ability and skill to read them does not come naturally; it must be cultivated. And I hoped that by immersing them in the stories of my heroes, people of deep faith, they would gain this wisdom, discover these maps, and that this discovery would be a powerful antidote to MTD and the "lock box" disease.

We continued climbing the stairs of the tower and eventually emerged through a small door onto the roof. Though not the highest point in Oxford, it affords a wonderful view of the city. This was close to the spot Cranmer stood to watch his friends burn. I thought of all the pilgrims, past and present, that have come to this city for myriad reasons. Cranmer and his two friends did not come here willingly. However, he was to learn some of his best—and most challenging— life lessons here.

Woodson, the jailer and a layman in the Catholic Church, spent time with Cranmer each day, attempting to convince him to recant and rejoin the Catholic Church. But Cranmer would not recant. Frustrated, Woodson stopped visiting him. This was too much for Cranmer. He had come to rely on Woodson's friendship, as it was the only emotional support he had. Finally, after days without a visit, Cranmer could not take it, and he requested a visit. When Woodson arrived, Cranmer asked him why he had not visited him in so long. The jailer got mad and said that since Cranmer would never repent he did not want to waste his time on a friendship with a heretic.

Cranmer, now emotionally beaten down, said that if the jailer would stay with him he would offer proof of repentance after supper. The jailer spent the day with him and after supper inquired whether he was ready to repent. Cranmer said he still needed more time; maybe tomorrow he could do it. Furious, Woodson accused him of dishonesty and bolted out of the cell. At that point the agony of nonconformity became too much for Cranmer, and he fainted under the strain of it.

When Cranmer awoke it was the middle of the night. The attendant in the room next door heard him sobbing and moaning and went to get help. He woke Woodson, who, when he got to the cell, told Cranmer that God was punishing him. At that moment, Cranmer, psychologically broken, wrote out his first recantation. He just could not withstand being ostracized by his only human contact. He was old, lonely and facing a brutal death. Could he be blamed for giving in?

Over the next two months, Cranmer signed six separate recantations, repenting of all his "heretical" views and submitting himself to the authority of the Roman Catholic Church and the pope. Many of these recantations were performed under intense pressure and duress. But could it also be that Cranmer saw this as one last attempt to save his life, even if he did not believe what he was signing?

Portrait of Thomas Cranmer by Gerlach Flicke

Mary and the Catholic officials were not pleased. This complicated their desire to execute him. While the Protestants claimed that the recantations were forged, Mary believed them to be insincere—Cranmer's attempt to avoid the stake. But having made them, Cranmer had every reason to expect clemency. After all, he had repented and rejoined the Catholic Church. Yet Mary, always cruel, did not see it that way. She decided to go forward with the execution. On March 9, she ordered the local officials to begin preparations for the burning.

As the day drew near, Cranmer appeared totally broken, no longer looking for a compromise to make his views compatible with Rome. His Catholic confessors now welcomed him with open arms as a repentant sinner and brother. Cranmer must have hoped that he might still be spared. But he could not bring this up or it would make his recantations seem insincere, a ploy to save his life. In the meantime, he enjoyed the new camaraderie of the Catholic officials who visited him, like a castaway experiencing human contact for the first time in months.

This newfound contentment would not last long, however. The execution date was set. Cranmer most likely heard the date of the burning a few days before it was to happen, on Saturday, March 21. He received the news calmly—he was no longer afraid to die. Yet he worried about his son, who, because of his conviction, could not inherit anything from him. He asked the authorities for an exception for his son but was rebuffed, another major disappointment. But it also made him angry. Something started to reawaken in him.

He began to use his last days to prepare for the end. With his confessors, he talked over the words he would say at the ceremony before his burning. Slowly, he began writing out a transcript of his speech. He would accuse himself of being a miserable sinner and repent of all his sins against the Church. He then would exhort those listening not to love the pleasures of the world, and to obey the queen gladly, to love their neighbors and give to the poor. After adding in a portion on the Lord's Prayer, he planned to conclude by renouncing all his false teaching and books written over the years and affirming all the teachings of the Roman Catholic Church. His Catholic counselors were satisfied.

The evening before his scheduled burning, he ate his last meal, appropriate for a Friday night during Lent—"spice cakes and bread, fruit and nuts and a dish of stewed prunes." He enjoyed a glass of red wine and lingered over prolonged conversation with his companions well into the night before going to bed. But Cranmer did not sleep through the night. At some point during the night, his counselors long gone, he awoke and secretly wrote a different ending to his speech.

Arising the next morning at 5:00 a.m., he was not sure which version of the speech he would use—the approved Catholic version or the revised nocturnal one. As he said goodbye to the jailer Woodson, assuring him one more time that his recantations would remain, Cranmer "had hidden in his bosom the Protestant version of the final speech."

It was raining, a typical autumn day. The preliminary proceedings had to be moved indoors, from the stake to the University Church of St. Mary. On the way to the church, Cranmer walked between two Catholic officials from the Bocardo. Inside St. Mary's, the sanctuary was packed with spectators, the air electric with suspense. The officials ushered Cranmer to a raised platform. He stood there, tears rolling down his face, the emotions of the past few months flooding out as the dam of self-control broke. After a sermon to justify why a repentant man was being executed—a slightly embarrassing and awkward moment—it was Cranmer's turn to make his prepared speech. Since the authorities had approved the talk, there were to be no surprises for them. And indeed, the talk began as planned and proceeded closely to the approved text.

Yet suddenly, as Cranmer neared the end, they realized that he was departing from the script. Unbelievably, he was recanting his recantations.

> All such bills which I have written and signed with mine own hand since my degradation, wherein I have written many things untrue. And forasmuch as my hand offended in writing contrary to my heart, therefore my hand shall first be punished; for if I may come to the fire, it shall first be burned.

All hell broke loose. The crowd was in an uproar. There was glee, but even more shock. The authorities panicked. They had to stop Cranmer before he did more damage to the Church and to the queen.

Holy Gash

From the tower we retraced our steps, walking four blocks back across Broad Street, past the Bodleian, across Radcliffe Square to the University Church of St. Mary the Virgin. Dating back to the thirteenth century, it was once both the seat of university government and the university's main place of public worship and ceremonies. Over the centuries many well-known people had preached there, including John Wesley, the founder of Methodism, John Henry Newman, leader of the Anglo-Catholic revival in Oxford before he converted to Catholicism, and C. S. Lewis, Oxford don and bestselling author.

We passed through the gift shop with its selection of mugs, books and postcards, a little overdone for a church, marring the sacred space and turning it into a tourist destination. We passed a sign asking for donations for the continuing restoration of the church. We then found ourselves standing in the sanctuary, the place where Cranmer's disputation, parts of his heresy trial and his last speech before his execution took place.

"Hey Dad, why does it smell like it does?" one of my kids asked.

"What does it smell like?" I asked.

"I don't know, it has that old smell. I like it."

We were looking for "Cranmer's Pillar," and we found it opposite the main pulpit. The stage that he sat on for the trial didn't quite fit the space between the pillars. Instead of redoing the platform, they cut a three-inch gash, like a shelf, into the pillar, on which one end of the stage would rest. Five hundred years later that gash still exists. Finding the marred pillar was fun for my kids. Like Thomas touching the wounds of Jesus, our kids felt the gash in the pillar. They seemed amazed that such a particular circumstance from history still existed. It was like the past had broken into the present. At that moment, I could see why so many pilgrims come here to see the pillar. It was living history, almost a sacred moment.

In his book *The Way of the Lord: Christian Pilgrimage Today*, Tom Wright says that visiting places where saints lived can be a means of grace. That means that places like St. Mary's "carry memory, power and hope." This memory can break into our lives, providing grace and hope.

Wright explains how he went from seeing pilgrimage as a bunch of "mumbo-jumbo," works-righteousness, and at times downright idolatry of places and people, to seeing pilgrimage as a helpful tool for spiritual growth and a means of grace. His transformation came about from reading the Bible and seeing the role that the land and the physical space plays in our lives. Pilgrimage, for Wright, is different than tourism. "Tourism," he says, "is the modern, secular version of pilgrimage, in which we go to famous places or to see well-known sights, not to meet God or to receive healing or blessing, but to see things that our culture tells us we ought to see, to expand our own horizons and experiences, to buy souvenirs to make us feel good when we're back home." But after we get back to our hotel, we check it off our list; "our reality must remain undisturbed," he says.

So how do we know if we are on a tour or a pilgrimage? According to Wright, "The test of whether pilgrimage is genuine is . . . the question, whether you're prepared for God to remake you instead, lovingly to break the brittle 'you' that you've so carefully constructed, to soften the clay in his hands" and to remake you in his image, not the one you imagined. For this remaking to happen, we must be willing to let God break in unexpectedly. This may include suffering, his fatherly discipline or an encounter with his surprising grace. Wright's distinction is one I would return to over and over again throughout our year, making sure our family's pilgrimage was just that—a pilgrimage—and not high-priced tourism.

The authorities rushed the stage. They knew they needed to silence Cranmer before he said any more. Their goal to make him the scapegoat for all the heresy and schism in England was unraveling. He had dramatically turned the tables on them, and they were furious.

Cranmer "was deadly pale, but a surge of energy had taken away his tears." Above the din, he continued to shout his convictions. Trying to avoid further damage, the authorities ripped him off the stage and dragged him out of the church. Cranmer shook off the hands that held him. He did not need help going to the stake. He went willingly, running to the place on Broad Street where six months

earlier his friends Ridley and Latimer heroically went to their deaths.
As he ran, some of his counselors tried one last time to get him to
recant his recantations. But he would not turn back again. He was
ready and willing to die for his beliefs.

Cranmer had spent the last two years of his life trying to avoid
being burned while staying faithful to his beliefs. He could not do
it—he was too weak. But at the last moment, like Samson regaining
his strength, he knew who he was, what he believed and what he
needed to do. Some say he was just trying to get back at Mary for not
pardoning him after his recantations. But I think his final motivation
was different. I think he returned to what he truly believed and went
running to the stake to seek divine forgiveness for his profound
weakness, for all the ways that he had compromised, played the prag-
matist, denied his deepest beliefs in order to stay alive. Now he realized that his only comfort was to throw himself on the mercy of
God and trust that God would still accept him.

At the stake, he said his goodbyes quickly. They stripped off his

From John Day's 1563 English edition of Foxxe, *Acts and Monuments*

shirt and chained him down. The fagots were lit, and though it was a wet day, the flames shot up. Cranmer stuck out his right hand, placing it in the flames as he had promised for "writing contrary to my heart." He withdrew it, maybe to wipe his brow or possibly because the pain was overwhelming. But he placed it back in the scorching flames, crying out: "This unworthy right hand . . . this hand has offended." The flames burned higher and more intensely. The end was to come fast, but not before he saw something in the distance.

As the flames consumed him, Cranmer cried out: "I see Heaven open and Jesus standing at the right hand of the Father." With these words, he breathed his last. He had reached his ultimate destination and had found the rest he wanted.

St. Mary's Tower

I kept Meghan in front of me in case she slipped and fell back. At about twice the height of the tower at St. Michael's, St. Mary's tower was a more challenging climb, particularly with my girls. The tower gets increasingly narrower at the top, the steps so steep and worn away that a rope is provided to grab onto for support and safety. The passage is so thin that the people at the top had to wait until we got up before they could start the descent. We kept shouting to them, "We are almost there; we have a four-year-old with us. Thanks for your patience."

When we finally made it to the top, the view was worth the climb. My boys pointed down to Radcliff Square. As we stood there looking at Radcliff Camera Library at the center of the square, built in the English Palladian style two hundred years after Cranmer's death, I tried to imagine Cranmer running through the square toward Broad Street. But then the height of the tower got to me, and I was overcome with vertigo.

"Don't look down," Michelle counseled me. "Look out to the horizon."

With my back pressing against the wall for security, I looked into the distance. I could see the University Parks, Wycliffe Hall and into the Oxford countryside, and I started to feel better. For a moment I felt like Christian in *Pilgrim's Progress* when he stands in the castle on top of the Delectable Mountains and looks to the gates of Celestial City, his true destination. It is that moment that settles his anxiety about his pilgrimage. Once he can see his destination, he has peace, and his hope is rekindled, rising up inside of him like an unquenchable fountain.

Pilgrimage is having a clear glimpse of our destination, which in turn helps us hold on to faith. Looking over the medieval city of Oxford with our journey just beginning, I realized that, like Christian in *Pilgrim's Progress*, we were not certain of the journey once we climbed down the tower. We knew our final destination, but we did not have every step planned out on this journey. In fact, I was not sure what we would do next week, never mind in six months. But we were doing our best (some days better than others) to trust the one who was leading us. And this calmed our anxiety. We would need that comfort in the days ahead when circumstances got tough, money ran low, our kids complained and we didn't know what direction to take next.

At the end of his introduction to *The Way of the Lord*, Wright's prayer for his readers is that they will come to see pilgrimage as a way of taking "fresh steps along the road of discipleship that leads from the earthly city to the city that is to come, whose builder and maker is God." It was that vision, the sight of the Celestial City, that my family and I needed a fresh glimpse of.

We had come to the center of Oxford to relive Cranmer's last days, but we had encountered so much more. We had discovered that our pilgrimage was about three things: finding our roots, that is, a consequential faith; learning that journey was a metaphor for our life and that we needed the right map to direct us; and, finally, that if we were to have comfort and hope on our pilgrimage we needed to know our destination. As we walked down the steps that afternoon, it was time to begin. Our first step was to rediscover our roots, and Oxford was the perfect place to begin. Yet before that could happen, I needed to find something that was lost.

two

IGNITING DESIRE

Sheldon Vanauken's Search for Meaning

Deep in the night, the call came from the hospital. His wife was dying. "How long does she have?" Van asked.

"Her pulse is slowing," said the nurse.

Though only forty years old, Davy had struggled with her health for a number of years—intense fatigue, swelling and shortness of breath. But since returning to the U.S. from Oxford two years earlier, where Van had been pursuing a second bachelor's degree, her health had deteriorated. Doctors could not tell her what was wrong. Some mysterious illness, they said.

With the top still down despite the winter cold, Van jumped into his MG convertible, his faithful dog, Flurry, beside him, and made his way through the dark, deserted streets. He had purchased the car months earlier, hoping it would help shake them out of their depression, a dreariness of soul that had hung over them like a dark cloud since returning from Oxford. They had left Oxford in the dead of winter in 1952, returning to Lynchburg College in Virginia, where Van was a professor. They immediately missed Oxford, their friends, the church bells and the civilized culture. They reacted adversely to Lynchburg—the flimsy buildings, the too-warm houses, the overly bubbly beer and the semi-illiterate students. They were constantly "homesick" for Oxford, wondering if life would ever regain the spark it had in the "city of dreaming spires."

Their general unhappiness began to take its toll on their marriage. They spent less time together—he focused on his teaching, she busy with her new job—and began to grow apart. Their interests went in different directions. She was ready to settle down, nurture a home, be a wife, do things like baking and hosting parties, and learn to serve other people, especially those who were lonely or less fortunate. He loved adventure, seeking new experiences, always wondering where they would go next. He was always on the move, a restless spirit. His focus was on love, living an intensely romantic life filled with poetry, literature and travel. Others were not as important for him. He loved Davy, and that was all that mattered.

But as much as they drifted apart, by the second year things had started to improve. The MG convertible that Van purchased had brought them closer together. They had taken long drives through the Virginia countryside together, enjoying picnics and exploring unknown places. They missed Oxford less and began to appreciate where they lived. Their love for one another also grew stronger; the romance returned, and their future once again looked bright.

But Davy's illness threatened all this. Van was scared. As the MG flew through the backcountry roads, he longed to be near her. What if he lost her? Could he go on? Would he hate God for taking her away?

A Pilgrim at the Trout Inn

A few feet from where I sat, the Isis, engorged by a recent rainstorm, rushed under the Godstow Bridge and flowed past me. Sitting under an umbrella with the birds singing and the sun shining through the rustling leaves of the mighty oak trees that had lined the river for thousands of years, I looked over my shoulder at the historic Trout Inn, made from sandy Cotswold stone. Though renovated many times over the years, the Trout dates back to 1625, built to provide shelter for pilgrims coming to visit the ancient Godstow Abbey directly on the other side of the Isis. The two-story inn was constructed in 1757; the cozy interior, with its flagstone floor, exposed beams and roaring fires, has been a favorite place for conversation and good cheer for hundreds of years. In the nineteenth century the pub was frequented by Lewis Carroll, famed author of *Alice's Adventures in Wonderland*, and in the twentieth by C. S. Lewis, J. R. R. Tolkien and the rest of the Inklings. Because of this heritage, it was also a favorite spot for Sheldon and Jean Vanauken (known as Van and Davy). It was a good place for a pilgrim to reflect and read, which is what I had come to do.

A few weeks had passed since our time exploring the Oxford Martyrs. Most mornings, after picking up fresh bread and sundry grocery items at the local market four blocks from our home, a singular pleasure, I enjoyed a leisurely breakfast with the family, often reading stories out loud together. It was nice to have a break from the frenetic school mornings back in the States, packing up for what felt like a day trip every day—lunchboxes, bookbags, snacks, gym clothes, extra sweatshirts, sporting goods and so on. Now, each morning after breakfast, Michelle began homeschooling and I rode my bike down Banbury Road to Wycliffe to spend time reading, getting to know my new study mates and falling asleep in my comfortable chair under the basement window.

Before we arrived in Oxford, a pastor friend of mine who had taken

The Trout Inn

sabbaticals over the years, told me that once I got to England I would be surprised just how exhausted I was. At the time, I thought he was exaggerating his point. But he was right. With the stress of the big move to Britain finally behind us and a decade of church planting in our rearview mirror, I was spent, almost too tired to do anything but sleep and rest. Maybe some light reading, a stroll around the city, but not much more.

Archibald Hart of Fuller Seminary's School of Psychology, who is an expert on stress-related problems, said that the two professions that suffer the most postevent adrenal letdown are trial lawyers and pastors. I buy it. I felt it each Monday morning when I woke up the day after preaching. Even so, I struggled to take a solid day off each week. I found it hard to relax, partly because of the 24/7 demands of pastoring but also because the adrenal letdown made me anxious, tired, lethargic. I discovered that I only felt better when I finally ramped up the stress for the upcoming Sunday and started the cycle again, sometimes as early as Monday afternoon. Even on my vacations, I still had to work to keep the adrenaline flowing. I was addicted to stress.

Now with the external stress inducers removed, I was able to let go, ignore my emails (fortunately there were few of them now) and just rest. And that is what I did. After a few weeks of this, I was beginning to feel more rested, not so fatigued, more normal. But as I got the rest I needed, what surprised me was how numb I felt inside.

John Eldredge says, "We abandon the most important journey of our lives when we abandon desire." I began to wonder if I had done this. Had I buried desire under the constant stress of leading a church—weekly sermons, administration and never-ending pastoral care? Had I been just going through the motions the past few years, unaware of how much my thirst for learning, the Scriptures and the vision of the church had become extrinsic, something I just needed to do each week? How would I get desire back? I knew this time in Oxford was the beginning of our pilgrimage, but I was having trouble getting started. Somehow I knew it had to start with desire, with a passion to love.

I reached into my pack and pulled out a book that decades ago, back in college, had taught me that Christianity is, in part, an invitation to desire—that deep inside of me was a desire to know who I am, what I was made for, what kind of journey I was on and where in the world this was all heading. It is a desire for the full life, the abundant life, as Jesus promised. Christianity was never about abandoning or killing desire because it got us into trouble (which it often did), but about healing it, transforming it so that it focused on the right object to love. I knew at that moment that I needed this, so I opened the front cover and began to read *A Severe Mercy*.

Van's struggles with Christianity began as a child. At fourteen, away from home at a military academy, he turned his back on the faith. Having grown up in a religious, somewhat devout home, he no longer could believe Christianity; it had become childish, "held only on adult authority." To him, there was nothing exciting, positive or relevant about Christianity. In his school he learned about the Greeks and their passion for beauty, the Romans and their conquests, the spaciousness of the cosmos, and reality of life outside the church. His childhood faith was not strong enough to sustain the onslaught of his studies. So he gave it up, relieved to be done with the do-goodism and rule keeping of the church that masked so much hypocrisy in the people he knew. Christianity was nothing more than moralism to him, and all it did was make him feel guilty. "Such a relief!" he said. "What freedom! And atheism was exhilarating: if the gods were dead, then man was the highest. Glorious! And it was a belief totally opposed to that impossible Christianity—a strong, bold creed!"

But he soon realized that atheism did not have a "strong, bold creed." In fact, it had no standard, no outside authority, no guiding light. So he quickly abandoned atheism for agnosticism, a belief in a creator of some sort, a type of deism. But in rejecting the tired, worn-out views of moralism in the church, the deadening of desire in religious rule keeping, his quest for more passion lead him to rule breaking of various kinds. At one military school he went AWOL for a few days, at another he attempted escape but got caught, and throughout his time in school he missed assignments and struggled academically. He had gone from moralism to antimoralism, all the while searching for a code to live by, one that was passionate, exciting, and big enough to give meaning and purpose to life.

During his freshmen year in college, he found one. He became "dedicated, almost religiously, to beauty." It was during this search for beauty that he realized that the people who had drank most deeply of it were those who had discovered a great love. Beauty was attached to romance, and he found this great love his junior year in college. Her name was Jean Davis, a college student at Butler, ten days older than Van with shining brown hair, beautiful eyes and a low, lovely voice. The connection was instant.

> If we were caught up in love, we were no less caught up in beauty, the mystery of beauty. Essentially we were pagan, but it was a high paganism. We worshipped the spirits of earth and sky; we adored the mysteries of beauty and love. . . . It was to us the greatest glory we had ever known.

They "attempted goodness" through being dedicated to one another and to beauty. They became partners in desiring the god of beauty. Describing their views, Van says, "There was a power—a god—of beauty. . . . Beauty was somehow at the very centre of meaning . . . our religion."

So they had found beauty, in the world around them and, most importantly, in their great love for one another. For many years, this was enough. Until one day a crack appeared in their love.

St. Margaret's Church

After riding for fifty minutes we needed a break. Dismounting our bikes, we looked out over Port Meadow, where horses have grazed since the eleventh century when the three hundred acres between Oxford and the Isis (the name of the Thames at this stretch of the river) were given to the Freemen of Oxford to graze their animals free of charge in return for protecting the kingdom from the Danes. My girls pointed at the horses in the distance.

"Daddy, when can we get one?" Lindsay asked, a look of pleading in her eyes, as if her very happiness depended on having a horse.

We could see Oxford's "dreaming spires" in the distance. Cumulous clouds dotted the sky. Turning around we saw a small gate that led down a wooded path. Near the gate was a sign: The Perch, a pub dating back to the thirteenth century. I knew we were getting

The children by the Isis River

close. I looked at our map again. We were in the little village of Binsey, a town with only nine buildings that all, save one, belonged to Christ Church (one of the oldest colleges of Oxford University). Riding alongside the Perch, we rode down Binsey Lane, passing only a handful of buildings and then fields on both sides. When the lane terminated we got off our bikes and entered the tree-canopied grounds of St. Margaret's Church. Established in the eighth century, it is, in many ways, the spiritual birthplace of Oxford.

We had come to this medieval church to tell our kids about the myth of Saint Frideswide (c. 680–735) and the mysterious origins of her healing well that have helped define and give shape to the Oxford identity and the people who journey here. Considered the patron saint of Oxford, Frideswide was an Anglo-Saxon princess who, upon

St. Margaret's Church

her conversion, had become a nun. When her fellow nuns in Binsey complained of having to fetch water from the Isis River, she prayed for a well. Frideswide's prayer was answered: a drinking well miraculously appeared.

My kids had no trouble finding the famous well. Before I could warn them, they descended the four or five stone steps down to the hole where the spring bubbles up. I told them to be careful and be respectful—for many pilgrims this is a holy site.

As we stood there, I mentioned that the well is often called the Treacle Well. In medieval times "treacle" often meant an antidote for healing poison. So this was a healing well. I asked my kids which famous children's book this well appears in.

"*Alice in Wonderland*," they said.

"Not fair, your mother has already told you this," I responded.

We had brought our kids to St. Margaret's in part because we wanted to awaken them to desire. And this church, with its ancient bricks, its graveyard, its massive trees providing nature's canopy, stirs something in the pilgrims who come here—a holy longing. As parents we knew that if our kids were going to develop a deep faith, they first needed to understand that they are creatures of desire. As St. Augustine once said, "The whole life of the good Christian is a holy longing. . . . That is our life, to be trained by longing." We didn't want them to grow up thinking that Christianity didn't meet their deepest desires and that they would have to look elsewhere. Everything they truly desired could be found in God's kingdom.

The spring before arriving in Oxford I had read James K. A. Smith's book *Desiring the Kingdom*. In it he says, "We are essentially and ultimately desiring animals, which is simply to say that we are essentially and ultimately lovers. To be human is to love, and it is what we love that defines who we are." He is not talking here about trivial love, like my love for the Boston Red Sox or In-N-Out Burgers, but ultimate loves. Our ultimate love is what we worship.

As we entered the sanctuary at St. Margaret's, I had to wonder, what if we began shaping our kids' desires, what they love and worship? Would this make a difference in their lives, their education and their faith? Would it give them a holy longing for the faith that would stand up to the corrosion of MTD, so prevalent around them?

In the spring of 1947 Davy sat in a New Haven park, close to Yale University, reading a book, occasionally glancing up to watch some children play. But as the hours drifted by, the children left and eventually she was alone. Suddenly she heard a cry behind her, then another one. She turned around and saw a man running toward her. She dropped her book and ran as fast as she could out of the park, outrunning her pursuer and returning home by the busy streets of New Haven. That night when Van returned from his graduate classes she told him what happened. Amazingly she was calm, trying to make light of it. Van, on the other hand, was furious at the would-be attacker. They did their best to put it behind them.

It had been a decade since Van and Davy met at a department store and fallen in love. They married, spent the duration of World War II serving in Pearl Harbor and, the year after the war, sailed around the Florida Keys. Now Van was studying at Yale. Over the years they had pursued beauty and love and had developed their own creed, which included, among other things, "the Shining Barrier," "the Navigators Council," "total sharing" and "total trust." Every fortnight they held a meeting, called the "State of the Union," to root out any "creeping separateness" or other challenges to their love. When hard decisions had to be made in the relationship, they would "Appeal to Love," the code that said whatever was done had to benefit their relationship, their great love. "The Appeal to Love," Van said, "was like a trumpet call from the battlements of the Shining Barrier, causing us to lift our eyes from immediate desires to what was truly important." For years their love had held strong, with no cracks in the "Shining Barrier." Until now.

One evening, a short time after the attack, Van left Davy at home, curled up with a book. Upon returning from the library, he found her crying; when he went to her, she clung to him and continued to weep. For Davy, the trauma of the attack had not gone away. But instead of being filled with rage and bitterness—a normal reaction to an experience like that—something unlikely happened: she was convicted of her own sinfulness and rebellion. "Her sins, she said, had come out and paraded before her, ghastly in appearance and mocking in demeanor." She was beginning to experience the "classical conviction of sin." At the time, Van did not understand what this was or what she was going through. If he had, he would have been alarmed. Davy was now afraid—afraid of the night, afraid of the darkness inside. She did not know it at the time, but the belief that their love for one another and the quest for beauty would save them and keep the fear of death at bay was beginning to falter. Davy's sense of sin and guilt did not leave her from that night on. At one point she painted a picture of it, which they called her "sin picture." It was to foreshadow events a couple of years later in Oxford.

THE HONEYMOON OVER

I knew eventually the honeymoon of travel would start to wear off for our kids, and it happened as soon as they had to buckle down and study each day. We had great plans and high hopes for homeschooling, but none of it was working as planned. The kids began to rebel, and as the weather turned drizzly gray, these Southern California children became depressed. Michelle struggled to get them to do math or writing or any of the subjects that took real work; they stalled, they played, they threw temper tantrums. Amazingly, our oldest, Jordan, was having the hardest time. He missed his friends and his home and his school.

One evening in late September I arrived home from Wycliffe flush with the excitement of meeting new people, reading inspiring books and strolling around Oxford, only to find the house in turmoil. From a homeschool perspective, it was not going well; Michelle was distraught and discouraged. She was at a loss for what to do.

"Jordan is really struggling; he refuses to do any math," she said. "And as Jordan goes, so goes the rest of the kids. He's got Jonathan depressed too. It was just a terrible day. All they want to do is go to Corn Market and buy stuff."

"Okay, I will go upstairs and talk to them," I agreed.

I sat down to listen, to find out what was going on in their hearts. Well, honestly, I wish I had done that. Instead, I did what most frustrated parents do: I began to lecture them, scolding them for messing up our plan for homeschooling. I threatened them with the fear of repeating the same grade and then offered the pièce de résistance: a warning that if they did not get their act together they would not get into a good college, have a good career and make enough money to buy what they wanted. Great. First I shamed them, then scared them and then appealed to their idols. A wonderful job of parenting.

Finally, I calmed down and remembered a more biblical way of discipline and exhortation—one that shepherds the heart, their desire. In the National Study on Youth and Religion, Christian Smith and his team discovered that the vast majority of young people were not interested in learning for its own sake, but only for what it could produce: a high school diploma, a college degree, a good job, lots of money, a successful career—the American dream. Gone are the days when education is connected to character formation or answering the big questions of life such as meaning and purpose. In other words, education is just a ticket to the cultural idols of the day that people pursue in place of God to bring meaning and purpose.

My lecture to my boys was built on an extrinsic view of education. From James K. A. Smith I learned that this was a false liturgy, a set of stories and scripts that focus our hearts away from the Creator and instead onto idols. These secular liturgies teach us, form us and capture our imaginations so that we love something other than the kingdom of God.

Sitting with my boys in their upper-story bedroom cluttered with a week's worth of dirty clothes, I had a talk with them about false liturgies and idols. We had had this talk before, so it was not new. But this time, I wanted to motivate them to study not by appealing to idols or a false liturgy, which I had just done, but by talking about desire.

According to Tim Clydesdale, the kids who *don't* put their faith in an identity lock box when they get to college are the ones that learned growing up to push back on the reigning liturgies and idols of the day. They understand how these false stories are trying to adversely shape them and thus are more open to being shaped by the liturgy of the Bible. This is what we were attempting with our kids, and home-schooling was part of it. I tried to get them to see that education, *their* education, was, in part, about giving them the tools to push back against these false liturgies and idols, and at the same time creating in them a desire for the true kingdom.

"I know you guys don't see this right now," I said, "but even your math and writing are part of this counter-formation. As parents we have about six to eight more years to shape and mold you so that your faith can stand on its own when you get to college. And what you are learning each day is part of this training."

"Does this make sense?" I asked them.

They nodded. Harmony was restored. But I was not under any illusion that my pep talk would automatically bring bliss on the homeschool front. I had a feeling we had more rocky roads ahead of us.

Van and Davy had arrived in Oxford in the autumn of 1950 to pursue a second bachelor's degree in literature. Upon seeing the "dreaming spires" for the first time, they "were to be numbered for ever amongst the lovers of Oxford," and England too. They "had begun to think," wrote Van later, "what we later found to be true: that coming to England was like coming home, coming to a home half-remembered—but home." It began to awaken a long-buried desire for another kingdom.

Right from the start the atmosphere of Oxford began to work on Van and Davy. It was a kind of counter-liturgy to the religion of romance and pagan beauty. The church towers and spires that pointed heavenward; the bells pealing

St. Mary's Church spire in the background

throughout the day; the names of the colleges—All Souls, Blackfriars, Christ Church, Corpus Christi, St. Peter, Magdalen, Jesus, Trinity, Wycliffe; the beautiful medieval architecture, so sublime and solid;

the great church music; and the transcendent splendor of the *Book of Common Prayer* worked their magic on them.

After just a few months, they realized that the vast majority of their new friends were devoted, passionate and lively *Christians*. How could this be? They had always dismissed Christianity as childish, joyless and unexciting. But these people were different. "The sheer quality of the Christians" they met "shattered" their "stereotype."

One afternoon that first autumn, a friend took Van to Binsey and St. Margaret's Church and the "Treacle Well" and the Perch for the first time. Late that afternoon, Van crossed Port Meadow to reclaim his bike in front of his college when suddenly he looked up and "there against the darkening grey sky was the tremendous uprush of the spire of St. Mary the Virgin." The spire had done what it was constructed to do, in part: to direct one's attention up to God. His "mind's gaze"—through the spire, as well as the other aspects of Oxford that spoke of its spiritual heritage—compelled him to give Christianity a second look.

Immediately, he turned around and walked a few hundred feet through the front door of Blackwell's Bookshop on Broad Street and purchased "an armload" of books about Christianity, most notably a handful by Oxford don C. S. Lewis, whom Van had heard about from his new Christian friends.

When Van got home that day, he told Davy of his decision to take a second look at Christianity. She was pleased and excited to start reading. Over the next few months they read voraciously about Christianity—Lewis, G. K. Chesterton's *The Everlasting Man*, books by Charles Williams and Dorothy Sayers. The study of Christianity absorbed them. They spent hours in dialogue with their new Christian friends. They told themselves that if these brilliant people could believe in God, there must be something there. Van and Davy continued to throw up every intellectual roadblock they could think of—the resurrection of Christ, the existence of God, miracles and ethics—but their friends had reasonable answers. Ever so slowly, Van and Davy started to believe; they began to see that Christianity made sense intellectually.

Davy made the step first. Her deep conviction of sin had remained, and her need for a Redeemer was evident to her. So she committed her life to Christ: "Today, crossing from one side of the room to the other, I lumped together all I am, all I fear, hate, love, hope; and, well, DID it. I committed my ways to God in Christ."

For Van it was not so easy. He struggled to believe. Intellectually, he had come to see the validity of Christianity, but emotionally he agonized over taking the step of faith. And the fact that Davy went ahead of him must have irked him. Undoubtedly, he felt betrayed. What happened to "total sharing"? He must have wanted to call a "state of the union" meeting, but how could he raise the point that she betrayed the "Shining Barrier" by believing in Christ and loving God more?

Around this time, Van wrote to C. S. Lewis, who was a tutor at Magdalen College. He admitted that he wanted to believe Christianity was true but just could not. Lewis wrote back and said that his conversion experience was the opposite: "You wish it were true; I strongly hoped it was *not*," wrote Lewis.

Van and Lewis exchanged a number of letters, and Lewis patiently answered all his questions. But finally Van admitted his real struggle. More than his intellectual doubts, the bigger issue for him was that "there is nothing in Christianity which is so repugnant to me as humility—the bent knee." Even if he knew Christianity was true, his real battle, he said, was against his pride. He simply did not want to admit that God was sovereign.

But Christianity kept pulling him in; he found it both "intellectually stimulating and aesthetically exciting." He was being drawn to Christ, but would he take the next step? Lewis kept at him: "Have you read the *Analects* of Confucius? He ends up by saying 'This is the Tao. I do not know if any one has ever kept it.' That's significant: one can really go direct from there to the *Epistle to the Romans*." Of course, this was the problem. Romans says that "all fall short of the glory of God." No one can keep the law, thus we need a redeemer. And Jesus is that Savior. Davy understood this. But Van kept wanting to find a way to believe in God and yet save himself through being good and committed to his desire for beauty. Lewis ended one of his letters in a manner that frightened him: "But I think you are already in the meshes of the net! The Holy Spirit is after you. I doubt if you'll get away!" But would he? And if he did not, what would this mean to the "Shining Barrier"?

FOLLOWING VAN

When author Will Vaus knocked on our Summertown door, I was already feeling guilty about leaving Michelle for the day. She was tired and worn out from homeschooling and bad attitudes.

"You go and come back and tell me all about it," she said like a sailor prepared to brave the storm alone. I would have stayed if I thought it would have helped. But my presence at home hadn't helped at all over the last few days.

Will, who was writing a biography on Sheldon Vanauken, was in town to speak at the C. S. Lewis Society, and he kindly gave me some of his time. Our goal was to retrace some of Van and Davy's steps in Oxford.

We began our day at the Perch, the seventeenth-century pub in Binsey, just down the road from St. Margaret's, where Van took Davy often. Sitting by the roaring fire, with the expansive stone hearth, the warm lighting, the old-style wooden tables and the traditional pub feel, I could see why people loved this pub. Lewis enjoyed it too, because it had not been "tarted up" like so many Oxford pubs.

"Why did you decide to be Van's biographer?" I asked him as I rubbed my hands together to warm them.

In his forties with sandy blond hair and a youthful appearance, he hesitated slightly before answering. "I was drawn to Van and Davy's passion for meaning, purpose and the good life," he said. "I am writing his biography because his book impacted me deeply."

From the Perch we walked a few hundred feet to the Isis and turned south. After about a tenth of a mile we arrived at the "humped-back bridge," which Van and Davy would take back across the river after a visit to the Perch. As we walked, Will and I talked about the other influences on Van and Davy: the Christian books they read, the conversations they had, their interaction with Lewis, their visit to different Anglican churches, and the beauty and grandeur of Cranmer's *Book of Common Prayer*. All of these things and more began to reshape Van and Davy, to challenge the Shining Barrier of pagan love that had no room for God. They were being challenged to see the world differently—to see that humility, the bending of the knee, is at the center of this new imagination.

Van and Davy

When we got back into Oxford, we made our way to Jesus College, where Van was a student and where his sighting of St. Mary's spire inspired him to take another look at Christianity.

I took Will to the Fellows' Garden in Exeter College, and we climbed the mound to some benches with one of the best views of St. Mary's. Just as we sat down, the bells began to ring. I once read somewhere that the biblical scholar Walter Brueggemann wrote that in worship, our hearts, our minds, our very imaginations are radically reshaped. Through the metaphors, stories and narratives of the Bible and worship, we begin to imagine a different reality and, slowly but surely, to live into this reality. The liturgy of worship reshapes what we love, what we desire and what we live for. Could it have been that when Van saw St. Mary's spire he was beginning to imagine the world differently?

Three months had passed since Davy had become a Christian. She, along with their friends, was praying for Van. After long days of gut-wrenching soul searching, his intellectual breakthrough came while reading the Gospel of Mark. Suddenly he realized that as hard as it was to move forward in belief, to jump the gap, it was just as impossible to move backwards to his former deistic belief in a vague creator and a do-good moralism. He knew too much now; belief in Christ, his life, death and resurrection was now credible. "Christianity now appeared intellectually stimulating, aesthetically exciting, and emotionally moving." He realized he could not reject Christ and thus flung himself over the gap toward Christ. Immediately, he wrote Lewis to tell him. "My prayers are answered," Lewis responded. But he cautioned him: "There will be a counter attack on you, you know, so don't be too alarmed when it comes. The enemy will not see you vanish into God's company without an effort to reclaim you."

In December 1952, after two-and-a-half years away, Van and Davy returned to Lynchburg for Van to resume his teaching career. The first year back was rough, summed up in the name they gave their home: Li'l Dreary. Right away "the counter attack" Lewis predicted began. Van started to struggle mightily with his faith. His old doubts returned, and his old paganism reared its head. Intellectually he was committed, he said, but he was holding something back. Davy, on the other hand, was not holding anything back—she was all in. This made it worse for Van, and he began to resent the new Davy, the one who loved God more than the Shining Barrier and commitment to pagan beauty. He wanted the old Davy back "for their own sakes"; he did not want them connected to God anymore. God was an intrusion. Van longed for pagan joy and a "schooner under the wind." He realized that he was still worshiping beauty, and Davy was worshiping God. His struggles caused them to drift apart; the Shining Barrier was not holding. Davy was finding joy in "the Obedience," as they called Christianity, and longing for Van to experience it as well.

By the second year in Lynchburg, they were doing better. Van had bought an MG convertible, and together they began to rediscover their love of the Virginia countryside. Along with their dog, Flurry, they spent days driving the back roads, simply enjoying the beauty, stopping whenever and wherever, soaking it all in. As their love grew for hay and hills, sunsets and sunrises, their love for each other returned, stronger than ever.

But then the mysterious illness took a turn for the worse, landing Davy in the hospital. By January 1955, she had been in the hospital for months, her liver almost gone, and had only days to live. Months before this point, Davy had a sense that she was dying. During one sleepless night, she spent the entire time in prayer, offering up her life in exchange for the fulfillment of her husband's troubled soul.

Then Van received that fateful call in the night. With the top to the MG still down, he raced through the cold, dark streets toward the hospital. Her pulse was slowing, the nurse had said on the phone. He had to hurry.

When Van entered the hospital room, Davy was awake, but her breathing was slowing down. They prayed together, and courageously, Van released her to God: "Go under the Mercy," he said to her. Moments passed. The sky became lighter. Van stayed by her side. Soon her breath became fainter. Then suddenly Davy said, "Oh, dearling, look." She reached up and touched his face. What did she see?

Every now and then Van said in a low voice: "I am here, Davy; I am with you." Finally, her breathing stopped, and she was gone. She had passed away, quietly. "She could not say it to me," wrote Van later, "so I said it, whispered it, to her: 'All shall be most well, my dearling.' Then I kissed her lightly and stood up." Her suffering was over. Yet for Van, the way of grief had just begun.

Could he go on without Davy? Should he end his life, joining her in death? Although they had discussed that before they had become Christians, after they were converted, he promised her he would not kill himself. But would he continue to love God, to remain in the Obedience? One thing was sure: Davy wasn't there to help. Whatever he would face in the future, he would face it alone.

In his profound grief, Van reached out to Lewis for help. He ad-

mitted how empty the world was without Davy and how God seemed
to have withdrawn too. He could not contain his anger against God:
"God could not be as loving as He was supposed to be" he raged. On
one particular night Van was overwhelmed with a sense of a cosmos
empty of God as well as Davy: "'All right,' I muttered to myself. 'To
hell with God. I'm not going to believe this damned rubbish any
more. Lies, all lies. I've been had.'"

Lewis, who by now had earned Van's trust and love, wrote in
candid terms that Van's problem was that he and Davy had made their
love an idol. They had made it an end in itself, instead of seeing romantic love as a pointer to a higher love. He wrote: "One way or another the thing had to die. Perpetual springtime is not allowed. You
were not cutting the wood of life according to the grain. . . . You have
been treated with a severe mercy. You have been brought to see . . .
that you were jealous of God."

Van took Lewis's strong counsel to heart. Davy's death had been a
"severe mercy." Lewis was right. By putting the Shining Barrier first,
they had excluded God. They had made their love an idol and a false
liturgy of life. Van realized too late that all created things, including
love, have the potential to become a rival to God. He had done this
with Davy and their quest for beauty. Her death was needed to bring
Van back to faith; if she had not died, he would have grown to hate
God or have damaged Davy's faith. Either way, he would not have
remained committed—unless God allowed Davy to die.

Van knew this, but would he take it to heart? Or would he allow
his grief and bitterness to turn him away from God for good? It would
take two decades to find out the answer.

Last Stroll in Oxford

It was early on a Tuesday morning, and Will, Michelle and I were
standing on Pusey Lane, a few blocks from the Eagle and Child Pub,
cobblestones under our feet, the old gas lamp now powered by elec-
tricity above our heads. We were looking for the location of Van and
Davy's studio—the cramped, damp but tremendously inviting flat

with a small fireplace that was both their home and the place of so much warm community and conversation with their friends. It was the place, more than anywhere else, that their desire was redirected, where they began to see the world differently.

From Pusey Lane we walked past the Martyr's Memorial and on to Broad Street, heading toward New College. Our goal that morning was to retrace Van's steps on his last day in Oxford, from the studio to the Eastgate Hotel, his last goodbye to the city that had meant so much to them, and one last meeting with Lewis. I was glad Michelle was with us. In spite of being an amazingly gifted and inspirational teacher, homeschooling was still not going well, through no fault of her own. Jordan was angry at being away from his school and friends. The other three were defiant and depressed, often following Jordan's lead. And Michelle was losing hope. I needed to find a way to ignite her passion for our pilgrimage, for the kids' schooling and for her own desire for the kingdom. I hoped this walk with Will would help. Just getting her a day off was a start. She deserved it.

As we came to New College and then Queen's Lane, we took our time, walking slowly. We were enjoying one of the quintessential medieval streets in Oxford, untouched in a thousand years save for some exhaust stains on the walls when cars were allowed to drive here. After we reached the Magdalen Bridge, like Van and Davy we turned around: "The High, gently curving ancient colleges on either side, may well be the most beautiful street in the world."

At the Eastgate, we ordered tea and settled into comfortable chairs with the High just outside the window. Will wanted to know why *A Severe Mercy* was important to us.

"That's easy," I said. "On a warm summer night, when Michelle and I had only been dating for a couple of weeks, we sat on a deck overlooking the San Gabriel Valley, high above the City of Roses, and read the first chapter of *A Severe Mercy* together. I wanted to share with her this book that had meant so much to me, and I thought if she fell in love with it, she might fall in love with me. A few weeks later, when she went with her family to Europe for a month, she took *A Severe*

Mercy along and devoured the rest of it on the long car rides between cities. She was hooked, caught up in the story, the pathos and the passion. It has been a favorite of ours ever since."

As we sipped our hot tea, we read sections of the book out loud, focusing on the "severe mercy" part and Lewis's strong, pointed counsel to Van that he had made his love for Davy into an idol and that one way or another his idolatrous love had to die. "That's strong counsel to a grieving man," I said.

"It's testament to Van's honesty that he included that letter from Lewis, a letter that doesn't flatter Van, in the book," said Will.

"What was God doing?" asked Michelle as she took another sip of her tea.

"Van was being tested," said Will. "He'd struggled with his pride and idolatry before he was a believer, and he continued to struggle afterward."

"Is it possible that God allowed this event to happen in his life, as painful as it was, to thwart his idolatry?" asked Michelle.

"Lewis sure thought that," said Will.

After Will ordered a dessert, I asked him about the real hero of *A Severe Mercy*.

"I think Van holds Davy up as the real hero," he said. "She had her allegiance right. She's the one who understood that salvation is total surrender. She's the one who experienced the retrieval of self—she became exactly who God meant her to be in all her glory." Davy had her desire pointed in the right direction, attached to the correct object. "But Van," he continued, "struggled with becoming who God wanted him to be. He was always looking for a new adventure, a new romantic journey. He wasn't content."

"Is it possible that Davy's faith had matured while Van's had not?" I asked.

Will nodded. "I think that's accurate. She had settled down; she was ready to be a wife, to serve the church, to be steady. She still believed in beauty, but now beauty was wrapped up in Christ. Beauty was connected to the Obedience, the response to grace."

"And I think she realized that suffering was now part of the equation," I added.

Will glanced at Michelle and then said, "Davy understood that the Christian life is not always exciting, that sometimes it feels mundane and is even filled with tears."

I then looked over at Michelle and saw her take a deep breath.

Van continued to struggle with life without Davy. Though he remained a professor at Lynchburg, he did not know what to do with his life, and he continued to look for things to fill the hole that she left. But nothing seemed to work, at least for long, and then he was on to the next thing like a bored child trying to find stimulation.

During the sixties, he joined the antiwar movement. He believed that Christ would stand for peace and be against the war in Vietnam. By the late sixties Van was so caught up in the peace movement that he had angered the president of Lynchburg College. It did not help that he had adopted the views of the liberal left on the issues of the war, feminism, reproductive rights and sexual ethics, and rural living. He had even stopped going to church.

However, by the early seventies, twenty years after Davy's death, God began to pull Van back to himself. In 1973 a friend sent him a book about C. S. Lewis, and as he read it, the following words jumped out at him: "If a man diligently followed his desire [for Joy], pursuing the false objects until their falsity appeared and then resolutely abandoned them, he must come out at last into the clear knowledge that the human soul was made to enjoy some object that is never fully given . . . in our present mode of subjective and spatio-temporal existence." Van was so affected by the quote that he typed it onto an index card and looked at it often. It was true, he must have thought. He had desired Joy and had pursued it first through Davy and then through so many dead ends of the sixties. But these things should have been pointers to the real object of Joy, not the final destination. Why had he not seen this before—or had he?

A short time later, he wrote the Bodleian Library, to which Van had given his Lewis correspondence, and asked for copies of the letters. Arriving home from class one day, he discovered the package from England. Not even bothering to take off his jacket and scarf, he sat down and read them straight through, tears dropping from his face as he thought wistfully of his friendship with Lewis and his profound love for Davy. Something was stirring in Van. A few months went by, the letters weighing on him. He took them out and read them again. In an instant, he knew he had to write a book about Davy. It would be called *A Severe Mercy*. It was the surest sign that Van had returned to the Obedience. The dark night of the soul, spanning twenty years, was over; he was back in the light. His desire, long distracted by idols and false liturgies, was once again directed in the proper direction—toward Christ and the worship of God. And he had a new calling as a writer.

In December 1975 he confessed his sins of the past twenty years to a priest, an old friend from his Oxford days. He then had his long-dormant membership transferred to a new church, St. Stephen's Episcopal Church, the church that Davy and he had loved for so many years from afar. She would have approved. He had returned to the Obedience. But would he get it right this time?

Eternity at the Eastgate

Our time at the Eastgate was coming to an end, but we continued our discussion of the book: how God used the tragedy of Davy's death to reshape Van and liberate his desire, to free it from the wrong attachments so that it could be directed to the right object, the right worship. We discussed the role of St. Ebbe's in Oxford and the Episcopal (Anglican) churches in Virginia that they attended and the importance of liturgy and the *Book of Common Prayer* in reshaping Van and Davy's desire. The liturgy of the prayer book became a counter-liturgy for them.

The waitress came with a refill of the hot water. We paused from our discussion to make another cup of tea. Will took a moment to ask

Michelle how she was doing with the transition to Oxford. Sitting there still wrapped in her jacket and scarf, she shared some of the trials of homeschooling and her feelings of failure as a mom.

We were down to our last minutes. Before we left I wanted to read one last section of the book, the description of Van's final lunch with Lewis and their parting for the time being:

> On the last day I met C. S. Lewis at the Eastgate for lunch. We talked, I recall, about death or, rather, awakening after death. Whatever it would be like, we thought, our response to it would be 'Why, of course! Of *course* it's like this.' . . . We both chuckled at that. I said it would be a sort of coming home, and he agreed. . . . Then it was time to go, and we drained our mugs. When we emerged onto the busy High with traffic streaming past, we shook hands, and he said: 'I shan't say goodbye. We'll meet again.' Then he plunged into the traffic. . . . When he reached the pavement on the other side, he turned round as though he knew somehow that I would still be standing there in front of the Eastgate. Then he raised his voice in a great roar that easily overcame the noise of the cars and buses. Heads turned and at least one car swerved. 'Besides,' he bellowed with a great grin, 'Christians NEVER say goodbye!'

I read the last line into a rich silence. When I looked up from the page, Michelle's eyes were filled with tears. Will leaned forward. "Michelle," he asked gently, "what about that touched you so deeply?" With the pub empty save for the three of us, Lewis's bold declaration had surrounded our little community with a sense of wild wonder. Trying to hold back more tears, Michelle smiled and then said, "I'm not sure. It just does."

In the twenty years since the widely successful publication of *A Severe Mercy*, Van had pursued the life of a writer. Retired from teaching since 1980, he wrote full time, turning out dozens of essays, journal articles and full-length books, including a novel. He had faithfully pursued the vocation God had given him, and he had done it well. He wrote with passion, he lived with purpose. He had remained true to the Obedience. True desire had met, finally, the true object of its desire.

Over the final six months of Van's life, Will exchanged fourteen letters and three postcards with him. He visited him at Vancot twice. Van said he felt a bond with Will as a brother in Christ. On Friday, October 25, Van wrote Will a postcard saying he was in the midst of two weeks of radiation treatment for his lung cancer, hoping it would help his breathing. He said he was trusting in Jesus as his final security. Three days later he was dead at eighty-two.

Over a million people have read *A Severe Mercy* in the years since it was first written, and it has touched countless lives. One of the scores of people affected by the book was a young Indonesian missionary child, just sixteen years old. Inspired, she wrote to Van in June 1978 not a letter but an "afterword" to the book, describing Van's death and arrival into heaven.

> Something in the air smelt very clear and sweet. It was the golden brightness, of course. He was sitting on the grass by the lily pond, Davy's hand in his. "Van," she said delightedly. "Welcome home!" He was just going to say, "But I've been here all along," when he remembered. "Oh, Davy!" he said, and he took her into his arms. "Why, it's spring," he said. "Of course," she said. "So it always is." Then, Aslan . . . and Jack were there too.

three

THE STRUGGLE WITHIN

The Case of Dr. Jekyll and Mr. Hyde

Dejected, Michelle pushed her chair away from the homeschool table and stood up. Taking a deep breath, she looked out the window at the early afternoon drizzle and thought, *Why can't I motivate them to learn?* A tear trickled down her cheek. It was the last week of October, and after two months of homeschooling, she was ready to quit, frustrated with the lack of progress. The gloomy weather, the shortened days and the absence of a car all contributed to her dour mood and the kids' cabin fever. Further, there were no homeschool groups in Oxford to provide friends, support and extracurricular activities—elements so important to successful homeschooling.

Some days had gone well and they managed to learn. But mostly, they struggled. The kids did not want to do math, grammar or writing, subjects that took some effort. They dragged their feet and distracted themselves with anything that would keep them from their work. Michelle attempted different ways to motivate them—pep talks, fun activities and even threats of punishment—but nothing worked.

Turning her attention back to the homeschool desk, she said, "Since we aren't getting anything done, let's walk to the library."

She bundled up the girls, making sure they had on "Wellies," those distinctive rubber boots that Brits wear in inclement weather, and handed them each a small umbrella. Shutting the door behind them, she hoped to close the door on the sad school day as well.

They headed south down Middle Way and turned right on South Parade, named for the location where Oliver Cromwell lined up his troops to fight King Charles I in the English Civil War. Nestled in the middle of pricey boutiques and trendy restaurants was a small 1960s brick building that housed the local library.

When they got inside, they stashed their wet umbrellas and then all went in different directions. The library was a happy place for them—an opportunity to get out of the house, hang around other people and discover new books. They had already taken out dozens of books over the first few months in Oxford. And read them all.

After a couple of hours of browsing and roaming the library, it was time to go. Michelle needed to get home to start dinner. She whispered to the boys, who were now playing on the computers, that they had to leave, but she got no response. A few minutes later, she told them again, this time with a little more aggravation in her voice. Jonathan turned off his game, but Jordan kept playing. She tried again. He still ignored her.

"Jordan, come on," Jonathan said, attempting to coax his older brother off the machine.

The rest of them went outside. Michelle remained outwardly calm, but inside she was fuming. "You've got to be kidding!" she said under her breath. She gave him one more chance, catching his eye through the window, but he still did not come. And then she did something that surprised even her: she turned and headed home with the other three in tow.

Conversations in the Kitchen

At the start of October, three weeks before Jordan's library episode, we knew that the homeschool experiment was in trouble. If we did not make some changes, the kids would lose out on a year of learning. Government schools were not an option; they already had long waiting lists. Private schools were too expensive. Homeschooling was the only option. But as important as our kids' schooling was, there was an even bigger issue for our family that had to be corrected.

Jordan, and for that matter each of our children, was struggling to obey. All our best parenting strategies were not working. Until we solved this problem, we could not move forward.

Michelle and I spent hours discussing our children, particularly Jordan's struggle for obedience. We had come to Oxford for a pilgrimage, and part of this was to rediscover our spiritual roots. But we had not anticipated this conflict over obedience stopping us in our tracks. After discussing it, we recognized this as an opportunity for growth, training our kids toward a consequential faith. So, as anxious as we were to fix homeschooling, we first needed to address the issues of motivation and obedience. If we were going to do more than just force them to obey, that is, motivate them by fear, we needed to understand how their hearts—and, for that matter, their faith—worked.

In *Soul Searching*, one of the books based on the NSYR, Christian Smith and Melinda Denton write that young people have no language to explain their daily spiritual experience. According to Smith and Denton, young people are *"incredibly inarticulate* about their faith, their religious beliefs and practices, and its meaning or place in their lives." And if they can't articulate their faith, the authors argue, it will never become real, as it is articulation that engenders reality. Part of the problem is that adults have failed to help young people understand and discuss their faith or to deal with the daily challenges of belief. When young people don't have this language, it inhibits their faith from being a vital part of their daily life, and eventually, when they get to college, they drop it into a "lock box."

To this point of articulation, whenever I asked Jordan and Jonathan, "Why did you do that when you knew it was wrong?" their response was always the same: "I don't know." And when I asked them why they didn't do the right thing, like doing their homework, they also didn't know why. Now, I realize that at eleven and nine they were not fully self-aware yet, but they struggled with articulating anything they were going through. And without this vocabulary they could not experience their faith on a daily basis. I worried that if we did not help them understand the struggle within, at some point in the future they would abandon the faith, claiming it as irrelevant to their life.

One afternoon, sitting in front of the open oven to keep warm, Michelle and I talked about our kids. We agreed that they needed to understand the reality of sin in the believer's life. After all, this teaching was a core doctrine of our faith. But how should we teach it so that it would become their own?

CHRIST CHURCH MEADOW

The first Sunday in October, we attended St. Ebbe's Anglican, our regular church and the fellowship that Van and Davy joined after becoming Christians. After a beautiful and meaningful service, we decided to go on a little field trip just down the street from the church.

With the sun shining, cumulous clouds speckling the sky and a cool breeze blowing, we exited the church and headed east toward St. Aldates Street. Just past the church, sections of the original city wall encircled ancient buildings. Inside the stone wall sat Pembroke College, built in 1624.

"That is where George Whitefield, the famous eighteenth-century evangelist, went to school," I said, as we walked along the ancient walls, which were partly covered by black soot from automobile exhaust. Whitefield entered Pembroke in the autumn of 1732 at age seventeen. From a religious family that was too poor to afford tuition, he worked as a servitor in exchange for free tuition. Being a servitor meant serving as a lackey to three or four students of high standing. He was required to do whatever jobs they requested, no matter how repulsive, like cleaning their rooms, washing their clothes or shining their shoes. He had to wear clothes that marked him as a servitor so that students of higher rank could identify and ignore him. His religious devotion also exposed him to ridicule. But the persecution inspired him to redouble his efforts. Along with morning and evening devotions, he prayed, sang the Psalms three times daily, fasted on Friday and took Communion each Sunday. He was committed. But he was also lonely and had few friends. He longed to be part of the

Holy Club, the Methodists who were famous around the university for their religious zeal. But because of his inferior rank he could not introduce himself, so he continued on alone.

As we crossed St. Aldates Street, we walked in front of Tom's Tower, one of the entrances of Christ Church. I mentioned that John and Charles Wesley, two of the most famous members of the Holy Club, had been students at Christ College. Since my kids knew by heart a number of Charles Wesley's hymns, having learned them in our Sunday school back home, they recognized his name. We continued down the sloping hill of St. Aldates in the direction of the river, toward the entrance of Christ Church Meadow on the south side of the college.

After a year at Pembroke, Whitefield's religious dedication finally caught the attention of Charles Wesley, who invited him to join their fellowship. Whitefield was thrilled to have new friends and a support network for his faith. He redoubled his religious efforts, taking on many of their strict spiritual disciplines, spending time in prisons like the Bocardo and in the poorhouses. But no matter how hard he strived to enter the "narrow gate" of salvation, he continued to lack spiritual peace. He knew he needed to be "born again." Anxious for his soul, he was overcome with his sense of sin. He thought that if he strove harder in his religious devotion, he could experience the new birth. He whipped himself into such a spiritual frenzy that he stopped eating and could not sleep more than three hours at a time; his studies suffered. Friends tried to intercede and moderate his religious striving, but it did not work. He was desperate; he needed to be saved.

Physically exhausted, he pushed himself harder, attempting to follow Jesus' example of praying in the wilderness "with wild beasts." As Andrew Atherstone, a professor at Wycliffe Hall writes, this was "a difficult environment to recreate in Oxford." So Whitefield took to lying under the trees in Christ Church Meadow.

By now, we had made it into Christ Church Meadow and I stood with my family under a tree, reading from Atherstone's account: "He lay on his face under the trees of Christ Church Meadow, praying late into the evening, and the gathering storm clouds reminded him of the Day of Judgment. Yet still he found no peace."

He had to wonder if he would ever know Christ. What more would it take?

Taking Sin Seriously

I had taken my family to Christ Church Meadow to learn about Whitefield's struggle with sin. His story provided an opportunity to discuss the power of sin and the need for a savior, something my kids might take for granted having been raised in the faith.

As pilgrims we were rediscovering our roots. Whitefield and the Puritans, unlike so many churches in the West today, took sin seriously, both in their hearts and in the world. They saw sin as rebellion against God's gracious reign and vandalism toward his good creation, and were quick to admit they were sinners. They preached the deadness of the human heart and its inability to keep God's law and thus earn salvation. They knew that without a Redeemer, they could never please a Holy God. Sin was such a serious matter to Whitefield that he spent his days trying to atone for it with all manner of spiritual disciplines. After years of moral and spiritual striving, Whitefield had hit bottom that second year at Oxford. Giving up, he threw himself on the mercy of God and, to his surprise, experienced the new birth. It not only changed his life, but many people think it changed the course of British history.

At times my boys were cavalier about sin and resisted confessing. So I would ask them, "If you don't have sin, why do you need a savior?" They understood my point. I wanted them to see that only when they admit their sin and daily turn to God for forgiveness will they be able to live without guilt and shame and at the same time have the proper motivation to obey. But I was having trouble getting this point across.

I remembered catching my boys in a lie a couple weeks earlier. Their first response was to cover it up. When this didn't work, they shifted their tactics to blame someone else. But they wouldn't admit their sin. Sometimes Jonathan would admit his wrong, but he often did it not because he was truly repentant but because he wanted to move on and avoid getting punished. So he would confess right away, even for things he did not do. Lindsay was similar. Meghan, like Jordan, refused to admit wrong. But regardless of their first response, they all struggled with repentance.

Closing the door to their room, I sat on the edge of their bed, toys strewn everywhere after a productive afternoon of play, and I reminded them of Adam and Eve.

"What did they do as soon as they were caught?" I asked, formulating my own catechism.

"They hid from God," they said.

"What else did they do?"

"They lied about it and blamed someone else."

"That's right," I said. "Isn't it amazing how quickly and spontaneously, like it's second nature, they lied to cover their exposure?"

As I was saying this to them, I knew they weren't the only ones who struggled with covering up sin. We all do it, calling it other names and refusing to admit we have done anything wrong. Yet guilt weighs heavy on our consciences. We deny its existence, but we feel its reality.

Back at Christ Church Meadow, the kids off playing in the garden, Michelle and I under a tree enjoying the cool shade, I thought if I could get them, especially Jordan, to admit their sin, we might begin to solve the problem of motivation and obedience.

Was this the key, I asked Michelle, that might unlock the problem? Michelle's eyes lit up. "I sure hope so," she said.

But in the weeks after our trip to Christ Church Meadow, even after long conversations explaining to Jordan his need to repent and getting him to finally admit, usually begrudgingly, he did something wrong, it still did not seem to have much impact on his obedience. At times, we resorted to the carrot and at other times to the stick, motivating him by rewards and by punishment. But even that did not always work. Some days he was good, and some days he was bad. We felt like we were dealing with Dr. Jekyll and Mr. Hyde.

TABARD THEATRE

Wednesday night, the second week of October, I boarded a bus for London. I had bought tickets to see a play at the Tabard Theatre in London with two friends: Ross Khuene, an ice hockey teammate from Gordon College who lives outside of Oxford, and Steve Turner, an author and journalist who is a denizen of London. I was looking forward to a relaxing time watching a play with dear friends. But as I climbed to the second floor of the Oxford Tube, I could not shake from my mind the struggle for obedience that was going on at home.

Ironically, the play we were going to see was *The Scandalous Case of Dr. Jekyll and Mr. Hyde,* billed as a modern adaptation of Robert Lewis Stevenson's famous book set in London in the nineteenth century. With his *Treasure Island* and *Kidnapped,* Stevenson was a Belcher family favorite.

As the bus crawled through rush-hour traffic in Oxford, I pulled from my backpack Claire Harman's *Robert Louis Stevenson: A Biography,* wanting to do some research on Stevenson before the play. Ever since I had heard Tim Keller, a pastor in New York City, link *Dr. Jekyll and Mr. Hyde* with the New Testament book of Romans, I have been intrigued by Stevenson. Keller mentioned that Stevenson had grown up in a Scottish Presbyterian home and may have been influenced by Romans 7.

As the bus bounced around the old streets of Oxford, I read Harman's biography, trying to keep the book steady. Stevenson's childhood, she writes, was conflicted. On the one hand his upbringing was idyllic, filled with happy memories, but on the other hand, it was terrifying, characterized by nightmares. He credits most of his good memories to his parents, who indulged him, and the bad memories to his nurse, Cummy, who took care of him. "But the strength of Cummy's religious views," writes Harman, "made her a very troubling influence." As a member of the Free Church, Cummy believed "the theatre was the mouth of hell, cards were 'the Devil's Books' and novels (meaning romances) paved the road to perdition."

She filled six-year-old Louis's mind with fears of hell, eternal punishment and damnation of his parents for breaking the sabbath. Most nights, he awoke with nightmares that "made much of the sick little boy's life a misery." He read his Bible, prayed and tried to be good in order to stave off nightmares and the constant fear of dying and going to hell. Cummy did her best to scare him away from hell, but in the process it caused him to loathe God as well.

In his late teens, according to Harman, Stevenson matriculated at the University of Edinburgh. Once free from his nurse and the oversight of parents, he threw off his piety and embraced the "precocious depravity" that was hidden underneath a veneer of religiosity: "Just as in childhood Stevenson had found himself drawn fascinatedly toward the wickedness that his puritan upbringing taught him to revile, so in the freedom of adulthood and the long hours of college truancy he quickly became a habitué of some of Edinburgh's most disreputable dives."

But it did not take long for his dissipation to lose its flavor. He "was often subject to fits of morbid melancholy during these years." But he could not stop. He led a "double life," according to his own words, "one of the day, and one of the night." He was plagued by this conflict and also intrigued by it at the same time. *Dr. Jekyll and Mr. Hyde* was Stevenson's attempt, contends Harman, to work out this "double life" and find a solution. "I had long been trying," he wrote, "to write a story on this subject, to find a body, a vehicle, for that strong sense of man's double being which must at times come in upon and overwhelm the mind of every thinking creature."

At that moment, the bus came to a halt, my backpack sliding off the seat next to me. We had arrived in London. As I got off the bus, I was left with a lingering question: did Stevenson find a solution to the double life? I tucked Harman's book back into my backpack and hailed a taxi. I was now curious to see if the modern adaptation dealt with the double life and if it provided an answer to it. Was there hope for the mind that is overwhelmed with this "double being," or is the human being stuck in this conflict with no escape?

Pub Talk

"So what did you think?" Ross asked as we exited the Tabard Theater, a London fog settling damply on our shoulders. Passing two-story Victorian row houses, many converted into shops and cafés, and crowds of people strolling the sidewalks, we found a cheery pub to discuss the play in.

When our hot chocolate arrived, Ross, an English major in college, asked excitedly, "What would you say the play got right? Let's talk about that before we critique it. Because it seems to me," Ross added, "that although the play took some liberty with the characters, overall it got the main theme of the story correct."

"That's right," I said, "it was accurate more or less."

For the next two hours we discussed the play, how Jekyll, frustrated by his inner conflict, devised a potion to live morally during the day as himself and to live immorally at night as Mr. Hyde. But after a few months, this delicate balance of the two natures crumbled; the dark side slowly took over, and he needed more and more potion each morning to return to Dr. Jekyll.

After dessert, we talked about the differences between the play and the book, the biggest being that when he no longer has any more potion, he must decide whether to live morally as Jekyll or immorally as Hyde. In the play, the choice is easy: Jekyll chooses a life of sin. Yet in the book it is different—he chooses to be moral and resists the dark side, producing great tension where the reader is encouraged to root for him to conquer the evil side. In the play this tension does not exist—of course anyone would choose the dark side, the play seems to say. But once the tension was gone the play became boring, watching Hyde commit one heinous crime after another. What was interesting about that?

"I was so ready for the play to be over at that point," I said, showing my frustration. "It completely lost my interest."

But even in the book, the three of us had to admit, Jekyll can't remain moral for long, despite the fear of the scaffold, and he tumbles back into Hyde.

Around 11:30, we left the pub, the exotica lounge music streaming from the speakers. As we spilled out onto the street, I was amazed to see the road filled with traffic and the sidewalks jammed with people, a city still alive. When I got into a cab to take me back to my bus, with the excitement of a night in London over and the reality of two bus connections in front of me, I was slightly depressed, that feeling one gets when a big event is over. I peered out the window and thought

Ross, Steve and Jim

about my question at the beginning of the night: did Stevenson find a solution to the double life, the conflict within? After the play and our conversation, it was clear that he didn't. Even the book ends on a hopeless note. Rather than face the law, Hyde takes justice into his own hands, judges himself and commits suicide. Undoubtedly Stevenson would have agreed with the apostle Paul: "Wretched man that I am, who will deliver me from this body of death?"

When I got to the bus, my thoughts returned to my family and the struggle with obedience at home. I had hoped the night might provide some insight for us. But I realized that Stevenson, while brilliantly describing the inner struggle (no small task), had no solution to offer, for the reader or my family. Even though Stevenson knew the immoral life was a dead end and that the moral life, propped up by self-will or the fear of punishment, was impossible to sustain, he was unable to find a solution in his own life. Until the end of his life, he sought an answer but couldn't find one. As I propped my head against the window of the Oxford Tube, ready to sleep for ninety minutes, I realized my search for answers to help my family would have to continue. But at that moment, it had to wait: I drifted off to sleep.

WYCLIFFE HALL

Still groggy from the late night in London, I biked to Wycliffe Hall the next morning and settled in at my desk. With my books and papers spread out and my notebook open, I was anxious to record my thoughts from the night before and come to some conclusions that might help my family. As a parent, I couldn't let my kids do anything they wanted. We needed to guide them to know what was right and wrong and to know that living rightly would bring blessing to them. But just telling them to try harder never seemed to work for long. There had to be another way.

In the middle of journaling, I thought of Keller's comment that Stevenson had been influenced by the apostle Paul. After last night, I was convinced that Keller was right: there had to be a connection between Jekyll and Hyde and the seventh chapter of Romans. Although Stevenson never mentions Romans, he would have known the text from growing up in Scottish Presbyterian circles. In fact, Stevenson could easily have been channeling Paul when he has Dr. Jekyll say, "I stood already committed to a profound duplicity of life . . . a perennial war among my members. . . . Man is not truly one, but truly two."

Moving over to my comfortable chair, I grabbed my Bible and opened it to the book of Romans. "For I do not understand my own actions," Paul writes. "For I do not do what I want, but I do the very thing I hate. . . . So now it is no longer I who do it, but sin that dwells within me" (Romans 7:15, 17). Paul wants to do good but he can't. And it tears at him. There is an irreconcilable antagonism inside of him, a deep split in his soul. What is interesting is that the more he tries to obey God's law, the worse it gets.

After the previous night, I realized that Stevenson makes the same point. At first the fear of the scaffold keeps Hyde locked inside and under control. Jekyll feels free from Hyde. But it does not last long. Stevenson describes Jekyll sitting on a park bench, people watching. As they walk by, he compares himself to them, thinking how morally superior he is to them, when all of a sudden, his body starts going through violent changes. Moments later, to his horror, he realizes, "I was once more Edward Hyde," this time without the potion. For Jekyll, obeying the moral law led to pride, another kind of hideousness.

His experience is straight out of Romans: "For apart from the law, sin lies dead. I was once alive apart from the law, but when the com-

Wycliffe Hall, Oxford University

mandment came, sin came alive and I died" (Romans 7:8-9). For Paul, the more he tried to obey God, the more prideful he got. I once heard Keller say that there are two ways to be self-centered: one way is to be very bad, breaking all the rules, and the second way is to be very good, which leads to self-righteousness. For Paul, to keep the moral law does not get rid of the hideousness within—it actually leads to more deadness. As if he had memorized Romans 7, Stevenson understood this point. He depicts Jekyll's badness both ways—as immoral hideousness in the character of Hyde and as moral hideousness in the good doctor. But both are hideous.

Feeling depressed, I set my Bible down and picked up Harman's book. I recalled something a critic had written when *Dr. Jekyll and Mr. Hyde* was published. After a few moments of flipping pages, I found it: "It is indeed a dreadful book," the critic wrote, "most dreadful because of a certain moral callousness, a want of sympathy, a shuttering of hope. Most of us at some epoch of our lives have been on the verge of developing a Mr. Hyde." The reviewer was not using the word "dreadful" to comment on the quality of the book; he was saying that in perfectly describing the splitness of the human condition, the book offers no solution and is "dreadfully" hopeless. After all, if on the one hand hedonistic relativism fails miserably to deliver a happy, content and meaningful life, and on the other hand religion also fails by making us prideful boors, then the human condition is without hope.

I put Harman down and checked my watch. It was well after 2:00 p.m.; I had been deep in thought for hours and now needed to get home. As I grabbed my bag and jumped on my bike, I thought of my boys at home. If I wasn't already convinced by the poor results, I was utterly persuaded now that to tell my kids to be more obedient to God or love their sisters more or follow my rules better was not the answer. It would only make the situation worse. So what was a parent to do? At that moment, I wasn't completely sure but I was determined to find out. And the next few weeks would provide a breakthrough.

LIBRARY RETURNS

Half a block from the public library, Michelle and the three kids stopped and turned around. It was now dark. They waited a few seconds, hoping that Jordan would exit the library. She wondered whether she should go back in and drag him out, but she decided against that. When he didn't come out, they turned and went home. No one said a word on the way home. For the first half hour, Michelle's frustration overruled her worry about Jordan's safety. But eventually she grew concerned. Should she go back and get him? Was he safe? She decided to wait a little longer. Fifteen minutes later, Jordan came through the door.

It was the final week of October, and while Michelle had been struggling with Jordan at the library, I had spent the day at Wycliffe. Over two weeks had passed since my time at the Tabard Theatre, and since then I had been in Cape Town, South Africa, for a ten-day conference, The Lausanne Congress on World Evangelization, and had just gotten home two days earlier.

When I returned home that evening from Wycliffe, still tired from my international travel, I greeted Michelle and got the whole library incident story. Michelle was distraught, at the end of her rope and out of answers. I went up to Jordan's room. He looked as if he had seen a ghost. I asked him what happened. "Why did you do it?"

"I don't know Dad," he said. "I just did." He told me that when his mom asked him to go he didn't want to leave, and the harder she pushed, the more he pushed back. He did not want to lose the tug of war.

"Why did you come home?" I asked.

"I don't know. I guess I was bored."

"Mom says you have not apologized," I said.

He agreed. When I pushed him on this, he tried to make excuses for his actions. When this didn't work, he tried to blame his siblings. I kept trying, but I could not get him to admit his wrong.

I sat him down and asked Jonathan to join us. I took out my Bible and read Romans 7, a chapter I had been dwelling on for weeks. As I had learned, I couldn't motivate them by more law. But I wanted them to at least see the struggle that goes on in each of us and that it is a normal part of being a Christian. Paul is writing Romans 7 not from his experience before he is converted, but after he becomes a Christian. I was hoping this might get the boys to drop their defensiveness and admit they were wrong, that they really loved God but struggled to obey him. But although they understood what Paul was saying, it was not hitting home.

"Jordan," I asked, "why is it hard for you to admit you are wrong?"

He paused, looked down at the floor and said, "I don't know. I guess I feel stupid."

"What?" I asked, curiously. He repeated himself. That's when a light went on in my head. Why had I not seen this before? It was now obvious to me. What Jordan struggled with was not guilt over breaking the law, though he knew when he was wrong. His problem was shame. And although they overlap, they are not the same. I could not get him to admit real guilt because shame—feeling stupid at his sin—was clouding his heart. So asking him to take sin seriously, like Whitefield, or to understand the dual nature, like Paul in Romans 7, was not hitting home. For people dealing with guilt, these topics are key, but Jordan already knew he was wrong; his conscience was sensitive. The problem was that he felt shame, so he covered it up. Therefore motivating him by forcing him to admit guilt or try harder to obey did not work. He needed to be liberated from shame. It was then that I remembered something Tim Keller had said, providing the insight I needed at that moment.

INSIGHTS FROM CAPE TOWN

As I sat there in the boys' room, I began telling them about a conversation I had had in Cape Town the week before, at the Lausanne Congress for World Evangelization, with bestselling author and New York City pastor Tim Keller. I had mentioned to Tim that I had gone into London to see *Dr. Jekyll and Mr. Hyde* and that it sparked my thinking on Romans 7. Tim had made the connection between Stevenson and the apostle Paul years ago, and when I mentioned this, his eyes lit up.

"You know," he said to me as we sat in the conference center's main auditorium, "the solution in Romans 7 to the conflict within is not trying to obey the law more, but to realize that we are no longer married to the law. This is the key."

Well, I got the first part of his statement, I told him. But what did he mean with the phrase "married to the law"?

Shifting in his chair, he continued: "Well, marriage, whether it is a healthy one or an unhealthy one, gives us identity. Our spouse, through what she says, has tremendous power to form our identities. When our spouse praises us, we feel good about ourselves. If she is abusive, we feel bad. In the same way," he said, "the law, when we are married to it, gives us our identity. When we keep it, we feel good about ourselves; we feel justified. But when we don't keep it, when we fail, we feel terrible. The law condemns us; it tells us we are bad, and our self crumbles under the weight of its accusations. What is the solution? To divorce the law and marry Christ."

Now, as I sat talking to Jordan and Jonathan, Tim's insight hit home. When Jordan kept the law—obeyed God and his parents—he felt good about himself. But when he disobeyed, he felt terrible about himself. Being bad formed his identity. He needed to divorce the law. He needed to see that he no longer got his identity from the law, especially the accusations. When he sins, which he will, he no longer needs to be controlled by shame. Jordan had an idea in his head of the kind of person he was, and when he disobeyed he failed his own standard. As Dick Keyes has said, "Shame is at root a loss of trust in yourself. You are not so glorious and heroic as you thought. Shame jars your sense of your own identity, your certainty about who you are at some bedrock level." He continues: "Shame strikes directly at our identity by showing us that we are not who we thought we were. It attacks our self-acceptance because at the center of it is the feeling of self-rejection. Shame shrinks your identity." You become that one shameful act.

According to Keyes, we need to see that sin, although real and something we must take responsibility for, does not define us. When we are born again, our core self, the image of God in us, which was shrouded in sin, bursts forth, able to realize its true identity. Yes, sin is still present around the core, trying to sabotage our growth, but it does not define us. The image of God does.

> So I find it to be a law that when I want to do right, evil lies close at hand. For I delight in the law of God, in my inner being, but I see in my members another law waging war against the law of my mind and making me captive to the law of sin that dwells in my members. (Romans 7:21-23)

Once we understand this, we can see the vital role of repentance in allowing us to achieve a certain psychological distance from our sin. Keyes explains: "My sin is mine, but it's not me. I have a power of sin working in me for which I am responsible [and need to repent], but which does not define me or exhaustively sum me up." We can stand back from it, objectivize it and separate our real self from it. As we accept responsibility for our sin and turn away from it, we can hate the sin and accept ourselves.

Jordan's sense of self depended on keeping a certain image of himself as a good person. Every time he sinned and got caught, he had to deny it in order to maintain his self-image. It was a losing and destructive battle. I wanted him to see that he was not married to "being good" or to the effects of "being bad." He is married to Christ, who has freed his inner, core self, which is the image of God, from the control of sin and its destructive power to determine his self-image. His image now comes from Christ and is not undone by the reality of sin that remains in his life, because it no longer controls or defines him: "He is a sinner who can face his sin because he has confidence that God has forgiven and accepted him in spite of it. The acceptance of God is the basis of self-worth."

This self-acceptance in Christ is also the key to motivation. When we know we are accepted no matter how dark our hearts prove to be, we are free to stop covering up. Now married to Christ, we want to love him by serving him. The law then becomes a way of being grateful and living the way God wants us to live—to his glory. In the days ahead this word *glory* was to take on new meaning for my family.

LESSONS FROM NARNIA

It was now October 30, a few days after my insights into the new self. We were huddled in the dining room, the only room on the first floor that had heat. When we left the room to go down the hall to the kitchen for some more tea or hot chocolate, we could see our breath. As we sat around the homeschool table together, Jordan was devouring Will Vaus's *The Hidden Story of Narnia*, underlining key passages. When Will discovered that our children were reading through the entire Narnia series, he sent them an autographed copy. That meant a lot to Jordan. We were enjoying our time reading, drinking tea and hot chocolate and listening to the BBC's classical music station. We had candles lit around the room, compensating for the broken fireplace. There was a calm in the air. But after a while the girls got antsy and began to complain; they were hungry and bored. Jordan and Jonathan joined in the whining: the house was too cold, the weather outside was depressing, the lack of friends was sad.

Here we go again, I thought to myself.

"Ah, ah, ah," Michelle said, trying to cut off their whining before it got worse. "Don't you remember what we talked about? About being grateful?" Michelle, a fabulous read-aloud teacher, had spent the morning enchanting the kids with one of the Chronicles and teaching them the spiritual meaning in the text. But the kids looked puzzled at her question.

"You know, what we learned about not falling under the spell?" Still no response.

"Stomp on the fire," she said.

"Oh yeah, the witch's green potion," said Jonathan, who has tremendous listening comprehension.

"What does *that* mean?" I asked.

Jordan, who had devoured the seven Chronicles, explained that in

Lewis's *The Silver Chair* the Queen of the Underland (the witch) puts a green powder into the fire and starts to play a mandolin. As the fumes rise from the fire and the music plays, the Queen tells the kids that there is no such thing as Narnia, the sun or Aslan. Like all children, they were just dreaming, says the Witch. The only thing real, she says, is the Underland. Slowly they start falling under her spell. But then Puddleglum, realizing the danger they are in, shakes himself from the impending sleep and stomps on the fire, putting it out and ending the witch's spell.

"Stomp on the fire," Meghan said.

At that moment I saw something I had not seen before. When we sin and break God's laws, we hide from our guilt and shame. We do it naturally. But when we do, we let guilt and shame define us. We are just wicked wretches incapable of good, we tell ourselves. And we live out this identity, not trying to obey.

But to believe this was to live under a false spell, to accept a reality that is not true. Paul says that our sin does not define us; it is in us but it is not our true selves. When we are justified in Christ, the image of God is restored in us. And it is glorious, because it reflects God's glory: "And we, who with unveiled faces all reflect the Lord's glory, are being transformed into his likeness with ever-increasing glory, which comes from the Lord, who is the Spirit" (2 Corinthians 3:18 NIV 1984). As John Eldredge says, "Our destiny is to come fully alive. To live with ever-*increasing* glory." And Paul writes, "Those whom he justified he also glorified" (Romans 8:30). In this life, God is transforming us, little by little, to live into this glory, the image of God, in us. He wants to make us fully alive, to reflect and experience his glory.

Yet so many of us don't understand this new identity and thus we remain caught in shame and guilt. This was true for Jordan, and for all of us at times. We don't see the truth, our new reality. We are under a spell; the green powder has done its job. But this is not the end of the story, thank goodness.

In *The Silver Chair*, just before the story of the green powder, Jill and Eustace discover Prince Rilian, who has been abducted by the Queen, put under a spell and made a prisoner in the Underland. He is convinced that the Queen is good and that she has saved him from some evil enchantment, when instead she has enslaved him in her dungeon. He thinks that the one hour each night he spends chained in the silver chair is his hour of madness, but in reality it is his hour of sanity. When the children realize who he is, they free him—with the help of Puddleglum—from the chair, and the spell is broken. Turning to his rescuers, he asks,

> "How long then have I been in the power of the witch?"
>
> "It is more than ten years since your Highness was lost in the wood at the north side of Narnia."
>
> "Ten years!" said the Prince, drawing his hand across his face as if to rub away the past. "Yes, I believe you. For now that I am myself I can remember that enchanted life, though while I was enchanted I could not remember my true self."

His true self has returned.

If this year abroad was about discovering our spiritual roots, then it certainly had to be about helping our children, and us, understand the battle within and how our old nature no longer defines our reality. We have a new self. God is restoring his image in us. And although the battle against the witch's green powder won't cease until the end of the age, we have been created for glory—to experience our true self, both now and in eternity.

Later that night, I shared my new insight with my family. And it was then that I knew what we needed to explore next—the weight of glory that rests on us. To do this, there was no better guide than the don from Magdalen College.

four

THE WEIGHT
OF GLORY

C. S. Lewis and the Power of Story

As winter cold penetrated the room, six undergraduates and tutors huddled around the hearth in the warm glow of the fire and clouds of pipe smoke. They told stories, laughed and enjoyed each other's company. But they were having a hard time; C. S. Lewis, whom they called Jack, remained grave.

Leaning over to his friend and fellow tutor Hugo Dyson, Lewis complained, "I am not a philosopher."

"Nobody said you were, Jack; you are a man of letters," said Dyson.

Lewis's sour mood had begun two days earlier, at the weekly meeting of the Socratic Club, which had been formed to intellectually defend Christianity against the best atheistic minds at Oxford. On February 2, 1948, Lewis, the club's president, engaged in a vigorous debate with Elizabeth Anscombe, a young tutor at Somerville College. Though a fellow believer (she was a committed Catholic), she had come to refute a key point in his book *Miracles*, published the year before. Anscombe was bigger than life. She smoked cigars, wore trousers (when the style of the day was skirts) and was already considered a brilliant philosopher. One day she would go on to a distinguished career at Cambridge University. She was one of the few people in Oxford who could match Lewis intellectually and charismatically.

It had been said that "nobody could put Lewis down" at the Socratic Club. But Anscombe certainly tried, and by many accounts she shredded Lewis's critique of naturalism. He was not ready for her strong attack, and even some of his supporters found his response weak. Afterward he was in low spirits and later he told a friend that his own "argument for the existence of God had been demolished." He believed that he had let his fellow Christians down, leaving doubt in their minds that Christianity could be defended rationally.

Lewis biographer A. N. Wilson contended that Lewis was so psychologically damaged that he gave up on apologetics books and sheepishly retreated into writing children's fairy tales, even turning Anscombe into the demonized Green Witch in *The Silver Chair*. Other critics also claimed that the defeat shattered Lewis's confidence in the reasonableness of Christianity, something he had defended since his conversion as a young professor almost two decades earlier. Had this debate shaken his faith and shifted his writing plans? Or was something else brewing in his life?

SEARCHING FOR LEWIS

We walked under the Tower of the Five Orders, adorned by pinnacles shaped like spires looking as if they could touch the heavens. We crossed the small quadrangle and entered the door of the library. As we climbed the wooden stairs to the Duke Humphreys Library, my boys started counting.

It was the first week of November, a couple of weeks after Michelle's parents, Fred and Marna Miller (who had stayed with my family while I was in South Africa), had returned to California, and Michelle sensed that we needed to lighten the mood in the family, especially with the boys. With the stress over homeschooling (still an unresolved topic of conversation) and the struggle over obedience, October had been an intense month for the boys. She believed that they needed some fun time with their Dad—to explore, to laugh together and to enjoy one another in a less charged environment. Michelle had strong intuition, and she knew when things were out of balance in the family, so I took her wise advice.

As I thought about the month, I reminded myself that this pilgrimage was about rediscovering our roots. Part of this rediscovery was to answer the questions "Who am I?" and "Where do I find meaning?" One of my goals for the fall in Oxford was to help my boys to know themselves so well that they never placed their identity in a "lock box" when they arrived at college. The "feel good, do good" religion of Moralistic Therapeutic Deism provides no resources for young people to develop a healthy sense of self rooted in the historic, orthodox faith. So when they get to college their weak identities crumble in the face of the liturgy of university culture.

After a month of talks on resisting the dark side of the self, I wanted to focus on the "new self," celebrating the transformation that the gospel brings to our lives. We are "new creations"; we have a new identity, and we are no longer defined by the old self. We need to experience this more.

Since my boys were already reading the Narnia tales and I was spending lots of time at Wycliffe rereading Lewis's books, I thought it would be a good month to explore his life and writings. Michelle had begun reading to the kids the children's biography *C. S. Lewis: The Story Teller,* and I began planning our Lewis pilgrimage for the next month.

"Sixty-one steps," Jonathan said as we got to the top of the stairs, winded from the climb.

A short gate blocked the entrance to the library. I handed my library card to the attendant at the desk and turned to my boys, admonishing them to whisper. As we went through the gate, I pointed to the ceiling, which was painted with open books and crests; medieval portraits covered the walls. Study desks joined to bookcases came out of the walls at right angles. The room smelled of must and slowly decaying old books. To write his *English Literature in the Sixteenth Century*, Lewis read every book in the library on medieval and renaissance literature. He loved it here, spending hours each day in the summer months researching books and preparing his tutorials. He thought it was "one of the most delightful places in the world."

Since my college days many years ago, Lewis has been one of my great heroes—a role model for my faith. Right after college, when I was teaching English in China, I read William Griffin's biography of Lewis, *A Dramatic Life,* and it brought Lewis alive to me. I enjoyed the experience so deeply that I would limit myself to just one of the thirty-nine chapters each day, milking the experience for as long as I could. On those warm autumn afternoons in China, Lewis became for me, in his life and writings, the picture of human flourishing and the true self that I longed to capture in my own life. I was twenty-three years old, testing and trying my faith, looking for role models to show me what my life could really be like if I lived it in Christ. Lewis became my example; his life of the mind, his power of imagination, his joy of living captured me like no one else. When I finished Griffin's book, I was sad, as though I was parting with a good friend.

So as I walked around the Duke Humphreys with my boys, I wanted Lewis to be a hero for them as well, a role model who understood the struggle within but also knew how to experience God's glory, a renewed sense of self that gives meaning and purpose. So often my boys, like all of us, struggled with the wrong model of what it means to be a Christian. They needed a new vision, a new story that would empower them to live obediently and experience their true selves. Lewis, through his life, the lessons he learned and the books he created—particularly his Narnia tales—provided just the stories in which to bathe our imaginations. I was excited about the month ahead.

When J. R. R. Tolkien and Hugo Dyson arrived at Lewis's rooms in September 1931, they were anxious for conversation. After dinner, the air unusually warm and still for this time of year in Oxford, the three exited the eighteenth-century neoclassical New Building and strolled across a footbridge over the Cherwell River to Addison's Walk. Weaving their way around the large deer park and acres of dense forest, the three picked up their conversation on metaphor and myth.

Over the last few years they had spent hundreds of hours talking about the great myths of literature, which they all loved, and how those myths related to Christianity. Tolkien and Dyson were believers. Lewis was not. Whatever semblance of faith Lewis once had, he had lost it as a teenager. Since then he had been an atheist, a believer in the power of natural reason. But cracks, however small, had begun to appear in his armor. The more he read of medieval and renaissance literature (with its "dynamic adventurousness"), the more his heart was stirred by ideas he was supposed to hate. And when he tried to read fellow atheists, he was left cold.

All this reading, and the conversations he was having with his friend Tolkien, a professor at Pembroke College, changed his mind about the existence of God. It led to a dramatic step in his life.

"You must picture me alone in that room in Magdalen," Lewis would write years later, "night after night, feeling, whenever my mind lifted even for a second from my work, the steady, unrelenting approach of Him whom I so earnestly desired not to meet. That which I greatly feared had at last come upon me. In the Trinity Term of 1929 I gave in, and admitted that God was God, and knelt and prayed: perhaps, that night, the most dejected and reluctant convert in all England."

But although he believed in God's existence, he still did not believe in Jesus Christ. He was a theist but not a Christian. The change brought new joys: he marveled at the beauty of creation and delighted in the natural world and its Creator. He was filled with a new gusto for life. But the more he tried to live a life pleasing to his Creator, the more frustrated he got. His pride, his selfishness and his sin got in the way. He was amazed at the wickedness of his own heart. Years later, he would create the character Eustace Scrubb in *The Voyage of the Dawn Treader*, who, after his pride turned him into a dragon, couldn't shed his dragon skin; only Aslan, the Christ figure, could do it for him. Lewis began to realize that the only antidote to his pride was Christ. But he had a problem. For Lewis, Jesus was a myth. He struggled the most with the resurrection of Christ, unsure how the death of one person so long ago explained anything.

As they meandered Addison's Walk with the wind picking up, they continued to talk about myth. Lewis contended that myths were for children, not adults. Myths were lies, even if they were beautiful, "breathed through silver."

Tolkien disagreed. He contended that, even if they were not completely true, they contained elements of the truth; they were still vehicles of moral and spiritual reality. Lewis countered that myths were wish projections, created by people to cope with life and satisfy a longing for joy. But Tolkien pushed back, asking him how a desire for joy exists in a biological animal made up of water and chemicals. Myth, said Tolkien, demonstrates that we are more than biological—we have longings for joy and love and meaning, and only myth can satisfy those longings, only myth can meet our deepest needs.

Lewis was not convinced; he brought up the doctrine of redemption in Christianity. Surely this was a myth too? He could not see how the life and death of someone else two thousand years ago could help now. He found the idea of sacrifice shocking.

But what was wrong with sacrifice? countered Tolkien. Nothing, said Lewis, when it is found in the pagan myths. But the idea seems out of place in the gospel. Why couldn't the story of Christ be construed as a myth, argued Tolkien and Dyson, but a myth that is true—that is, a myth that moved them deeply in the same way as the others, but this time

Addison's Walk, Magdalen College, Oxford

with an important difference: that it really happened?

Around midnight, with rain threatening, the three friends returned to Lewis's rooms and talked till 3:00 a.m. Lewis was becoming more certain that the Christian story had to be seen in the same way that he saw other myths and that it was—as he said later in a letter to his friend Arthur Greeves—"the most important [of them all] and full of meaning."

After Tolkien went home to his wife, Dyson, who was spending the night, went for another walk with Lewis. Passing up and down the colonnade under the New Building, Dyson kept pressing home the point that Christianity, though a story, was a true story, and that Lewis was being asked to join the adventure. By the end of the night, Lewis was close to believing and would make the step a week later. As he said twelve days later in a letter to Greeves, "I have just passed on from believing in God to definitely believing in Christ—in Christianity." And "my long talk with Dyson and Tolkien had a good deal to do with it."

Along with a newfound faith, he had a new calling: to spend his life defending the faith and helping others move from rationalism to belief in the true myth, the story that really happened—Christianity. In the years ahead, this calling would take some unexpected twists and turns.

After his conversion in 1931, Lewis's days were filled with tutorials, academic lectures and scholarly essays. He also wrote books. With the publication of *The Allegory of Love: A Study in Medieval Tradition* in 1936 and *A Preface to Paradise Lost* in 1941, he distinguished himself as a world-class scholar and popular lecturer at the university.

When World War II arrived, many saw it as a disruption of their lives. Lewis, however, saw it differently: "I daresay," he wrote Arthur Greeves, "for me, personally, it has come in the nick of time: I was just beginning to get too well settled in my profession, too successful, and probably self complacent."

Unlike many in Europe at the time, he recognized right away the evil of Hitler and the need to stop him. Too old to enlist, he joined the Oxford City Home Guard Battalion, patrolling Oxford with a rifle every Saturday from 1:30 to 4:30 a.m, looking for German paratroopers. In 1941, he volunteered to lecture the men and women of the Royal Air Force. This post took him all over the country and took up a great deal of his time.

Yet it was a book he wrote at the very start of the war, in the autumn of 1940, that affected his life the most. When Dr. James Welch, director of religious broadcasting at the BBC, read Lewis's *The Problem of Pain*, he immediately wrote Lewis and asked him to go on the air. From 1941 to 1944 Lewis gave over three dozen live talks on the basics of Christianity, which were widely successful. George Sayer recalled, "I remember being at a pub filled with soldiers on one Wednesday evening. At a quarter to eight, the bartender turned the radio up for Lewis. 'You listen to this bloke,' he shouted. 'He's really worth listening to.' And those soldiers did listen attentively for the entire fifteen minutes."

But Lewis found it difficult to work with the BBC, particularly recording live at night in London and having to return to Oxford by train. He often got in well after midnight, waking still exhausted the next day, and the fatigue began to take a toll on his health. He was also inundated with letters from listeners—"a daily cascade of letters from angry, worried, confused, bemused, curious and grateful listeners." This deluge would continue to the end of his life. When the burden became too great—he sometimes answered thirty-five letters a day—Lewis asked his brother, Warren, to help with the correspondence.

While giving talks for the BBC, lecturing for the RAF and patrolling Oxford each weekend, he continued to write books. From 1942 to 1945, he published *The Screwtape Letters, The Abolition of Man* and *The Great Divorce,* and his thirty-three broadcast talks as *Mere Christianity*. These books brought him greater fame and additional letters, squeezing his time and energy even more. He still had a full load of tutorials, academic lectures and writing. Though he enjoyed the fame and the thrill of being one of the most famous defenders of the faith, he began to reach a breaking point.

Not only was he physically exhausted, often struggling with painful, chronic sinus infections, but the fame was perilous for his soul. He had reached astonishing heights of fame for a college professor. He had become the voice of Christianity for his generation, explaining it, defending it and representing it to millions of people. But for someone who struggled with pride, it was a dangerous place to be.

Magdalen Chapel

On November 24, the weather wet and cold, we sat in Magdalen Chapel and waited for Evensong, led by the famous Magdalen College Boys Choir. Michelle, Jordan, Jonathan and I were with Michael Ward, the well-known Lewis scholar who was chaplain of St. Peter's College and the author of the groundbreaking *Planet Narnia*. At forty-two, he exudes charm, grace and a passion for all things Lewis, even reciting Lewis's poetry at any opportune time. Michael and I had just spent a couple of hours walking around Oxford talking about Lewis. Michelle and the boys had taken the bus to meet us.

Smaller and more intimate than most college chapels in Oxford, the Magdalen Chapel was built in the 1470s. Its chancel has five bays with projecting buttresses surmounted by pinnacles. There are three sections of pews facing each other on either side, the middle section of which was filled by the boys' choir. I could see our ten-year-old neighbor James, who was part of the choir, out of the corner of my eye.

As the boys sang liturgy, their young voices echoing off the ceiling, I was surrounded by whispers of the transcendent—the voices, the lighting, the soaring architecture of the chapel. They sang from Psalm 131:

> O LORD, my heart is not lifted up;
> my eyes are not raised too high;
> I do not occupy myself with things
> too great and too marvelous for me.
> But I have calmed and quieted my soul,
> like a weaned child with its mother;
> like a weaned child is my soul within me. (Psalm 131:1-2)

As Michael reminded me, Lewis loved worshiping in this chapel. He attended morning prayer each day at 8:00 a.m. and many evenings participated in Evensong. Daily worship grounded him, particularly the reading of the Psalms, which reminded him who God was and what the Christian life looked like. The Psalms, especially Psalm 131, reminded him that he shouldn't think too much of himself.

In the early 1940s Lewis knew he was struggling with pride. We get a glimpse of this in his BBC talk "The Great Sin," during which he says, "I wish I had got a bit further with humility myself: If I had, I could probably tell you more about the relief, the comfort, of . . . getting rid of the false self, with all its 'Look at me' and 'Aren't I a good boy?' and all its posing and posturing." In diagnosing pride, Lewis's keen insights into the human condition seem to have come from firsthand experience—from someone who knew his own heart well and understood that often he posed and postured in order to be accepted and prove to God that he was worthy of his favor.

I had been trying to show my boys the danger of pride. I pointed out that shame is at the core of our struggle to confess wrong. We just don't like admitting that we are the kind of person who would do such a thing. But this shame is really pride masquerading as humility. How do we overcome pride though? Michelle and I tell our boys to practice being humble or to serve their sisters even when they don't feel like it.

"But I feel fake when I do something I don't want to," Jordan says. "I just don't want to fake it."

Now, I appreciate the boys' desire to be authentic, to avoid hypocrisy. But they were missing the point. Or maybe we weren't being clear. When Paul says to "put on Christ," we should do it even when we don't feel like it; because we are already "in Christ." Though we don't have the feelings, we put on Christ out of obedience and commitment.

Lewis understood this. In one of his final BBC talks, "Let's Pretend," he referred to "dressing up as Christ." We play the part even though we don't feel like it, and as we do, we begin to take on the role as our true selves. "Even though you don't feel like it," Michelle said to the boys, "serve your sisters, and before you know it you will not only enjoy being a servant but it will feel like second nature. This is how godly habits are created."

Yet Lewis pointed out that our ability to develop humility or other virtues does not come from our own moral effort. He was not an Aristotelian. When you "put on Christ," Lewis said, he "is actually at your side and is already at that moment beginning to turn your pretense into a reality." That is how we change, how we become virtuous. What Christ is doing is "killing the old natural self in you and replacing it with the kind of self He has." Thus the more we "pretend" in faith, the more Christ remakes us into the most authentic people possible. This is the paradox I wanted my boys to see. "The more we get what we now call 'ourselves' out of the way," Lewis said in one of his final broadcast talks, "and let Him take us over, the more truly ourselves we become."

But as Lewis knew, this "losing" was not easy. He admitted as much in his BBC talks. He was struggling to live what he believed about pride and the self. And the circumstances in his life—the rigorous schedule, his exhaustion and his newfound fame—were not helping the matter.

We were halfway through Evensong. The boys' choir was singing Psalm 132: "Remember, O LORD, . . . all the hardships . . . endured." I thought of Lewis's hardships and was reminded that God often uses our trials as a way to wake us up and move us to depend on him more. "God whispers to us in our pleasures," said Lewis in *The Problem of Pain*, "speaks in our conscience, but shouts in our pain; it is His megaphone to rouse a deaf world."

My boys were finding this out in their struggles in Oxford, just as Lewis discovered it in his famous debate with Anscombe.

Lewis's contribution to the war effort did not stop with Guard Battalion, lectures for the RAF or radio talks for the BBC. Like many people outside London, Lewis and his brother, Warren, took in children who'd been evacuated from London for the duration of the war. The Kilns, the name of Lewis's house, had received four girls the day after Germany invaded Poland. From then on, they had a steady stream of young children staying in their home. Although Jack had no children of his own, he learned to love these children and discovered how to communicate with them, something that would come in handy after the war was over. But in the meantime, the in-

The Kilns, Lewis's home for three decades

creased housework at the Kilns from taking care of these children added to his burden. He was often sick and had to work despite chronic pain.

He also wrote a new book on a subject that was often an obstacle to belief. But unlike his other books on apologetics, *Miracles* was not a success. According to his friend George Sayer, the "main argument is suspect." In the book, Lewis argues that naturalism is self-contradictory—its faith in reason runs counter to its belief that human thinking is the product of irrational causes. "If this is true, Lewis pointed out, then human thought itself is irrational and so too naturalism."

During the famous debate in 1948, Anscombe contended that the argument, though not completely wrong, was flawed. The audience was divided on who won the debate, but commentators have said Anscombe defeated Lewis, at least on this one crucial point.

Some have argued that Lewis was so devastated by the debate that he never wrote apologetics again. "Lewis had learnt his lesson," said Humphrey Carpenter. "For after this he wrote no further books of Christian apologetics. . . . Though he continued to believe in the importance of Reason in relation to his Christian faith, he had perhaps realized the truth of Charles Williams' maxim, 'No one can possibly do more than decide what to believe.'" But Carpenter's words aren't completely accurate. Lewis did not abandon apologetics entirely. Two years after the debate, he reworked the argument in *Miracles* and later republished it, responding directly to the points made by Anscombe. He also wrote a number of articles defending the faith, and he continued to speak weekly at the Socratic Club.

But even if it is wrong to say that Lewis abandoned apologetics—for clearly he did not—he was certainly humbled by the debate with Anscombe. As Sayer wrote years later, "The debate had been a humiliating experience, but perhaps it was ultimately good for him. In the past, he had been far too proud of his logical ability. Now he was humbled. He had been cheered on by the crowd of admirers at the Socratic Club, often young women who regarded him as the great defender of Christianity, almost like a knight of the Round Table."

It is possible, then, that he was coming face to face with his pride. He had to internalize his own lessons from his BBC talks. But something else was at play, something bigger than just relearning lessons on humility. "It seems almost certain," writes Alan Jacobs, "that at some point in these dark years Lewis remembered how he himself had become a Christian. Argument played a role, to be sure, but a largely preparatory one." Arguments may have cleared away intellectual objections, but what he had really wanted was a "positive vision of a story that he could inhabit." He must have remembered that it was his long conversation around Addison's Walk with Tolkien and Dyson that softened his hard heart. Jacobs writes, "He became a Christian not through accepting a particular set of arguments but through learning to read a story the right way. And maybe others could move closer to Christian belief by the same path."

So he returned to an idea that had been brewing in his mind for years: writing children's stories. He would still be doing apologetics, but it would be more like pre-apologetics. It would give him a chance to tell the story of Christianity in myth and legend—to awaken the imaginations of his readers to the glories of the Story. For Lewis, who was tired and discouraged, it meant a return to the kind of stories he had loved since he was a child, a return to delight.

Ironically, Jacobs believes, it was the war and the presence of the evacuees at the Kilns that provided the inspiration, years before the debate with Anscombe, to write children's stories. When the evacuees complained of how bored and unhappy they were, Lewis realized that because they had never had the great fairy tales read to them as children, their imaginations had been malnourished. They were incapable of entertaining themselves. And without robust imaginations they were certain to become the "men without chests" he describes in *The Abolition of Man*. What these children lacked was a moral education. Lewis decided he could provide one through stories.

THE EAGLE AND CHILD

We ducked through a narrow door, passing under a painted sign that depicted a bird carrying a baby swaddled in a sheet. Down the wood-paneled hallway, past two cramped but cozy rooms, we emerged into the heart of the Eagle and Child pub. It smelled of beer and fish and chips, and it was full with university students. It was December 8 and we had brought our kids for dessert at one of the key spots on the Lewis trail. Jordan had finished the Narnia series, Jonathan had read four, and the girls had seen the first two movies in the series, so it was a good time to make a pilgrimage.

On our right was the bar, serving a range of local brews. On our left was a small sitting area, framed by a fireplace on one wall and a row of pictures on the other. The photos captured the pub's most famous patrons: Lewis, Tolkien, Charles Williams and other members of the Inklings, a group of Oxford professors and writers who gathered to enjoy good beer and stimulating conversation every Tuesday morning. A plaque indicated that this was the exact spot where the Inklings gathered.

I pointed to the pictures of the Inklings, including one of Tolkien. Although my boys had not yet started *The Lord of the Rings* trilogy, they had seen parts of the movies. It is well known that Tolkien was

The Eagle and Child

not a big fan of the Narnia books (he contended that Lewis wrongly combined figures from different mythologies, for example, placing Father Christmas in *The Lion, the Witch and the Wardrobe*). Yet he and Lewis shared similar views on the purpose of myth. They both believed that good fairy tales and myths baptize our imaginations, especially when we're children. As Lewis wrote, "Fairy land arouses a longing for [a child] knows not what. It stirs and troubles him (to his lifelong enrichment) with the dim sense of something beyond his reach and, far from dulling or emptying the actual world, gives it a new dimension of depth."

Lewis believed fairy tales begin to work on our hearts and minds, calling us to grander things; they stir a longing in us for heaven, our true home. Baylor Professor Ralph Wood, who teaches and writes on Tolkien, says that many of his students "have confessed that they feel 'clean' after reading *The Lord of the Rings*." What they are referring to, says Wood, is "not chiefly to the book's avoidance of decadent sex but . . . to its bracing moral power: its power to lift them out of the small-minded obsessions of the moment and into the perennial concerns of the ethical and spiritual life."

We continued past the Inklings' spot down a long hallway. Years after the Inklings met here, the pub expanded to make room for more patrons. As we settled into our seats and scanned the dessert menu, we began talking about the movie *The Voyage of the Dawn Treader,* which we had just come from seeing.

"What was your favorite character?" Michelle asked.

"Reepicheep," said Meghan, who adores animals of any kind and asks me almost every day when we can get a cat or dog. Michelle thinks Meghan will be a veterinarian someday. She may be right. "He is so cute," Meghan said about the sword-wielding mouse.

The others agreed. We talked about his duel with Eustace and the funny things Reepicheep says and how over time he becomes a mentor and friend to Eustace. The Chronicles make it easy to initiate conversations about all kinds of meaningful topics. Lewis knew this. Myth had captured his heart, and led him to see the gospel story as the most truthful and meaningful myth of all. For this reason, he filled the stories with meaningful scenes that capture children's imaginations.

He also knew that when he was a child, the obligations of church and the pressure to believe certain things aroused in him resistance, both to authority and to the clinical nature of church teaching. But stories broke through these defenses. "I thought I saw," he wrote, "how stories of this kind could steal past certain inhibitions which had paralyzed much of my own religion in childhood. . . . But supposing that by casting all these things into an imaginary world, stripping them of their stained-glass and Sunday School associations, one could make them for the first time appear in their real potency? Could one not thus steal past those watchful dragons?" Lewis believed they could and thus wrote seven books with which he hoped to baptize the minds of children around the world.

MOVIE NIGHT IN OXFORD

I read somewhere that as much as the *Dawn Treader* is about the transformation of Eustace Scrubb, it is also about the great virtues and how we obtain them. Gilbert Mielaender writes that the Narnia tales "are not just good stories. . . . Rather, they serve to enhance moral education, to build character. They teach, albeit indirectly, and provide us with exemplars from whom we learn proper emotional responses."

Moral education, writes Bill David, needs instruction, role models and habits. The three areas are connected. Moral instruction, which includes the theological foundations of Christianity, is the first step. But these foundations are best taught not in abstract terms but through role models. Christian Smith, in his in-depth study of youth, discovered that parents are the most important teachers in children's spiritual lives because they serve as role models. But role models can also be other adults in the church or characters in books or movies. When instruction is communicated or embodied in a role model, it shapes the imagination, which leads to new habits and dispositions, ways of acting that become "second nature." The goal of moral education, Lewis taught, was to train proper emotional responses or habits.

As I sat there watching the movie a few hours earlier, seeing the characters in various situations, I was reminded of how hard it is to respond in the proper emotional way to life's challenges. And if this is true for adults, it is even truer for kids. Throughout the movie, the children are challenged to respond appropriately, to forge the correct emotional responses until they become habits. Many times they fail, and this was good for my kids to see. That is where forgiveness and grace come in. The Bible is filled with role models, but they don't always do the right thing. In fact, many of the characters in the Bible fail miserably. Yet in their failure they learn to rely more on grace. Stories like the Narnia tales can teach us in a similar way. As Gregory Bassham points out, the goal of good moral education is to surround our children with stories that "engage our moral imagination, provide vivid moral exemplars and activate our affections in ways that instruction or reasoned discourse (especially when directed at children) often does not." I agree.

Lucy has always been my favorite character in the Chronicles. I am inspired by her joy in coming to Narnia, her ability to see Aslan when the others cannot and her desire to stay in Narnia. In the *Dawn Treader*, the Narnians are captured by invisible people who force Lucy to sneak into the mansion, locate the Magician's book and find the spell that will make them visible again. Amazingly, she is willing to do it, to sacrifice for others, making the decision as if it was second nature. When the others protest, Reepicheep, the fearless mouse, affirms her decision like a good mentor.

After some time searching she finds the magic book. She opens it, discovering its magnificent beauty, which stirs her deepest desire and imagination. After a few moments of flipping through the enchanted pages, she comes upon a spell that will make her beautiful. Lucy has always struggled with being less beautiful than her sister, Susan, and here is a spell that will give her what she always wanted. She knows it would be wrong to say the spell, that she is being tempted with an idol, but she wants to say it anyway.

At that moment in the movie I hoped my kids were paying close attention. They needed to learn this lesson. But frankly, so did I. Like Lucy, I had struggled with my identity and wanting to look better in the eyes of others, whether it was through my career, my writings or in my family. I was riveted to the scene.

Lucy resists the temptation, but only temporarily; she tears out the page and stuffs it under her cloak. Then she hears a lion roar.

"Lucy, Lucy," a deep voice says in disappointment and warning.

"Aslan? . . . Aslan?" Lucy asks.

Then Lucy turns the page and the movie goes in another direction. How would they resolve this, I wondered. I did not have to wait long. A few scenes later, when she is alone in her room on the *Dawn Treader,* she takes out the page and she says the spell. As she gazes at her new beauty in the mirror, she pushes on the mirror and discovers that it opens, like a door, into a new world. She is now Susan, surrounded by adoring fans and her two brothers. But immediately, she discovers that no one knows Lucy; she does not exist. Horrified, she wakes from the dream. Aslan is standing beside her.

"You wished away yourself," Aslan says. "Your brothers and sister would not know Narnia without you. You discovered it first."

"I am so sorry," she says.

"You doubt your value," says Aslan. "Don't run from who you are."

It is a powerful scene, well written and shot. But it's only half true. Yes, she fails to see her value and runs from herself. But the movie gives the impression that she can generate these qualities herself—a kind of feel-good self-esteem lesson. Just believe in yourself. The book, however, does not portray it that way. When she is tempted to say the beauty spell, she sees Aslan's face on the page and hears him growl. She turns the page, frightened by Aslan and chastised for her moral lapse. Right then, she discovers a spell "for the refreshment of the spirit." It's more a story than a spell, going on for three or four pages. After a while she realizes she is living in the story as if it were real. She wants to relive it but the pages only turn forward, not backward, and this makes her sad. Finally she gives up, finds the spell to make all things visible, and says it. To her surprise, Aslan appears.

She asks him, "Shall I ever be able to read that story again? Will you tell it to me, Aslan? Oh do, do, do."

"Indeed, yes," he says, "I will tell it to you for years and years."

Oh, tell me the old, old story, the hymn writer once said. Lewis makes clear that experiencing this story is the key: once Lucy realizes that she is a child of God, adopted into his family, forgiven and redeemed, she will know that in Aslan's eyes she is the most beautiful girl in the world. She is made for glory and she can experience it now. Aslan wants her to be so captivated by the message of Narnia that she can resist temptation and, as if it is second nature, accept herself and live as she is meant to live—in the magic of God. Only the Story, heard, internalized and practiced over and over again, can truly change us and make us into moral creatures. The movie misses this powerful point.

As I watched the rest of the movie, I realized how deeply grateful I was for Lewis's fairy tales and the impact they were having on my kids, allowing the truth of the stories to "steal past those watchful dragons" put up by the "old self."

THE KILNS

Arriving at the Kilns around noon on December 1, I dropped my bags at the house and headed out for a walk, wanting to avoid the snowstorm due later that afternoon. I headed over to Shelly's Pond, a place where Lewis loved to go skinny-dipping on warm summer mornings. I walked around the pond and headed up the small hill, trying not to slip on the icy snow. From the top of the hill, I headed up a wooden path that went "further up and further in," dissecting two farms, passing a few horses. Eventually I arrived at Shotover Hill Park, a destination that often drew Lewis. Standing there looking down toward Oxford, I thought of how much he enjoyed his walking tours, some of them four or five days long covering as many as twenty miles a day. He soaked in the beauty of God's creation and the company of friends on these tours. Lewis loved God, he loved nature, and he loved his friends. And the more he became his true self, the more he enjoyed the life God had for him. He had discovered true delight. As Lewis once wrote to his dear friend Arthur Greeves, "My happiest hours are spent with three or four old friends in old clothes tramping together and putting up in small pubs—or else sitting up till the small hours in someone's college rooms, talking nonsense, poetry, theology, metaphysics over beer, tea, and pipes. There's no sound I like better than male laughter."

When I returned to the Kilns, the sun already setting at 3:00 p.m., Debbie Higgens, the warden of the Kilns, made me a pot of tea and passed me a plate of her homemade cookies. Her hospitality was on display in every room, making the Kilns warm and inviting. We talked for hours about this house, what it meant to Jack and his brother, Warnie, and what made it so special today for the scholars in residence and others who have the privilege of visiting it. "There is just a feeling one gets," she said, "when one is here. There is goodness here."

Later that night as I sat alone in the common room, a place where Jack and Warnie passed many an evening, I came across a letter Jack had written shortly after moving into the Kilns: "This house has a good night atmosphere about it: in the sense that I have never been in a place where one is less likely to get the creeps: a place less sinister. Good life must have been lived here before us. If it is haunted, it is haunted by good spirits, perhaps such things are the result of fantasy, yet the feelings are real." His sentiments rang true for me that night.

As I sat by the fireplace, I thought of Lewis's words in *Mere Christianity*, "Until you have given up your self to Him you will not have a real self." It was in this house that Lewis learned that it was "no good trying to 'be myself' without Him." He had lost his life only to find it in God. Becoming the self that God intends—this is the journey I have been on for over two decades, and it is the reality I am trying to impress on my kids.

While thinking about these things, I went to the kitchen to refresh my tea. The pot sat on the old stove, staying warm. As I walked back to the common room to keep reading, I realized that it was in this house, the place where so many of Lewis's best books were penned, that the old ache of longing had been met for him. I reached over to the side table and grabbed a copy of his essay "The Weight of Glory," originally preached in St. Mary's church. No essay of his has meant more to me. My eyes alighted on this paragraph: "We want something else which can hardly be put into words—to be united with the beauty we see, to pass into it, to receive it into ourselves, to bathe in it, to become part of it." To become part of it, I thought—this is what happens when we flourish in Christ, when we are reborn daily with him; we become part of this beauty. And along the way, we experience our true selves. We become who he created us to be in all our individuality. I continued to read: "What would it be to taste," he ponders, "at the fountainhead that stream of which even these lower reaches prove so intoxicating? Yet that, I believe, is what lies before us. The whole man is to drink from the fountain of joy."

What we seek, however, can only be found in the recognition or approval of God. Lewis writes:

> It is written that we shall "stand before" Him, shall appear, shall be inspected. The promise of Glory is the promise, almost incredibly and only possible by the work of Christ, that some of us, that any of us who really chooses, shall actually survive that examination, shall find approval, shall please God. To please God . . . to be a real ingredient in the divine happiness . . . to be loved by God, not merely pitied, but delighted in as an artist delights in his work or a father in his son—it seems impossible, a weight or burden of glory which our thoughts can hardly sustain. But so it is.

So this is the key to the true self, to human flourishing: finding our acceptance in God and being approved by him. It is the source of freedom, joy, contentment. It is the way we become ourselves, safe in God's divine approbation, living life to the fullest under his fatherly care. I was being reminded that night in the Kilns that God's glory, his approval, is what sustains us and what transforms us; it is what makes us virtuous: "God became man to turn creatures into sons: not simply to produce better men of the old kind but to produce a new kind of man. It is not like teaching a horse to jump better and better but like turning a horse into a winged creature."

It was now after midnight. The Kilns was quiet. As much as I did not want the night to end, I knew I had to get some sleep. I turned off the lights in the common room, switched off the Christmas decorations on the mantel and headed up the narrow stairs to Jack's bedroom, my room for the night. I got into bed and lay there for about forty-five minutes, looking at the ceiling and thinking about how Jack had looked at this same ceiling for thirty years. In the morning there would be a wonderful breakfast prepared by Debbie, more reading of

Lewis's bedroom at the Kilns

Lewis's writings and then a walk down the back alleys to Holy Trinity Church, where Jack and Warnie worshiped and where they are buried. But right then, I did not want the moment to end. I could not come this way a second time.

Before drifting off, I remembered that Jack was plagued by nightmares, sleep not always the most pleasant experience, and I thought of a passage from his BBC talks, now part of *Mere Christianity*:

> What we have been told is how we . . . can be drawn into Christ—can become part of that wonderful present which the young Prince of the universe wants to offer to His Father—that present which is Himself and therefore us in Him. It is the only thing we were made for. And there are strange, exciting hints in the Bible that when we are drawn in, a great many other things in Nature will begin to come right. The bad dream will be over: it will be morning.

Earth will have become the real Narnia. Suffering will not be the last word; morning will be eternal, and our true selves and all of creation will be made right. I rolled over and went to sleep, comforted with the thought that someday all our bad dreams will be no more and that fairy stories still come true.

five

THE CALL

*William Wilberforce and Two Conversations
That Changed History*

When a well-rested and much-changed William Wilberforce, member of the British Parliament, returned in September 1785 from a year of traveling in the French Riviera with family and a good friend, he was in great emotional turmoil. Once the life of the party, he now refused to go to the theater, turning down invitations. That October, tormented by thoughts of a squandered life—wasted youth, wasted years at Cambridge and, up to this point, wasted time in Parliament—he began to rise early, no longer sleeping the mornings away. He spent time alone, meditating, strolling the gardens, contemplating his future, overwhelmed with the reality of his sinfulness, his lack of stewardship. "For months I was in a state of deepest depression," wrote Wilberforce.

For three months he remained in seclusion at his estate in Wimbledon, avoiding all contact with friends or associates, afraid of what they would think about him, as if he had become a social pariah. When William Pitt, the prime minister, invited him to visit, he declined. When Pitt unexpectedly showed up in Wimbledon, Wilberforce fumed.

Finally, at the end of November, he could not continue this way any longer and wrote to his friends, explaining in detail what had happened to him while on his lengthy trip, a trip that resulted in the great change in his life. One recipient threw the letter into the fire, disgusted with the content. Another wrote back, contending Wilberforce was just depressed and needed to spend more time with people. But the letter he got back from his dear friend Pitt, magnanimously sympathetic, assured Wilberforce that nothing could change the bond they had and led to a cascade of events that would affect the lives of millions of people.

THE GREAT HALL

Sensing that our kids were slightly depressed by cabin fever, a friend from St. Ebbes, a student at Christ Church, invited our family to be her guest for the Sunday brunch at the Great Hall. So the first Sunday in December, we climbed the grand stone staircase of the Hall, the kids immediately recognizing it from the first Harry Potter movie as the place where Mrs. McGonagall meets Harry and the other new students, ushering them into the Hall for the Sorting Hat Ceremony. We entered the Hall, passing a portrait of Lewis Carroll on our right. Our friend pointed out the brass characters in the grand fireplace that are featured in *Alice's Adventures in Wonderland*. But our kids were more interested in Harry and his friends.

They looked at the long tables. "There are only three," said Jonathan, "but in the movie there are four long tables for the four houses."

"That's right," I said, explaining to them that the moviemakers modeled Hogwarts after this Great Hall, but since the books describe four schools and four tables, they had to build a much larger dining hall for filming.

After walking around the Hall, my kids giddy with excitement, we went through the buffet line, piling our plates with steaming food, a variety of cuisine that was usually beyond our tight budget. We sat down to eat, still talking about Harry Potter. In the past six weeks, Jordan had read through the entire series, almost nonstop, and the day he finished, he began reading them to Jonathan, completing them inside a month. Michelle also read the series and spent hours discussing them with the boys; the books produced wonderful talks about character, consequences of bad choices and the trials of growing up. She located hundreds of Christian themes in the books, undoubtedly the result of J. K. Rowling's Anglican background, her current church attendance and her deep knowledge of Western literature.

Though I have only read the first book, I was struck with Harry's dramatic, almost biblical, experience of calling. Raised by his nasty relatives after the death of his parents, tormented by his mean cousin, his life is altered forever when mysterious missives start arriving one day. His calling, Pamela Dolan wrote,

> comes to him not from a Burning Bush or a heavenly messenger, but from a giant named Hagrid, who also arrives with a pink umbrella, an owl, and a birthday cake. And this is only after Harry's household has been deluged with letters, letters that his mean uncle confiscates and keeps from Harry. Whoever is sending the letters knows they are being intercepted, and their means of delivery become ever more urgent and ingenious. Bunches of letters shoot down the chimney and turn up hidden inside a dozen eggs. It turns out, of course, that the letters contain an invitation for Harry to begin studying at the Hogwarts School of Witchcraft and Wizardry.

Harry had been called. For the first time he learns about his true identity, where he comes from and who he is. It is a life-changing moment. But now that he knows his identity, his real education begins. "Harry needs to go out into the world," Dolan continues, "and learn to become the person he now knows he was created to be. He has to build up his knowledge and his skills, develop friendships, experience challenges and losses and great joys that are all a part of the journey." In other words, he needs to become educated, to learn all he can about his mysterious call and the implications it has for his life.

Harry's example was timely for our family. We were at a crossroads. We had to make a decision about homeschooling; we could not put it off any longer. Michelle and I had been discussing for months what we hoped to teach our kids that year. We were sure about the themes of pilgrimage that we wanted them to learn; but what about the basics? Surely this year could not just be one extended field trip. Or could it? Where did the basics—reading, grammar, math—fit into the "end" of education?

Part of the struggle was that Michelle was a tremendous teacher. She had taught in public schools and charter schools and home-schooled our kids. She knew what kids needed to learn and when they needed to learn it, and had come prepared with lesson plans, books, schedules. So when the kids were not motivated or refused to study, she was not only frustrated but worried: each day missed was one more day the kids fell behind. I understood her fear; I shared it. Our kids needed to master the basics—reading and writing are important.

Jonathan and Jordan in the Great Hall, Christ Church

But Harry Potter got me thinking. What if education is more than the basics, as important as they are? What if reading and writing are just tools, like a hammer and nails—useful for building something, but not the end product themselves? The hammer and nails are not the goal; building furniture or a house is the goal. Likewise, is it possible that learning to read, write and do math are not the ultimate end, as we are so often told by the education establishment (think testing and standards of No Child Left Behind), but are merely tools to be used for constructing something larger?

A few days earlier, I had read a quote in C. S. Lewis's *The Problem of Pain*: "Here at last is the thing I was made for . . . the secret signature of each soul." *Okay*, I thought, *what if education was more about discovering "the secret signature of the soul"—what we were made for—than about standardized tests, memorizing facts and regurgitating answers?* If, as Dolan says, Harry needed to "learn to become the person he now knows he was created to be;" and if accomplishing this meant learning more than the basics and in fact meant growing in knowledge, character, friendship, living through trials and experiencing the great joys of life, then maybe education is really about calling, about becoming the person God intends us to be, about being prepared to live gratefully in obedience and action. Maybe these are the true ends of education, and the basics are just tools.

As we were leaving the Great Hall, I realized that Harry had become a good role model for my sons. In fact, for my oldest son, he had become his best friend, as if he made up for Jordan's friends back home. But I wanted to introduce my kids to one of my real-life, historical friends, William Wilberforce. Wilberforce was someone who had experienced a dramatic call, agonized over what it meant to live it out and experienced the great joy of a life lived in obedience. It was time to begin telling his story to my children. In the meantime, I hoped that it would shed light on the decision Michelle and I needed to make about the next six months and how we wanted to educate our kids and whether we would stay in Oxford to do it.

William Wilberforce was born into a prosperous merchant family in Hull. In the summer of 1768, just before his ninth birthday, Wilberforce's life changed dramatically with the sudden, tragic death of his father. His mother, unable to cope emotionally or physically, sent young William to live with her husband's childless brother, William, and his wife, Hannah, in Wimbledon, a wealthy suburb of London.

Grieving and forlorn, William settled into the sprawling five-and-a-half-acre estate named Lauriston House, on the south edge of the Commons. His dashing and successful uncle and his attractive and warm aunt treated him like a son, showering him with love and affection, taking care of his needs, even making him their heir, and he flourished under their care. But there was something about them that stood out: they were committed evangelicals, having come to faith under the influence of the famous evangelist George Whitefield as part of the Great Awakening sweeping across England, led by men like Whitefield and John and Charles Wesley. Being an evangelical was considered socially unacceptable, especially for aristocrats like William and Hannah, but they did not care. They began to bring young William up as an evangelical, cheerfully taking him to church, daily reading the Bible to him and introducing him to John Newton, the ex–slave trader and author of the famous hymn "Amazing Grace." Newton was a frequent guest at Lauriston House, and young William loved to hear Newton's stories of ships, maritime adventure and narrow escapes from death at sea.

After just two years at Lauriston House, William was thriving under the care of his uncle and aunt. But then, something happened: his mother got word of William's new religious fervor, and she decided to put an end to it. Against his wishes she ripped him away from his happy home. Devastated, he returned to Hull, dearly missing his aunt and uncle, who over the past two years had become as parents to him. He wrote them frequently, sometimes without his mother knowing, telling them how much he longed to be back at Lauriston House and how he was trying to stay faithful to his new faith. But over time his newfound ardor began to cool; his mother did her best to drum it out of him, introducing him to all the pleasures of society, fashionable friends and approvable vices, attempting to undo the influence of her brother and sister-in-law.

By the time he went to Cambridge University in 1776, he had long forgotten his boyhood faith and spent his days running around with a corrupt crowd of wealthy aristocrats who did nothing but gamble, drink and carouse. His studies held no meaning to him, and as he admitted years later, he wasted his time at Cambridge in frivolous activities. Even when he did study to pass his exams, he had little interest in real learning or character building. It was a means to an end: to finish school and make money.

But it was during this time at Cambridge that his conscience began to catch up to him; he began to feel guilty for all the time he was wasting and the activities he was involved in. Toward the end of his time there, he distanced himself from the crowd he had been running with, recognizing they were no good for him. Slowly he began to apply himself to his studies. He even found new motivation to work hard: he had become inspired with the idea of becoming a member of Parliament, possibly after meeting classmate William Pitt, whose father was a former prime minister and who had himself been groomed to be the prime minister someday. Wilberforce thought being a politician was the best way to make a name for himself. By choosing politics, he was also turning his back on the family business, deciding that the life of a merchant was not for him. With his speaking skill, his ability to impress crowds and his general likability, he re-

William Wilberforce

alized he was better suited for the House of Parliament than the house of a merchant.

In 1780, at the age of twenty-one, and against all odds, he won a seat in Parliament, representing Hull, his hometown. Four years later, in March 1784, just months after Pitt became the youngest prime minister in the history of England, Wilberforce took another risk: he ran for the important seat from Yorkshire and won, in the process helping to secure Pitt's hold on power. As John Pollock says, "Yorkshire made Wilberforce a man of power and significance who might one day become Prime Minister himself. Welcome in the highest circles, privy to Cabinet secrets, the closest friend of Pitt, Wilberforce had a future."

But even with all this success, he was still not happy. Power, wealth, connections—none of these brought purpose or meaning. By this time he had inherited his uncle's home in Wimbledon, but it brought no further contentment. Unfulfilled, he decided to take a lengthy vacation in the south of France, hoping to distract himself from the inner turmoil.

MORNINGS WITH WILBERFORCE

To share the story about Wilberforce, I read each morning from the short biography of Wilberforce in John Piper's *The Roots of Endurance*. In the afternoons, Michelle rounded up the four children, cranked up the heater, cooked some popcorn and read them *William Wilberforce: The Freedom Fighter* by Bingham Derick. The kids found his story interesting. In many ways, Wilberforce's early life is similar to the lives of many young people in the West today. Though most are not as rich as Wilberforce, they nonetheless struggle with the same lack of direction and purpose in their education and their personal lives. They have unlimited freedom but have no idea what to do with it. They spend years learning to stand on their own but have no idea where to go once they are standing. They lack a larger purpose in life, something to inspire them, to pull them in the right direction. And like Wilberforce, with no clear direction and no calling, they look to entertainment and consumerism to fill the void; the American dream becomes the ultimate goal. But like Wilberforce, so many young people (and older folks as well) find this life empty. The problem is that most don't know the alternative. Is there something bigger worth living for? Does life have meaning beyond material comfort or, in my kids' case, video games?

One of those mornings while reading Piper's story of Wilberforce, a conviction grew inside of me. I looked up at my boys. I didn't want them going off to college thinking that the purpose of life was the accumulation of material goods. Material things are gifts from God, but they are not the ultimate goal. I worried about our children because the pull of materialism is so strong in the West. Could we teach them a story that could trump the story of the consumeristic West? I believed we could. I looked down at my book and kept reading. The story was about to get even more interesting.

At the time he was preparing for his long vacation in 1784, Wilberforce had begun to think that, just like his years at St. John's College,

Cambridge, his first few years in Parliament had been a waste of time. "The first years I was in Parliament I did nothing—nothing that is to any purpose," he wrote years later. "My own distinction was my darling object." He had become a Member of Parliament for recognition, to make a name for himself, to bask in the glory of victory. Yet now he had a name and tremendous recognition, but he was still empty. What were all this power, wealth and glory for? Did it have any meaning?

Wilberforce's grand vacation plan was to travel to Nice, in the French Riviera, in two horse-drawn carriages. Since the first carriage was filled with his mother, sister and cousins, there was no room for William. He would travel in a second carriage, and to make this more enjoyable he decided to invite a lively friend for conversation and companionship. When his first choice could not go, he encountered, quite unexpectedly at the Scarborough races, his former boyhood tutor, Isaac Milner, who taught at Cambridge and one day would become a Fellow of the Royal Society (of Science). Wilberforce invited him to be his travel companion, and Milner accepted. A short time later, Wilberforce discovered, to his chagrin, that Milner was an evangelical, the kind Wilberforce had been running from since the time he lived with his aunt and uncle. But it was too late to rescind the invitation, so in October 1784, the party set out on their journey, reaching Nice on November 30. Over the next few months, Wilberforce had many opportunities to question Milner about Christianity, often poking fun of it and dismissing it out of hand. Exasperated, Milner replied: "Wilberforce, I don't pretend to be a match for you in this sort of running fire; but if you really wish to discuss these topics in a serious and argumentative manner, I shall be most happy to enter on them with you."

In February 1785, after months of enjoying a leisurely life, staying "in a house separated from the Mediterranean only by a grove of Orange trees," eating fancy dinners and enjoying the company of other British nobility, Wilberforce received a letter from Pitt with an urgent request: return immediately for parliamentary business. With the carriage packed and a promise to his party to return by summer,

Wilberforce was heading out the door when a book resting on an end table caught his eye: *The Rise and Progress of Religion in the Soul* by Philip Doddrige. He scooped it up and asked Milner what he thought. "It's one of the best books ever written," replied Milner. "Let us take it with us and read it on our long journey."

As the two men set out on the long, perilous and snowy journey across France, they read together and discussed *Rise and Progress*. This classic book was the perfect book to challenge Wilberforce. It was intelligent, well argued and charming, the kind of book that would be popular in polite society. The book was called "a reasoned, elegant exposition" of Christianity and, along with Milner's engaging personality (who could intelligently and winsomely explain any element of the faith), made for a potent combination. Wilberforce was having a hard time dismissing Christianity, and he began to take it more seriously. A great change was taking place in his life. But these important conversations with Milner would have to be put on hold for a few months; there was work to do in Parliament and fun times to have with Pitt and their friends.

Talking with Os

By mid-December 2010, the record-breaking freezing temperatures, the black mold growing in our house and the lack of sunshine had all caught up with my Southern California family, bringing sicknesses of various sorts: colds, sinus infections and headaches. My idea of taking them on a Wilberforce pilgrimage was out of the question; they were not going anywhere.

Around that time, with the kids sick at home, I made my way into town to hear a lecture at the Oxford Center of Mission Studies, located inside a former Anglican church. My friend Bill Prevete, who was a tutor there, invited me to hear a guest lecture by Os Guinness. I had known Os, a writer and speaker, since my college days, and when I found out he was in town I emailed him and asked him to tea. After his wonderful lecture, we meandered back to his office a few blocks away.

Seeing Os reminded me of a time back in college when I was on a semester program in Washington, D.C., wrestling with God about my purpose in life. One of my professors said I should talk with Os, who worked in the city. It was a significant discussion for me because I learned about something I had never heard about before: the biblical doctrine of calling. A year later, after I graduated from Gordon College, I was still thinking about what I learned. And I was still struggling to discover my calling. That first autumn, I went to China to teach English, but I could not find any peace. In agony, I spent many afternoons pacing the roof of the school building, pleading with God to tell me what I was called to do, desperately wanting a sense of purpose in my life. I needed to know.

I wish I had known during those rooftop walks what Os would write many years later: that we are called first to God, through Christ. This is the primary call. But we also have a secondary call, a call to serve God and his kingdom in every area of our lives. Secondary calls—whether in the media, law, education, business or homemaking—matter to God, but they matter only because the primary call matters the most. It was this secondary call I wanted to discover. While I had not heard of Wilberforce at the time, I was trying to avoid making a mistake similar to the one he made. He had been called to Parliament, but he had no idea why or by whom. As a result, his job felt worthless. It had no purpose, and neither did he.

We had arrived at Os's office and settled into some comfortable brown leather chairs, the kind you find in a lawyer's office. When I mentioned my family's studies of Wilberforce, Os said, with an approving smile, "That's brilliant." Wilberforce was one of Os's heroes, and Os had written about him in his book *The Call*.

In *The Call*, Os discusses two important distortions people in the church tend to make when it comes to calling, which he refers to as the Catholic distortion and the Protestant distortion. The Catholic distortion elevates the spiritual over the secular and creates a dualism in favor of the clergy or missionaries as being more obedient to God. The Protestant distortion elevates the secular over the spiritual, in the end eclipsing the spiritual. The Catholic distortion highlights the primary call but does not leave room for secondary callings, and the Protestant distortion elevates the secondary calling above the primary calling.

Jumping right in, I asked Os to clarify what he meant by the two distortions. I had this sense that they might be relevant to Wilberforce and what I was struggling with.

"Well," said Os, "the church has made two big mistakes in the area of calling over the years. Wilberforce made one of them and almost made the second."

"What do you mean by that?" I asked.

"Right," he said, pausing just slightly before answering the question. "He made the first mistake in his early years of Parliament, and he almost made the second mistake when he returned from his extended vacation." The first, he said, is the Protestant distortion.

"And the mistake he almost made?" I asked.

"The Catholic distortion," said Os.

My interest piqued. I was eager to hear more.

Parliament was supposed to adjourn in May 1785 but instead ran all the way to June, frustrating Wilberforce's and Milner's return to the south of France. By then, the Riviera was sweltering. Wilberforce and Milner joined the travel party in Genoa, Italy, planning to go to Turin, Geneva and Interlaken. "We went thither by way of Switzerland," he wrote sometime later, "and I have never since ceased to recur with peculiar delight to its enchanting scenery, especially to that of Interlaken, which is a vast garden of the loveliest fertility and beauty stretched out at the base of the giant Alps."

From the start of the journey, Wilberforce and Milner resumed their conversations on Christianity. Together, they read the New Testament in Greek, which he discovered taught "the same Christianity as Doddridge, a conclusion that Milner pressed on him with alacrity." They spent so much time in rigorous debate and intense conversation that the women started to feel ignored. While Wilberforce found it more and more difficult to counter Milner's arguments, he nevertheless continued to share his doubts and fear about his inability to live up to the ideals of Christianity. But these doubts were evidence of the change taking place in Wilberforce. After months of reading and dialogue, observing the beauty of God's creation, and searching his soul, he finally came to "a settled conviction in my mind, not only of the truth of Christianity, but also of the scriptural basis of the leading doctrines which I now hold."

Soon, however, these new convictions began to run up against his settled way of life. He experienced this clash most strongly when he returned to England in October 1785. He desired to live a Christian life but had no idea how to begin. He wrestled with the implications of what he now knew and what he did for a living, wracked by remorse over his past life: "The deep guilt and black ingratitude of my past life forced itself upon me in the strongest colours, and I condemned myself for having wasted my precious time, and opportunities, and talents." He longed to find forgiveness, knowing it only came in Christ. "My anguish of soul for some months was indescribable," he wrote later, "nor do I suppose it has often been exceeded." Not only did he struggle with personal guilt, but he also wondered about his profession: could a practicing Christian remain in the sordid and often corrupt world of parliamentary politics, where bribes, lies and loose living were the norm? Should he resign, quit politics altogether and join the clergy?

After three months of agonizing seclusion, frantically desperate for answers, on Saturday, December 1, he wrote to Pitt, explaining the great change that had taken place in his life and the possibility that he might quit Parliament. Even if he did stay, though he would remain a dear friend, he said, he could not guarantee his unyielding support as in times past. Pitt wrote back the next day assuring his best friend that nothing could alter their friendship, even Wilberforce leaving politics, but counseled him not to take any bold action until they could meet. Pitt said he would visit Wimbledon the next day so they could talk this over. Could he convince his friend not to drop out of public service?

TWO DISTORTIONS

Back in Os's office we continued our conversation about Wilberforce's mistakes. Os said that, knowing his Caller and wanting his work, whatever it was, to have meaning and purpose and be done for God's glory, Wilberforce was convinced he needed to quit politics and do something more spiritual. Gripped for years in the vice of the Protestant distortion, he was about to make the opposite mistake—the Catholic distortion.

"If you look at the history of calling," Os said, "it was derailed by thinkers like Bishop Eusebius in the third century when he said that the Christian life could be divided into two categories—the 'perfect life' and the 'permitted life'—in other words, the sacred and the secular. This is what Wilberforce struggled with that dreary fall in 1785. There were people in his life who were counseling him, telling him that the 'perfect life' was spiritual, dedicated to contemplation and lived best by the clergy. For him to stay in public life (or for others to be farmers, soldiers, bankers, etc.), though 'permitted,' was less than ideal; in fact, it was secular."

Os continued: "But this two-tier view of life perverts biblical teaching by only focusing on the primary calling and neglecting the legitimacy of the secondary callings. The Reformation, particularly Luther and his break from the monastic life, shattered the Catholic view of calling. Luther called for the abolition of all orders and abstention from all vows. There were no higher or lower, spiritual or sacred callings. All secondary callings, if they come from God, are legitimate and noble and important. It was an explosive new doctrine."

It was now close to 6:00 p.m., and I needed to leave. After thanking Os for his time, I headed home to our sickbay. While I was gone, Michelle had shown the kids the movie *Amazing Grace,* the story of Wilberforce and his heroic deeds, which stimulated some good conversations about calling, purpose and meaning. What struck me

about the movie, I mentioned to my kids, was the image of Wilberforce reading books. Having wasted his youth and college, it was as if
he was attempting to make up for what he had missed the first time
around: an education that prepared him for a life of joyful, obedient
and active service to his Caller. For the rest of his life he was an avid
reader and voracious learner. I told my kids I hoped they would be
the same way—lifelong learners who crave knowledge that will help
them live out their callings. I went to bed that night excited about my
trip to London the next day, sad only that they could not join me.

Monday, December 3, 1785, Prime Minister Pitt traveled to Wimbledon to meet Wilberforce. The night before he had written an impassioned letter urging his friend not to do anything hasty until he
got there. Undoubtedly Wilberforce reread the letter as he waited for
his friend to arrive. In it, after affirming their friendship, Pitt suggested that his friend had received bad advice about his career: "But
forgive me if I cannot help expressing my fear that you are nevertheless deluding yourself into principles which have but too much
tendency to counteract your own object, and to render your virtues
and your talents useless both to yourself and mankind." Pitt was
eager to converse candidly with Wilberforce, to hold nothing back.

When Pitt arrived, they talked for two hours. For the first time, in
the presence of a dear friend who was as a brother to him, Wilberforce
"opened his soul to someone." At first Pitt played the skeptic, trying to
argue Wilberforce out of his new convictions. But he was not successful; Wilberforce had spent too much time working through the
reasonableness of the faith, and his resolve was too strong for Pitt. At
the end, they had to agree to disagree. But one of the points Pitt had
made in his letter, and undoubtedly pressed again on his visit, rattled
Wilberforce. In the letter, Pitt wrote: "If a Christian may act in the
several relations of life, must he seclude himself from them all to
become so? Surely the principles as well as the practice of Christianity
are simple, and lead not to meditation only but to action." Wilberforce

struggled to counter this point. For the next two days, he thought about it constantly. He now knew who he had to talk to next: the famous evangelist John Newton. Wilberforce was convinced that Newton would confirm his leanings to leave Parliament. But would he?

FROM CARRIAGE HOUSE TO CHURCH

Steven Tomkins, a Wilberforce biographer, and I stood facing the historic carriage house, looking at the blue plaque indicating Wilberforce had once lived there. The red brick carriage house was the only part of the original estate still in existence. As the rain came down, the Commons shrouded in fog, Steven and I discussed Wilberforce's important meeting with Pitt, taking place 225 years earlier to the month. Having recently completed his book *The Clapham Sect: How Wilberforce's Circle Transformed Britain*, Steven talked about how important friends and community were for Wilberforce. He relied on them for every major decision in his life, valuing their friendship and camaraderie but also seeing them as a key source for wisdom, as seen in his meeting with Pitt and his seeking out Newton. Over the years

The coach house of Wilberforce's former home in Wimbledon

he would look to his friends to inspire him, to sustain him in his calling and to learn together.

Steven's comments got me thinking about events back at home. Earlier in the day, Michelle and I had been talking about what to do with our kids' education. And then it dawned on us. We took our kids out of the only school and church they knew; we took them away from teachers, mentors and friends; we took them away from their learning environment in our home. No wonder they struggled. And as much as we tried to re-create the learning environment in Oxford, our kids could not do it without a homeschool network of other families to add support, community and learning experiences. Maybe we were expecting too much from them; maybe we needed to dial things back, to choose a course of study that was more manageable, making learning fun again so that they were not individuals pursuing their separate coursework but a community learning together, at least for a season.

After lingering in Wimbledon for an hour, it was time to get to St. Mary Woolnoth, the church that Newton pastored. When we arrived, we ascended the steps and pushed open the heavy wooden door, discovering a warmly lit interior, decorated for Christmas with a lighted tree and ornaments. Gazing at the open, spacious interior built in 1716 in the English baroque style, Steven said, "This is where Wilberforce encountered Newton for the first time in fifteen years since his childhood in Wimbledon when Newton was a guest at his aunt and uncle's house." He continued: "When Wilberforce arrived at the church he delivered a sealed letter to Newton, asking for 'some serious conversation' and to keep the contents of the letter and meeting secret. Newton, who was in between worship services, agreed to a meeting but could not meet then; he asked, could Wilberforce come to his house that Wednesday?"

Wilberforce agreed. And what they talked about that day would change Wilberforce's life and the slave trade forever.

When Wednesday arrived, two days after his meeting with Pitt, Wilberforce was nervous. "Something about going to Newton," writes Kevin Belmonte, "represented a sort of spiritual Rubicon to him." He must have known that after this meeting there was no going back. People would find out, and his standing in society would be ruined. But why would it matter? After all, he would no longer be in elected office.

When he got to Charles Square, the twenty-six-year-old aristocrat, who habitually took on the most powerful members of Parliament, was scared to knock on the door, afraid of what this meeting might bring. To calm his nerves, he walked around the block two times. Finally, he knocked and went in.

Wilberforce and Newton talked for two hours. When the meeting was done, he was in a settled state. In his diary the following day, he described his reaction to the meeting: "He told me he always had entertained hopes and confidence that God would sometime bring me to him. . . . When I came away I found my mind in a calm, tranquil state, more humbled, and looking more devoutly up to God." Newton, sharing from years of experience, gave him advice that he did not expect. And it was advice that would one day affect millions of people around the globe.

NEWTON'S TIMELY COUNSEL

I said goodbye to Steven and thanked him for his time. It was late and he needed to get back to his family. Though I was eager to get home as well, I had one more person I needed to talk to—someone who could shed light on what Newton had said to Wilberforce that so dramatically altered his course of action.

After a ten-minute tube ride and a short walk, I arrived at Barkston Gardens, a tawny neighborhood of fancy apartment buildings, high-priced condos and genteel townhomes all towering over a small, enclosed garden. I was there to talk to Jonathan Aitken, a former member of Parliament and Cabinet member whose meteoric career was cut short when he perjured himself. Sent to prison in 1999, he served seven months. Just prior to going to jail, he attended the Alpha Course, a ten-week introduction to Christianity, and became a believer. In prison he began studying theology and, upon getting out, enrolled at Wycliffe Hall. Now in his seventies, he had recently penned a biography of John Newton, subtitled *From Disgrace to Amazing Grace*, something Aitken knows only too well.

Tall, strikingly handsome, and smartly dressed in slacks and a sweater, Aitken possessed the air of a 1940s Hollywood movie star. He walked into the room carrying a serving tray and handed me a cup of tea. After he took a sip of his tea, I asked him, "What was it that Newton told Wilberforce that was so life changing? It must have been pretty persuasive to shift his thinking so dramatically."

"Well," he said, pausing slightly, "it was not so much *what* he told him but what he did *not* tell him. Usually a minister, when approached by someone who wants to join the club," said Aitken, "welcomes him with open arms. The predictable response would have been to tell Wilberforce to quit politics and become a pastor. But to say, in effect, 'My boy, stay where you are and serve God in Parliament' was unexpected. In fact, Newton advised Wilberforce not to withdraw from politics, but to serve God (as a Christian statesmen) like Daniel, Joseph and other Old Testament leaders had done."

As we talked, Aitken was clearly excited, for he admired Newton. Looking right at me he said this conversation with Wilberforce was Newton's finest hour. Instead of doing the predictable thing, he told Wilberforce to stay where God had placed him and combine the life of the Christian and the life of the politician and do it for the glory of God. Newton would have taken pains to convince Wilberforce, like Pitt had tried to do, that it is possible to be a faithful Christian in dark places such as Parliament and that God needed his servants in these places to bring transformation. Newton helped Wilberforce avoid the mistake of thinking he needed to do something more "spiritual," such as be a pastor.

Sitting there by Jonathan's fire, I thought back to what Os had told me the day before: that biblical calling provides the best antidote to the two distortions, the Protestant and the Catholic. Clearly Wilberforce, by God's grace and providence—and some tremendous mentoring from John Newton—avoided both distortions. He understood rightly that his work had meaning because he had a Caller.

St Mary Woolnoth, John Newton's London Church

As I left Jonathan Aitken's flat, I popped up my umbrella as a shield against the wet snowflakes that had begun to fall and headed to the tube station to make the long two-hour trip back to Oxford. I had much to think about.

Once on the bus, I took out my journal to make some notes. I remembered Os saying somewhere that calling was a metaphor for the life of faith. I liked the sound of that. My mind drifted back to my family and our struggle over homeschooling. If what Os had said was true about calling being a metaphor for the life of faith, that meant that calling is linked to our entire life. I sketched a few questions in my notebook that related directly to my family. Number one: "If we are going to grow in our faith, grow in our calling, then wouldn't it be true that our education, our learning about God, about ourselves, about the world, is linked to our calling and our entire pilgrimage of faith?" Second question: "Wouldn't a truly educated person be the person who knows her Caller and that she has a secondary call, what C. S. Lewis called the 'secret signature of the soul'?" I thought about those for most of the trip home to Oxford. And by the time we rolled back into the bus depot, I had come to an important conclusion: for the person with a calling, education plays an important role—it prepares, it shapes, it guides and it empowers.

As I waited for the local bus, I started to come to a new resolution:

even if we took the next six months off from school basics, it did not mean we were taking a break from *the* "basics." In fact, by spending the next six months doing nothing but learning about the calling of faith, "the secret signature of the soul" or what we had been calling "pilgrimage," we were pursuing the true end of learning. The basics, like math and grammar, are nothing but tools for this true end anyway. Over the past five months, we had been experiencing the best that true education had to offer, and we needed to continue to take advantage of it. As I came to this conclusion, I knew that my kids would be thrilled (what child likes grammar and math anyway?). I also knew that it was the right thing to do. There would be plenty of time in the future to catch up on math and reading, but we could never redo this trip.

Besides, I thought as my double-decker bus arrived, Wilberforce had reminded me that once people are inspired by their calling, they are inspired to learn. Once Wilberforce understood his call, you could not pull the books out of his hands; in fact, he went back and retaught himself many of the basics he had missed growing up. The true end of education—discovering our secret signature—engenders love of the basics. It is never the other way around, as any grammar-hating schoolchild can attest.

By the time I reached our house, I was settled in my mind. It was time to start spending our days, for the next six months, immersed in history, literature, theology, the arts, museum visits and deep conversations about our learning. Michelle would welcome this change. But we had a problem. We had already studied and experienced most of my heroes in Oxford. Was it time to move on from the city we loved so much, the city of dreaming spires?

Over the next twenty years, Newton continued to mentor Wilberforce, encouraging him in the battle, comforting him when things got tough and praying for him when he was spiritually spent. Wilberforce leaned on Newton as a father. But he also came to rely more and more on his new friends that formed a unique community, centered around Henry Thorton's home, Battersea Rise, on the edge of the Clapham Common. The group, known as the Clapham Sect, utilized their prodigious wealth, wide-ranging connections, business and political acumen—all combined with a strong calling to transform themselves and all of England. Over the next three decades they started Bible societies, created organizations to evangelize England, founded hospitals and schools, and worked toward prison reform, relief of the poor and the protection of animals. Wilberforce himself was personally involved in more than seventy charitable organizations. The members of the Clapham Sect may have been involved in two hundred or more ventures to reform the spiritual and moral decay in England. The group was, as John Pollock writes, "proof that a man can change his times, but that he cannot do it alone."

But their biggest reform, one that took twenty years to see results, was the most dramatic: to end the slave trade. It took years of sacrifice. Almost every year, starting in 1787, Wilberforce put forth a bill in Parliament to end the selling of slaves, and every year there was more delay, more danger, more defeat. On two occasions after the bill was defeated, Wilberforce was so physically incapacitated, emotionally drained and spiritually discouraged that he wanted to give up. His life had been physically threatened and he often had a bodyguard with him. But Newton and his friends at Clapham rallied around him, restored him to health and encouraged him to fight on, which he did. And then, in 1807, after twenty long years, they finally believed they had the votes to defeat it. On the night of February 24, with Parliament packed, Wilberforce and his friends sensed that history was about to be made.

SNOWY PARLIAMENT

On Saturday, December 18, three days after my visit to St. Mary Woolnoth and my conversation with Jonathan Aitken, I took the bus back into London to visit Parliament amidst a heavy snowfall. My bus was the last one to leave Oxford that morning before they suspended service, and we arrived in London in whiteout conditions. The city was at a standstill, and I wasn't sure I would make it home that night.

An hour after arriving, Stephen Tomkins and I sat in Parliament, drying ourselves off by the heaters near the wall of St. Stephen's Hall, which sits on the site of the former St. Stephen's Chapel, burned to the ground in 1843 in the great fire. In the original chapel, amidst the stained-glass windows, mosaics, paintings and neo-Gothic architecture, great battles were fought over abolition. Here, almost every year for two decades, Wilberforce put forth his bill and made impassioned speeches—some of them lasting for four hours—on the evils of slavery, calling for its abolition. Year in and year out the bill was defeated. And yet somehow, through the support of his Clapham circle and the power of his call, he persevered.

"What happened here on February 24, 1807, that changed the world?" I asked.

"It was pretty amazing," said Stephen. The quest for abolition had finally gained some momentum over the previous year and was coming to a head on that night. As Wilberforce's motion was being discussed, as it had been year after year, it started to become clear what was going to happen. Excitement began to grow in the chamber. Sensing that history was about to be made, one MP after another jumped to their feet to support the bill, not wanting to be left out, all extolling Wilberforce and the evils of slavery. The end to the dark night of the slave trade was near. As Solicitor-General Sir Samuel Romilly came to the closing remarks of his now-famous speech, he compared Wilberforce with Napoleon, describing what it was like for each at the end of that very day. Napoleon would return in pomp and power, in adulation and adoration, in fame and fortune, yet his sleep that night would be tormented by dreams of bloodshed, destruction and tyranny. But Wilberforce would return home after the vote that night "into the bosom of his happy and delighted family" and lie down content and happy, a clear conscience, aware of "having preserved so many millions of his fellow creatures."

At that moment, the House of Commons exploded in applause, with cheers of "hear, hear." The gavel thundered: "Out of order, out of order." But over the sound of the gavel came three more loud cheers: "Hip hip hoorah! Hip hip hoorah! Hip hip hoorah!" Through all the celebration, Wilberforce sat slumped on his bench, head down, tears streaming down his face. At 4:00 a.m., the vote came: 283-16; the slave trade in Great Britain had been abolished. The long national nightmare was over. Wilberforce and his friends had done it.

Parliament enveloped in snow

Sitting in the same spot where MPs stood that fateful night in 1807, remembering this great man and recalling his momentous day, I thought of my own calling. Nostalgically, my mind returned to that afternoon pacing the school roof in China so many years ago. It was there, as I prayed to God, that I finally sensed God's secondary call on my life. Although I did not pen a famous "two objects" entry into my diary or do something as monumental as abolish the slave trade, it is remarkable that what God called me to that day on the roof—to pursue a calling of teaching, preaching and writing in order to help Christians understand the gospel, how it brings wholeness to all areas of life and the need to understand our secondary callings—was exactly what I was still doing. Overcome with gratitude, I said a silent prayer of thanks.

But I also realized right then that part of my calling was to educate my children, teaching them to live a life of faith, to discover their calling and to live into the pilgrimage that God calls us to take: experiencing our roots, preparing ourselves for the journey, knowing our destination. After five months in Oxford, we had learned about our roots—from Cranmer, the Vanaukens, Lewis and Wilberforce. It was now time to learn about the journey and about our destination; and for that to happen we had to reluctantly leave Oxford. But it was not all sad. Though we adored Oxford—its beauty, architecture, history— the cold was killing my warm-blooded family, and there were four more months of dreary winter ahead of us. They would not make it. I needed to take them to a new location, a sunnier place. The choice was not hard to make: we would go to the south of France, making a stop in one of the most beautiful cities in the world.

After a long day in London (I had to wait four hours before the buses resumed) I headed home, grateful for the insights gained and the decisions made. The snow had subsided, and the bus crawled back to Oxford through unplowed and clogged roads, cars stalled and stranded everywhere. I arrived back only to find the local bus service suspended. Happily, I was forced to make the long walk through the fresh snow, a sublime silence having enveloped Oxford, Christmas lights adorning the front of buildings like a scene from a Dickens novel, all the while thinking how much I wanted to be back home—in the "bosom of my happy and delighted family." Pure contentment.

INTERMISSION

"A re you bringing that on the bus?" the driver asked incredulously. "If that's okay," I said.

"All right, come on," he said as he waved us on board. As Jordan and I walked onto the bus each holding part of a Christmas tree, many of the passengers stared in disbelief. It was two days before Christmas, and we had gone in search of an artificial tree. When we got to the store they were sold out. After some negotiation, we managed a great deal on the floor model, with ornaments and lights already on the tree. We split it in two, and Jordan and I carried it onto the bus and then home through the snow-covered streets of Oxford, trying not to slip. Instantly it brightened the mood in our home.

Over the next week, we prepared for our pilgrimage to Europe. In Oxford we had been able to take our learning month by month, but we couldn't do that in Europe. Since we had to have housing lined up before we went, that meant we had to plan the order of our travel and the topics we wanted to focus on. While in Oxford, we had rediscovered our roots, looking at desire, the struggle within, the weight of glory, and the self and biblical calling. It was now time to focus on the other two pillars of pilgrimage: the journey (and the maps we needed) and the importance of destination. And like Oxford, our goal in Europe would be, in part, to discover a deep faith, establishing a foundation in our kids' lives that would help them avoid the identity "lock box." But it would also be a time to listen to God, being open to him breaking into our lives in new and profound ways and in the process learning to trust him more and as a response to his good gifts, to live lives of greater obedience, joy and freedom.

So one morning in early January, while Michelle read some Harry Potter to the kids and I fought off the worst sinus infection I had ever had, I began jotting down the topics I thought we should cover and some of the many heroes we could study. I came up with at least a dozen and then narrowed it to six or eight. Once I had the themes and heroes, I spent hours on Google Maps attempting to link topic to hero and to work those into a reasonable travel schedule. I would often get theme and character to match, only to realize the proximity was off. Or I would get the travel to make sense, only to have the themes out of order. Sometimes I would get all three to work, only to realize that I had not factored in some other important detail. Round and round I went. It was like a big puzzle. Finally, I decided that, like life, all the pieces of our travel might not fit perfectly, but we had to move forward anyway, even if that meant driving hundreds of miles out of the way to pursue a particular topic; we would just do it.

Once we figured out the themes, heroes and countries we wanted to experience, I tackled our housing and transportation. I labored online researching RVs, minivans and vacation rental apartments throughout Europe. I broadcasted our need for housing to friends on Facebook, and it worked. An American pastor in London connected us to an American pastor in Paris, who invited us to come speak and stay for two weeks at his church. A friend in Pasadena arranged for his South African uncle to lend us his flat in Provence. And a missionary friend got us a massive discount on another flat in the Luberon Mountains of France. I then booked a twenty-eight-foot RV for three weeks in Germany—big enough to sleep six—and with that we had our housing needs covered for the next three months. Finally, for the last piece, I leased a minivan in Paris for six months.

With the travel details done, I then focused on repairing our house, getting it ready so that we could get our huge security deposit back: painting smudged walls, fixing broken light fixtures and mowing the lawn (yes, in the freezing cold). While I worked on the house, Michelle, having mastered driving on the left side of the road, rented a car and took the kids to Warwick Castle, an amazing example of living history.

Finally, when the house was ready, I joined the rest of the family for two days of field trips outside of Oxford. The first day we explored Stratford-upon-Avon, introducing our kids to Shakespeare, and on the second day we wandered around the Cotswalds, enjoying the picturesque villages that seemed to have been frozen in time. Our last few days of travel only confirmed what we had learned soon after arriving six months earlier: we would forever be lovers of England, one of the most enchanted countries in the world.

When the day arrived to leave Oxford, it was bittersweet. After having thanked my colleagues at Wycliffe Hall and giving huge hugs to Bill and Ky Prevette, the truck from the local charity showed up and took away all our furniture and appliances. We were paying it forward. That evening we said a teary goodbye to our house (though not the black mold) and taxied to London to spend a few days there before our train to Paris. When we got to London, I will never forget how excited my kids were at the prospect of more travel; they were giddy with joy.

We spent two days enjoying the London sites and our friends Andrew and Rachel and their two girls, who introduced us to the crumpet. Finally the big day arrived. With twelve duffle bags and six backpacks and a whole lot of trepidation about the months ahead, we took the fast train to Paris to begin our next adventure. We would begin to explore the second pillar of pilgrimage: journey and the need for a map. Our first theme would be beauty. And the window through which we would explore beauty would be the life of one of the most famous painters of all time, an artist who during his lifetime sold only one painting: Vincent van Gogh.

Part Two

LIFE AS JOURNEY
AND THE NEED FOR A MAP

six

BROKEN BEAUTY

Searching for Vincent van Gogh

The situation was intolerable. After a year of sharing a flat in Paris, Theo could no longer live with his older brother. "There was a time I loved Vincent and that he was my best friend," Theo wrote to his sister, Wil, in the spring of 1887, "but that is now in the past. I wish he would go and live by himself, and I will do my best to make that happen."

Twenty years had passed since Vincent van Gogh and his brother Theo, four years younger, had shared a room in the family parsonage where their father was a pastor in the Dutch Reformed Church. But in the two decades since, much had changed. Theo, the pride and joy of his parents, was a successful art broker in the international Goupil Company, with its Paris branch located in the Montmartre section of the city, a trendy neighborhood of cafés, nightclubs and studios, long the favorite of artists, entertainers and Bohemians. Over the same period, Vincent had failed miserably at everything: boarding school, working at Goupil, teaching at a boys' school, training to be a pastor, serving as a missionary, and dating. Even in his painting, his last resort to find an honorable calling and sense of dignity and worth, he had failed to find commercial success—not one painting sold in six years. His parents heaped shame on him, cajoled him to change his lifestyle, browbeat him to dress better and exhorted him to surround himself with better company—in short, to make something of himself. Growing up, Vincent and his father argued, sometimes for hours each day. Bitter accusations, hurt feelings, unresolved tension—all mounted until his father succumbed to a heart attack. His father went to his grave unreconciled with his oldest son, and deep down, Vincent believed he killed his father.

Through it all, Vincent clung to his art as the key to his success: to show the world that he would amount to something, would be famous. But as the years passed and success continued to elude him, he spiraled into depression and anger. During those hard years, he consoled himself with the thought of one day living with his brother. If he couldn't be successful, Vincent told himself, at least he wouldn't be lonely.

Now Vincent was finally sharing a flat with his brother, rekindling the camaraderie they had had as boys. It started out so well, the brothers spending every night together enjoying each other's company. But within months, the relationship turned sour. Vincent stopped bathing, ate terribly and dressed like a hobo. He retreated into himself, becoming sullen, surly, depressed. He pushed his brother away. When Theo brought friends home, Vincent picked fights with them, insulted them and drove them away, never to return. At night, the brothers fought over Vincent's philosophy of painting, with Theo contending that it was too dark and gloomy. Vincent defended his style, claiming it represented the harshness of life. The arguments raged deep into the night, depriving Theo of peace and sleep. Six months after Vincent arrived, Theo had reached his breaking point.

Vincent van Gogh: *Self Portrait,* Paris, winter, 1887-1888

But Vincent vowed to change his behavior, and slowly he did, taking baths, dressing better and being more civil. He even agreed to change his painting style. Following Theo's advice, Vincent mimicked the style of the new impressionist painters living in the neighborhood: working in the same locations around Paris, slavishly following their techniques—long brush strokes, thinly applied paint, using a particular size of canvas—and imitating their color palette of bright, clear colors and the ever-present depiction of light that made the impressionists famous. Theo was thrilled, telling Vincent his success was simply a matter of time. Theo no longer wanted Vincent to move out. He liked his brother again, realizing he could live with him after all. They went out in public, enjoying the camaraderie that Vincent had sought for years, frequenting the well-known restaurants and cafés, and keeping company with other famous painters like Monet, Manet, Pissarro and Gauguin.

Yet with his relationship with his brother again secure, his artistic career trending in the right direction and his commercial success just a matter of time—all things that Vincent had sought in vain for years—he did something inexplicable, if not unimaginable: in February 1889, two years after arriving, he abandoned his brother and left Paris for good, returning to a life of loneliness. Once again the self-described pilgrim had set out on his own.

CLIMBING MONTMARTRE

"C'mon guys, we can do this," Michelle said with her usual boundless excitement for travel, doing her best to coax the children up the stairs and away from the warmth of the metro station. I looked at Lindsay and Meghan, dressed in heavy coats, scarves, hats and mittens, looking more like arctic explorers than pilgrims. From the look in their eyes, I could see they didn't want to move. I wasn't sure I did either. Finally, after much persuasion from Michelle, we all stepped out into the seventeen-degree weather of Montmartre, a burst of late January cold hitting us in the face. Michelle looked down at her map, getting oriented, and then led the charge.

It was January 27. Two days earlier we had arrived in Paris and were staying in the one-bedroom guest apartment of the American Church. Over the next three weeks, we hoped to enjoy as much of Paris as possible—its history, its architecture and art, and its beauty. But we were also there to focus on the second stage of our pilgrimage: journey and the need for maps. Van Gogh was our first historical character of this stage. Since college he had been my favorite artist, and I looked forward to digging deeper into his life, exploring his faith and reveling in his art. And I hoped my family would appreciate it as well.

After exiting the metro, we walked briskly to the tram at the base of the butte, taking it to the summit where the magnificent Sacre-Coeur Basilica sits, built in the late nineteenth century around the time Vincent was in Paris. Though it is considered to have the best view of the city, on that day fog partially clouded our view of Paris, as if it were inside a steam room. I could barely make out the Eiffel Tower and Notre Dame Cathedral in the distance. Nonetheless, we paused long enough to take in the view and asked a tourist to take a family picture. When the kids got cold, we moved on.

From the Basilica, we journeyed west a few blocks, in search of Rue Lepic, the street where Vincent and Theo once lived. We strolled through the Place du Tertre, a cobblestoned square where artists huddled around their stalls selling their art, much the same way impressionist painters did a hundred years ago. Many of the original impressionists like Pissarro, Monet, Renoir and Cézanne lived and worked in the surrounding neighborhood. They were refugees from the center of Paris, having fled to Montmartre in search of cheap flats and inexpensive studios to work in. For almost fifty years, it was one of the most famous artist colonies in the world.

We hurried down the sloping Rue Lepic, stopping at the Moulin de la Galette jutting out above the cafés, shops and studios. The windmill, once used for crushing grapes, was now the sole proof that at one time this area rivaled the Bordeaux region of France for fine wine. Vincent painted the Moulin de la Galette a number of times; it may have reminded him of the windmills of his native Holland and that he was just a pilgrim in Paris.

At that moment, I thought of Vincent and the lessons my family could learn from him about pilgrimage as a metaphor for life. "I am a traveler," he wrote a few months after leaving Paris, "going somewhere and to some destination." He grew up "seeing a journey in every road and a life in every journey." He loved the line from Thomas à Kempis "if you want to persevere and make spiritual progress, look upon yourself as an exile and a pilgrim on this earth." He adored Bunyan's *Pilgrim's Progress*, seeing in the allegory shades of his own life: "Our life is a pilgrim's progress," he once preached in a sermon.

We continued down the gently sloping Rue Lepic, the sharp wind cutting through our layers of clothing, our eyes watering and our nostrils frozen. Lindsay, wafer thin, looked frozen, as if she were a tiny ice cube. I spotted a toy store and suggested they go inside to get warm while I continued looking for the flat. I stopped to study my map.

Over the months ahead, maps would be important for us. Without them we would get lost. The same is true in life. We need maps to direct our pilgrimage. Without a map to guide us—one rooted in the virtues of beauty, goodness and truth—we would not only lose our way but also miss out on the best of human flourishing. If we did not want this to happen for us, and our kids, we needed to discover these maps and learn to let them direct us and set our desire on fire for the kingdom.

That morning, before we left our flat, I had been reading Roger Scruton's *Beauty* to help me understand the role of beauty in our lives and to explain it to my family. In the book, Scruton decries the sorry state of aesthetic education in the West. Teaching our kids to appreciate beauty, writes Scruton, "matters more today than any previous period in history" because beauty has been rejected as a standard to live by and as a map to guide us. Yet without the map of beauty, he contends, "we risk falling into a world of addictive pleasures and routine desecration, a world in which human life is no longer clearly perceivable." I remembered highlighting the phrase "addictive pleasures and routine desecration" and wondering about my kids' education, and my own.

After walking some more, at last I found the location, a plain fourstory building with a plaque on the outside marking the spot. I imagined Theo alone, forlorn after Vincent had left for Provence, surrounded by his brother's art—paintings that captured the beauty of Montmartre. Michelle and I wanted our kids to see some of those paintings, to learn to appreciate their beauty. But with so many media distractions—video games, movies and YouTube—demanding my kids' attention, all of which seemed so much more exciting than paintings, would they appreciate his art? I wasn't sure.

But like Scruton, I agreed about the importance of aesthetic education and that the road map of beauty was vital for our children. I was hopeful that Vincent's life and art would lead us into a deeper love of beauty. But what I did not know at the time was that an insight from an argument I would have with my son in Provence would provide the key to unlock the secret of this appreciation and enjoyment, not just in Vincent's art but in all of creation.

No sooner had Vincent stepped off the train in Arles, an ancient Roman garrison on the banks of the Rhone dating back to 46 B.C., than he missed his brother. Now he was alone in a remote, Provençal town. But as much as he hated leaving Paris, he knew it was the right thing to do; he did not want to be responsible for the death of a family member again. In his final nine months in Paris, having tragically lost his way, Vincent had led his brother into the darkness of the bohemian lifestyle, embracing the *nostalgie de la boue* (nostalgia for sordidness), drinking from late afternoon deep into the night. Vincent's "reckless pursuit of pleasure, his heedless surrender to temptation, and his encouragement for Theo to follow that had wreaked havoc on Theo's fragile constitution. He was killing his brother—just as he had killed his father."

But if Vincent left Theo for his brother's own good, he also left him for another reason: to keep alive the only person in the world willing and able to support his art. Vincent depended on the monthly support of his brother, so he needed to keep Theo alive for at least as long as he lived. It was a race against time, though, for deep down, Vincent knew that neither of them would live much longer.

Arriving at the train station, he waded through two inches of fresh snow and then checked himself into a hotel. Immediately he got to work, energized by the scenery, the deep blue sky, the picturesque city scenes and the uniqueness of Arlesian people. For the next four months he turned out canvas after canvas—as many as two a day—painting fields, roads, a drawbridge, street scenes and

Café at Night, Place du forum; Rijksmuseum Kroller-Muller

every kind of tree imaginable, experimenting in the many styles he learned in Paris, searching for his painting voice to keep alive his dream of commercial success. Years later, many of these paintings would become famous, but at the time, nothing worked for Vincent. No matter how hard Theo tried, he could not sell a single painting.

As months passed without any commercial success, Vincent plunged deeper into depression and bad health. Not willing to change his lifestyle to achieve what he wanted most—a guilt-free conscience, peace with his past, reconciliation with his Creator—he physically and emotionally deteriorated: "Stomach disorders, fevers, and general weakness plagued him. . . . He complained of absentmindedness and spells of mental fogginess that sent sparks of panic through his letters." At times he felt like he must be going mad. His body was falling apart fast for a man in his mid-thirties, and he felt old inside.

His agony made him cantankerous. He verbally fought with his neighbors, merchants, everyone he came into contact with, saying "foolish and vicious" things in the heat of the moment. That spring, he could not go outside without an angry confrontation. The local teenagers taunted him, uproariously laughing at his hobo clothes and his strange ways, forcing him to retreat to the safety of the Yellow House. "Loneliness, worries, difficulties, the unsatisfied need for kindness and sympathy—that is what is hard to bear," he wrote Theo, revealing his deepest fears about the future. He was estranged from everyone, including God.

Ironically, having given up years ago the "infectious foolishness" of religion, Vincent still sought consolation in his art, trying to capture the "it," the often illusive feeling that he "fit," that he belonged in the world. He tried to find a place free of guilt, regret, sadness; he was searching for a type of redemption through beauty. But could his art meet his deepest need? He had hoped it would. And it was the Yellow House, the place he envisioned as an artist studio, which rekindled this hope.

PROVENCE

"I worry about our kids," Michelle said, repeating a fear she had about our kids being addicted to media. It was the second week of February, and our children were watching something on the laptop. Michelle and I were standing in the kitchen of our third-floor flat that overlooked the cobbled stone streets and boutique shops, the fancy restaurants and cozy cafés of Lourmarin, a tiny hilltop town in the Luberon Valley in the heart of Provence.

"Don't you think this is how it starts?" she wondered.

As a family we were not anti-media. Michelle and I watched movies and had our favorite TV shows. We let our kids enjoy video games and watch stuff on the laptop. Like many parents we set boundaries and limited their time, and Michelle and I tried to spend more time reading books than watching movies ourselves. But in the months ahead, two things were going to challenge our boundaries: lots of time in the minivan and a fluid daily structure. To pass the time traveling we knew our kids would ask for media time and we would be tempted to use it as a babysitter when we didn't know what to do or were out of energy. We didn't want to be one of those families out in public where every member is tied to a media device.

That particular day had started well; we had wandered around the town, enjoying the shops while my girls chased cats down narrow streets. "Mommy, can I pet the cats?" Lindsay, who is allergic to cats, asked plaintively.

Michelle told her she could play with them as long as she didn't touch her face and promised to wash her hands as soon as she got back to the flat. Lindsay agreed, and for thirty minutes she and Meghan had a wonderful time with the cats.

Eventually we moved on, climbing a slightly sloping street, and stumbled upon the former home of Albert Camus, the famous French writer. At that moment a woman stopped and told us that Camus's daughter still lived in the house. My kids didn't know who Camus was, but they found the woman's story interesting.

Soon it was time to return to the flat for lunch. Afterward, the kids got restless, so they put on a DVD.

"Don't get too comfortable," I said. "We're taking a road trip."

They protested vehemently. I wanted to go to Arles and pick up the van Gogh trail, but they wanted nothing to do with my idea. Instead they wanted to stay home and watch *Little House on the Prairie*. That's when our conversation about media addiction had begun.

"Just tell them to turn it off," Michelle said to me. "I don't want them to grow up addicted to the stimulus of TV and video games."

I froze, halfway between the refrigerator and the sink. *Stimulus. Addiction.* Where had I heard those words before? I snapped my fingers as I remembered. Roger Scruton's book *Beauty*. In his discussion of art and the "flight from beauty" he mentions "stimulus addiction": "the hunger to be shocked, gripped, stirred in whatever way might take us straight to the goal of excitement." Many artists are addicted to this not only in their art, he said, but also in their personal lives, and often the two reinforce each other.

Scruton's description made me wonder if this is what we all love about media: it provides excitement and temporarily fills our "hunger to be shocked" and desire to be "gripped." Now, there is nothing wrong with being "gripped"; all good stories do this, and it is why we are drawn to them. We are wired for story, and good books, plays and movies touch us at the deepest part of our being. But Scruton seems to be talking about something entirely different, not so much the power of story to grip us but the quick rush that media like video games provide—the kind of rush that bypasses, in his words, "thought and judgment," so necessary for our learning, and that goes right to the "pleasure switch."

Now, as I stood there in our kitchen eating some cheese and fresh bread, I realized that not every kid who has an obsession with video games and movies grows up with a serious stimulus addiction. It does happen and more and more these days, but when I thought about my kids, I wasn't too worried about this. What I was worried about were missed opportunities, not just for my kids but for Michelle and me as well. Would the time we all spent watching movies and other media at night take away from appreciating beauty in other areas? How do we limit media so we don't miss out on other important things in life? For me this was the important question.

As we headed down the steps of our flat, my conversation with Michelle sparked another thought. "What if," I said, "instead of just setting boundaries, which are good, or instead of just saying too much media is bad, which it is, we did something different? What if we learned as a family to fall in love with real beauty, to learn to really appreciate it and enjoy it—the kind of beauty that makes most media feel shallow, fleeting and a waste of time? What if we did that?"

"I agree with you," Michelle said. "But how?"

As we drove through Provence, the beauty all around us—rolling hills, cropped grapevines, gray stone farmhouses sprinkling the countryside—I was deep in my thoughts, trying to answer Michelle's "how" question. How *do* we learn to appreciate real beauty? As we passed another vineyard, I thought of Nicholas Wolterstorff's contention in *Until Justice and Peace Embrace* that God wouldn't have gone to such effort to create so much beauty if it wasn't for our benefit as much as his. Wolterstorff quotes John Calvin as saying that God gave us beauty "for delight and good cheer," that is, he made it "attractive to us" in order to delight our eyes and stimulate our noses. Beauty was for our pleasure, to enjoy and delight in. God didn't need to make creation so beautiful, but he did. And he did it for us just as much as for himself.

I looked over at Michelle, who was peering out the window, enjoying the view of the countryside. Michelle has always been good at seeing beauty. She often tells me to slow down to notice a garden or a tree. I tend to live much more in my mind, not aware of the beauty around me. But at that moment it dawned on me. If I wanted my kids to have a better eye for beauty, I needed to develop one too. I started to look around as I drove, to notice nature more. It really wasn't hard once I tried; it was all around me.

We arrived in Arles just after 1:00 p.m. After finding a parking space and walking to the visitor center to get a map, I was excited to go in search of the van Gogh trail, but my kids were still not excited by that prospect. I tried to increase their enthusiasm about touring the city by talking about going in search of the locations of Vincent's art like a detective, but they were not having any of it.

Just as Michelle pulled me aside to talk, the kids ran to a merry-go-round near the visitor center to play. "Look," she said, "I know you want to find van Gogh landmarks, but I think the kids are tired from the drive to Arles and just need some time to play and unwind. So why don't I take them to run around the Roman bullfighting arena, where they can let off some steam, and you can go find Vincent's art?"

After I left them at the ancient arena much happier than they had been minutes before, I went searching for the Yellow House, a ten-minute walk down the hill toward the Rhone, just outside the old Roman gate. I was anxious to find the house. I knew it was important for him, a symbol of comfort, community and finally feeling at home on his long pilgrimage of life. And I wondered if this yellow house could help my family to learn the same things about beauty, how to enjoy it more and how it guides us on our pilgrimage.

Vincent had found new hope. If he could not find success on his own, he thought to himself, he might find it in community, forming a brotherhood of artists to support, encourage and love beauty together. Two months after arriving in Arles, Vincent discovered the "Yellow House," a dilapidated building just outside the city walls on Place Lamartine, a small park on the north side of Arles, adjacent to the Rhone. In mid-March 1889, he moved in and began fixing it up—

painting it, buying furniture, decorating its walls, doing his best to turn it into an artists' studio, a colony of artists sharing "their warmth, their fire, and their enthusiasm."

The first artist he invited was Paul Gauguin, a poor, struggling painter offering him financial support, certain commercial success

The Yellow House, Arles, September 1888; Amsterdam, Rijksmuseum Vincent Van Gogh

and a utopia of brotherhood. He wrote him a letter extolling the virtues of Arles, a veritable Eden in the south of France. While waiting for Gauguin's response, Vincent spent long days in the burning heat, the *mistral* mercilessly pouring out of the north, scorching the earth and Vincent's hatless head, turning it a bright red. But he did not care. Time was running out on his dream; if he failed this time, it would be the end.

Vincent was beside himself, wracked by anxiety and thoughts of death. In his muddled madness, his thoughts turned to religion. "When in a state of excitement," he said, "my feelings lead me to the contemplation of eternity and eternal life." As a way to find comfort, he attempted to paint Christ in the Garden of Gethsemane under the starry night. But whether because of guilt or lack of artistic skill, he failed to do it. He destroyed the canvas. Instead, he painted the *Starry Night Over the Rhone*. "I must have a *starry* night," he wrote Theo. When "I have a terrible need of—shall I say the word?—religion," he wrote, "then I go out at night to paint the stars." The stars had become for him a substitute Christ, something he looked to in order to end his loneliness, his guilt, his shame. Vincent longed for redemption but could not find it. "Is this all," he asked, "or is there more besides?" The stars represented hope of redemption, no matter how impossible it seemed.

Finally, in late October Gauguin arrived. But from the start, it was a disaster, the two painters fighting over everything from money to women to perspectives on art. After two months together, life was a living hell for both of them. The dream of an artists' commune, a brotherhood of artistic souls, was coming to an end.

Vincent's inner agitation reached a boiling point on December 23. After yet another contentious fight, Gauguin took a drastic step: he stormed out of the house, leaving Vincent, perhaps for good. In a panic, Vincent—his dream over, his life in ruins, his mind spinning out of control—took out a razor, grabbed his ear and sliced off the bottom half. Blood rushed everywhere. He bandaged his ear, attempting to stem the flow and then wrapped the severed part of his ear in a towel and went in search of Gauguin. He had to make Gauguin see what his desertion had engendered. Thinking he might be at the brothel next door, Vincent tried to enter, but the owner refused to let him in. He left his severed ear with the doorman, returned to the Yellow House, climbed the stairs to his room and collapsed on his bed, bleeding to death.

HOTEL DIEU

"He was a crazy man who cut off his ear. What could you possibly learn from him?" The question posed to me by an American college student the week before rattled around my mind as I stood outside the entrance of the Arles Hospital, the place they took Vincent after the police found him in his room. As I walked through the large archway into the center courtyard, I noticed the sign over the door: *Hotel Dieu*—God's house. Likely built in the sixteenth century, "the hospital looked like a prison, with high stone walls pierced by small windows and few entries." Soon after Vincent was brought there, his condition stabilized. Yet his mad hallucinations, his screams, his violent outbursts, forced the staff to lock Vincent into an isolation cell.

Standing in the large garden in the center of the former hospital, I tried to imagine Theo searching the hallways, looking for his brother locked away in some far off room. I imagined his quick meeting with Vincent, his brief talk with the doctor in residence, assuring Theo that Vincent would recover. I imagined Theo's glad getaway, just nine hours after arriving, determined to rejoin his fiancée in Amsterdam, undoubtedly annoyed that Vincent had spoiled his holiday with his untimely mental breakdown. Yet I also imagined how guilty Theo must have felt, abandoning his brother in his time of need. In fact, days later, to assuage his guilt, he wrote: "His suffering is deep and hard for him to bear," but "nothing can be done to relieve his anguish now."

Vincent was a brilliant artist but a tortured soul. It is this dichotomy between his art and his life that makes it hard for many Christians to know what to think. Sadly, many discount his art because of his troubled life. I wonder if some dismiss his art because they don't like dealing with his suffering—and Vincent really suffered. Some of it was self inflicted—his cantankerous nature, his inability to forgive, his careless lifestyle—but much of it was caused by his illness (doctors were just starting to diagnose it as a nonseizure type of epilepsy), which led him to make bad choices and for which no medication existed at that time. Is it right to blame him for a reality that was often out of his control?

I turned left to make my way around the courtyard, where I saw a gift shop. Along with some great prints of his work, there were shelves and shelves of trinkets and souvenirs, every imaginable object printed with a van Gogh image: wine glasses, paperweights, pencil holders and key chains. Kitsch. I was reminded again of Scruton's book. Kitsch, he writes, is a major enemy of beauty. It exists, he says, "when people prefer the sensuous trappings of belief to the thing truly believed in," when "emotion is directed away from its proper target towards sugary stereotypes, permitting us to pay passing tribute to love and sorrow without the trouble of feeling them." In kitsch we want to avoid the real thing but "retain its comforts."

Those trinkets in the gift store sparked a thought. If our goal as a family was to appreciate and enjoy beauty, not only did this mean avoiding stimulus addiction, it also meant avoiding kitsch, where we sidestep the real thing but "retain its comforts." That was easier said than done, especially in our Disney-style culture that tells us to have faith but never provides the content. Just believe.

This kind of shallow sentimentality has affected the Christian world of art as well. So often modern Christian art is saccharine and shallow, the painting of a house sitting on a hill, illuminated from inside, giving off the impression of perfect comfort and peace. But there is something wrong with the picture. There is never any disorder in the picture, never any suffering, not even the slightest bit of paint peeling from the house. It's not real. In his essay "Beauty, Sentimentality and the Arts," Jeremy Begbie writes that so often Christian art is mired in sentimentalism; it hearkens back to a time before the Fall, a time free of sin and evil when there was no suffering. The late artist Thomas Kinkade once said, "I like to portray the world without the Fall."

As Christians we are tempted to like art that only makes us happy and that does not remind us of sin or evil or suffering. We want our art to show us the lost Eden and stir our desire to return. We don't want to be told that we can't go back to paradise, that instead we must go forward as pilgrims. This is too hard for us. So we take our

The Garden of the Arles Sanatorium (Hotel Dieu)

beauty like our coffee: with lots of sugar. It is an idealized type of beauty, a Hallmark card kind of beauty that is not the real thing. We want a sentimental feeling without the suffering.

As I fumbled with a tacky van Gogh key chain, something else dawned on me: it wasn't just the gift shop that struggled with kitsch, but ironically, Vincent as well—not in his art but in his life. With his idea of utopia, a new Eden of artists, the Yellow House was like kitsch. He wanted the feeling of community, the dream of utopia, but not the real thing, which was often difficult and demanded sacrifice and commitment. He wanted community but never the forgiveness that sustains it. He wanted the idea of fellowship, not the reality. But it never works that way.

As I headed back to meet my family in the park, I was excited to share what I had learned from Vincent's life, what his struggles had taught me about the "flight from beauty." If my family and I were going to appreciate real beauty and let it guide us like a map, we first needed to know what to avoid. That was true. And Vincent's life had lots to teach us about what to avoid. But I didn't want to learn from him only by negative example. I believed he also had much that was positive to teach us. But these insights, I would learn, would be mingled with suffering.

Vincent was scared. Almost four months had passed since that December attack, and he remained in the hospital. Since then he had had two more attacks, each followed by recovery, the resumption of painting, the desire to return to normal life, and then by renewed anxiety and mania and the inevitability of another attack. That spring, after his third attack, he realized he was not ready to live on his own. He was terrified that one more attack would tip him over the edge into complete madness and he would end up babbling in his room like so many patients he encountered in the hospital.

So on the advice of his doctor, on May 8 he transferred to the asylum of Saint-Paul-De-Mausole, an eleventh-century monastery established for pilgrims who "sought succor for the troubled minds and infirm spirits." With its location in the village of Saint Remy, twenty-five kilometers outside of Arles, in a snug valley at the foot of the Appilles Mountains, the place looked more like a resort than an asylum. Vincent hoped that it was here, under the care of kind doctors and in an atmosphere free from stress and worry, that he could find solutions to his illness.

While he waited for a cure, he began having nightmares, terrifying visions of the future, as if his fear of insanity and death were visiting him in his dreams. Many of them were laced with religious themes, which was strange. Since his break with his father years earlier, Vincent had rejected the institutional church and turned his back on his former religious experience. So what prompted these dreams?

Perhaps one explanation was that around June, "Theo [in a letter] unthinkingly praised a Rembrandt drawing of an angel." From that moment on, "Vincent began to see religious imagery everywhere." Long held back by denial, anger and resentment, the water of religion—not just the religion of the starry night but the religion of

Christ—began to pour back into his life. Over the next six months, interrupted by more attacks, each lasting longer than the last, he painted *The Pieta, The Raising of Lazarus* and *The Good Samaritan*.

Vincent had returned to religion; there was no denying it. He had a strong sense that his life might be cut short by madness, and thus clung once again to the religious truths of suffering and healing, the reality of death, and the hope of the resurrection, all themes from his earlier life when he was a missionary. "He identified with the suffering of the dying Christ, the victimized Samaritan, and the decaying Lazarus," contends Kathleen Powers Erickson, conveying this identification artistically "by replacing the face of Christ in *The Pieta* and the face of Lazarus in *The Raising of Lazarus,* with his own." Vincent was beginning to see that beauty was more than nature; it was more than the individual capturing the "it"; rather, it was people serving others in the midst of suffering. It was sacrifice. In these religious paintings, particularly the *Raising of Lazarus*, he also demonstrated something new in his art: that suffering and decay in this life would not have the last word (no matter how depressed he was about his illness); rather, resurrection, rebirth and recreation would one day win out. He still believed in beauty, but now it was a broken beauty, a beauty mingled with suffering.

In June, with another attack imminent, he desperately clung to the hope of this new day of redemption, a day when his suffering, and all suffering, would be no more. He painted a small village, importing a Dutch Christian Reformed church, the church of his youth, foreign to the Provencal landscape. He made the church devoid of light within, showing that the Spirit of God no longer resided there, and instead resided in the adjacent homes, illuminated by light. But unlike his first *Starry Sky over the Rhone*, where he left out Christ, unable to come to grips with the reality of Jesus, in this painting, *The Starry Night*, the viewer's eye is drawn to a sun/moon in the right-hand corner, a symbol of Christ who will one day end all suffering and make all things new. A new heaven and a new earth. Vincent made it clear that as much as he was at home in this world, especially nature, he was also a pilgrim longing for a new day.

SAN REMY

"Sorry, but the van Gogh room and gift shop is closed for the winter," a middle-aged woman said to us before ducking into a side office. I hated to take no for an answer and miss our only chance to see his room, so I went to find the director of the hospital, hoping he might take pity on us. It took some effort to find him, but after a short meeting, he kindly made an exception and let us in. When we entered Vincent's second-floor room, it was spartan: a bed pushed against the wall, a small desk placed next to the bed, an easel standing next to the window. As Michelle walked over to the window and looked out, I imagined Vincent standing there painting as he gazed intensely at the rolling fields and the rugged Appilles in the distance. For many months Vincent had to remain in his room, not allowed to walk the grounds or paint outside. His window was his only portal to beauty.

After exiting his room, we walked around the grounds of the hospital. I pointed out to my kids the large reproductions of his art hanging on garden walls and the sides of buildings. I wanted them to see beauty—not a sentimental beauty, but a broken beauty marked by suffering, while still retaining

Pieta; Amsterdam, Rijksmuseum
Vincent Van Gogh

hope. Jordan surprised me and stopped and looked intently at *Starry Night*. "That's the painting that hangs in the girls' room," he said. "I have always liked that painting."

As we were leaving, we paused one more time at the bronze statue of Vincent in the garden, a look of sadness on his face. While all the conflict and suffering in his life shaped his art, forged a broken beauty, and one day would bring his work untold commercial success and fame, I knew from the letters he wrote Theo that he wanted something even more: personal peace.

Vincent was always after the "it," the heart of beauty, which he tried to breathe in and softly exhale onto others through his work. But he could never find it. He didn't find it in his art or his artist colony or his relationship with his father. None of these could deliver the "it" he so desperately longed for. And there were times when he despaired that what he was looking for even existed.

What Vincent didn't realize was that what he was after all those years was actually the biblical concept of shalom. In Hebrew, shalom is a fourfold concept encompassing peace with God, peace with self, peace with others and peace with the created world around us. This shalom was the thing he most desired. But it could only come from one place, which Vincent couldn't see. Why? This was the question that haunted me as I stood in front of his statue.

At that moment I recalled a heated argument I had had with Jordan the day before, when we first arrived in Arles. When he and Jonathan ignored our instructions not to climb on the merry-go-round, I lost my patience (not unusual) and yelled at him—more like shamed him. He was really hurt and got mad at me for singling him out and letting Jonathan off the hook, which I often did even though it wasn't fair. We found a section of pavement behind some trees to sit and talk, but it turned into a stalemate, he arguing his case and me, mine. For forty-five minutes, the blame went back and forth, each of us trying to win our case, justifying our actions. Then, as if the scales had just fallen off, I was struck with a realization: this was exactly what Vincent did with his father every day for two years before his father died. Arguing for hours on end, neither Vincent nor his father would admit wrong or ask for forgiveness. The result was always more bitterness and more arguments. Was this what was happening to Jordan and me? Was Jordan going to grow up bitter toward me like Vincent was toward his dad? The thought frightened me. So right then I took the first step; I asked Jordan to forgive me. Then he did the same with me. What followed was a sweet moment of reconciliation, the experience of shalom.

Back at the statue, I thought about that moment of reconciliation with Jordan the day before. I realized then why Vincent couldn't see where shalom, the "it," comes from. It came down to forgiveness, something Vincent struggled to do. My mind returned to his art. I did a quick survey of his religious art. Is it possible, I thought, that in spite of all the wonderful religious themes Vincent painted, there was one image missing that was most needed? He never painted the image that represents divine forgiveness: the cross.

By now Michelle had joined me in front of the statue of Vincent. I told her about my insight from the day before when she asked me something important: "Why do you think he ignored the cross in his art?"

"I'm not sure," I said. "But I have two theories. Do you want to hear them?" I began telling her my theories. The first was that the absence of the cross in his art had to do with his religious up-bringing. His father, who was a pastor, was a follower of the Groningen school of thought, a liberalized theology that saw Jesus as only a moral example, not an atoning Savior. Vincent had grown up hearing that Jesus could inspire us to live better lives, but he could not forgive our sins.

Then I mentioned the second theory, which has to do with his pride. Vincent never wanted to admit he needed forgiveness from God or his friends or his family, especially his father. If only he could have seen that divine forgiveness would have reconciled him not only with his heavenly Father but also with his earthly father. If he had had peace with God, he might have had a chance to have peace with others, something he so desperately wanted.

I started to walk away from the statue and stopped. I looked back one more time at Vincent. "What breaks my heart," I said to Michelle, "is that Vincent's guilt, his shame, his regret tortured his heart to the very end. I wish he had found in his personal life what he had found in his art: the broken beauty of shalom. Forgiveness. But I am not sure he ever did."

As Michelle and I walked down the garden path toward the exit, I had to wonder, when Vincent left St. Paul's that spring in 1890, did he leave behind his last and best chance to experience this shalom?

Vincent was "cured." At least that is what his doctor wrote on his asylum record on May 16, 1890, almost a year after he had been admitted. Just weeks after recovering from an attack lasting two months, this one more violent and destructive than any previous attack, Vincent decided to leave St. Paul, to attempt a normal life one last time. He worried that if he had one more attack like that he would end up in St. Paul's forever, unable to paint or even to talk, a silent, brooding, ghost of a figure like so many others there. So on May 17 he took the train to Paris, and after spending three days with Theo, his wife Jo, and their new baby, he traveled an hour outside of the city to Auvers. Theo had arranged for the prominent physician Dr. Paul Gachet, an amateur painter and doctor to other famous impressionist painters over the years, to oversee Vincent's care. When Vincent arrived, he immediately deemed the village beautiful. Running along the length of the right bank of the River Oise, the population squeezed in the gap between the river and the ridged, sloping sides of the Vexin Plateau, Auvers has been called the cradle of impressionism. Cezanne, Pissarro and Daubigny all spent time there painting its scenic landscapes.

Although Vincent found the village beautiful and managed to stay productive, painting seventy-plus paintings in seventy days, life was anything but idyllic. "He had arrived in May holding on by the thinnest thread: terrified by the possibility of another attack, still racked with guilt over the money diverted from Theo's new family, haunted by the stacks of unsold paintings in Paris." But he continued to paint—he had to. It was the only thing that kept his mind occupied, holding off another attack, and made him feel useful, called. But his hope was failing. "I am far from having reached any kind of tranquility. . . . I feel a failure, . . . a lot that I accept and that will not change. . . . The prospect grows darker, I see no happy future at all."

He sensed that his life was slipping away, that his time on earth was limited. He felt old and tired. His mother wrote him on the five-year anniversary of his father's death, heaping more guilt on him for the role he played in the death. By July, his relationship with Dr. Gachet had soured and ended badly. He could not count on him in an emergency. Vincent had no friends in town, repelling them with his eccentric ways, the ghastliness of his severed ear, his tramplike appearance, his unkempt beard and his "wild eyes in which there was a crazed expression."

At the beginning of July, he received the letter he had feared for years. Theo was running out of money; there was just not enough to take care of his new, growing family and support Vincent at the same time. The partnership between brothers that had lasted for almost a decade was about to end. Fear seized Vincent at every turn, and his art turned dark and foreboding. Instead of painting landscapes of rolling countryside dotted by warm and inviting houses, he now painted "vast fields of wheat under troubled skies" or his *Wheat Fields with Crows*, trying "to express sadness and extreme loneliness." "My life is threatened at the very root," he wrote shortly after receiving Theo's letter cutting off support. "My steps are wavering." He was in a state of panic. There was no way out of this dilemma, no more utopian dreams that could make this nightmare turn out all right. For

Wheatfield with Crows; Amsterdam, Rijksmuseum Vincent Van Gogh

two weeks, he painted, trying to stay busy, trying to hope for the best. The end was near.

Then on July 27, after a meal at the Ravoux Inn, he went back out to paint, his bag of paints and brushes around his arm, his easel slung over his back. Hours later, he staggered back without his paint supplies, his easel or his freshly wet paintings. "[He] was holding his belly and seemed to be limping," recalled one of the patrons enjoying his dinner on the Inn's terrace. He had been shot. Vincent passed the terrace and stumbled up the stairs to the first floor, climbed into bed and waited to die.

Auvers

"It looks the same as when van Gogh lived here, doesn't it?" the manager said as he showed me around the Ravoux Inn, assuring me that nothing had changed in over a hundred years. It was now late February. Three weeks had passed since I took my family to St. Paul's in San Remy. I was on my way back from a week speaking in Vancouver and had scheduled an extra day in Paris in order to spend an afternoon in Auvers. I wished my family were with me. I had come to Auvers to draw together some conclusions on the role of broken beauty as a map, a guide in the pilgrimage of life. But I had also come to enjoy beauty: the beauty of Auvers and the beauty of the art Vincent created here.

From the Ravoux Inn, I made my way to the tourist office, picked up a map of the van Gogh sites and headed up the famous steps toward the church. At the top of the steps, I turned around to see the valley and river below. Vincent called it "gravely beautiful." He was right. After visiting the church, the cornfields where Vincent painted *Wheat Field with Crows* and the graveyard where he is buried (two headstones, one for Vincent and one for his brother Theo, who died six months later, sit side by side), I had descended back downhill to the center of the village, and I was now standing in the spot where he painted *Chestnut Trees in Blossom*.

Vincent loved the blossoms in the spring. He loved to paint them because they reminded him of the new heaven and new earth. I thought of the prophet Isaiah: "For behold, I create new heavens and a new earth, and the former things shall not be remembered or come into mind. But be glad and rejoice forever" (Isaiah 65:17-18).

People adore Vincent's art, I was coming to understand, because it brings them joy; they experience an aspect of shalom through it, a sense that for one moment in time things fit together. In some sense, even if they don't realize it or want to admit it, they are worshiping, giving God his due for the way things fit together.

How is this possible? Perhaps the simple answer is that God is the source of beauty. As theologian Bill Dyrness contends, "The splendor of beauty, its attractiveness, is grounded in the fact that it is inherent both in God himself and, by extension, in the creation that he has made and that bears his mark (it is, by God's standards, 'very good')." This means that when we admire God's good creation we are honoring the one who gave it to us. And when an object is created that honors or fits with this larger creation, it is good to delight in it. In doing this we are giving the Creator his due.

When I made it down the hill I found on an easel the reproduction of his *View of the Oise with Bridge*. Vincent loved bridges, I think, because they reminded him of Bunyan's *Pilgrim's Progress* and the journey of life. For Vincent, bridges take us places; they take us over obstacles and provide unobstructed views of the road ahead. They are a metaphor for the journey of life.

I could see the bridge Vincent had painted off in the distance. As I stood there looking at it, my thoughts turned to the role of beauty—to art as a pointer on the road of life, a standard to order our moral imaginations, a guide to the good life. Beauty rightly understood—broken beauty—I had come to conclude over the past month, has the ability, when we perceive it, experience it and learn from it, to steer us between twin dangers: decadence (stimulus addiction), seeking shalom apart from beauty, and sentimentalism (utopian visions of life), looking to beauty to return us to a lost Eden.

But broken beauty can do more than stir us away from these twin dangers. It can also point to a greater beauty—the shalom of God, a place of profound comfort, the reality that we belong in the world, with God and others, and to a day when there will be no more pain or suffering or evil. In this sense, broken beauty is, at its core, redemptive, showing us where forgiveness and reconciliation come from. "Broken beauty," writes art historian E. John Walford, "is not only true to the human condition, but it can embody the essence of the gospel of redemption, or, at very least, manifest its fruits. . . . A broken beauty can be a redemptive beauty, which acknowledges suffering while preserving hope."

Searching for Vincent, my family and I had learned that broken beauty is beauty marked by suffering but infused with hope. It's like a powerful story where conflict and suffering and brokenness are overcome. It is a hope for a better future. But it's not just about hope; it's also about our lives right now. We can experience and enjoy broken beauty in this life. We can be inspired by it, compelled toward a reality so much fuller and richer and deeper than the cheap imitations of addictions and sentimentalism offered to us by our culture. And we can enjoy a beauty beyond our wildest imaginations. This is the promise of broken beauty, rooted in Christ, his redemption, his beauty. It is what we all long to experience.

Slowly I walked back to the inn and thought of all we had learned over the past month. Back at our flat when I had asked Michelle if it was possible to not just limit media in our lives but also develop an appreciation for beauty that trumped all imitations, I was hopeful we could discover it. Now, walking van Gogh's trail, drinking deeply of his art and soaking in the beauty of Provence, we had come closer to our goal. At the very least, we now had a better idea of what we were looking for, the kind of broken beauty that can move our souls, point our hearts in the right direction and inspire us to know better the real source of all beauty. We also knew that this broken beauty would take a lifetime to pursue and that, ultimately, whatever we experienced in this life would not be complete until the arrival of the new heaven and earth. We are still pilgrims and will remain so to the end of our lives. Our time here is marked by suffering but also hope. I think deep down even Vincent knew that. I recalled a sermon that he had preached in his early twenties:

> It is an old belief and it is a good belief that our life is a pilgrim's progress, that we are strangers on the earth, but that though this be so, yet we are not alone, for our Father is with us. We are pilgrims, our life is a long walk or journey from earth to Heaven. . . . And the pilgrim goes on sorrowful yet always rejoicing—sorrowful because it is so far off and the road so long. Hopeful as he looks up to the eternal city far away, resplendent in the evening glow.

I was now back at the Ravoux Inn, where I had started. Soon after Vincent returned to his room there, a doctor was summoned. After examining the wound, the doctor determined that Vincent was shot from some distance away. Vincent disagreed. He shot himself, he claimed. But regardless, there was nothing the doctor could do to save him. A telegram was sent to Paris, summoning Theo. When he arrived the next day, Vincent was still alive but was bleeding to death. Theo held him in his arms, trying to comfort him. Just after midnight Vincent's breath became weaker. "I want to die like this," Vincent said. For the next thirty minutes he struggled for air until finally he breathed his last. "He has found the rest he was longing for," Theo wrote his mother. "Life was such a burden to him. . . . Oh Mother! He was so my own, own brother."

Vincent's funeral took place in the restaurant under the inn. A number of his artist friends came from Paris and creatively lined the walls of the inn with Vincent's art. Appropriately, *The Pieta* hung at the head of the casket. Vincent would have approved. After all his suffering with poverty and illness, so much of it beyond his control, he finally had the rest he desired and longed for. His pilgrimage was over.

As I walked back to the station to take the train back to Paris and then another one to Provence, a kind of melancholy settled over me. I grieved at the tragic end of Vincent's life. But I also grieved that my time with Vincent was over, at least for now. He had affected me so much. I saw beauty differently, and the role it would play in my family's life would forever be changed.

As the train rattled out of the station, my seat providing a great view of Auvers nestled on the hillside, I was reminded of a line from a hymn that Vincent knew by heart:

Come home, come home! You are weary at heart,
For the way has been dark, and so lonely and wild. . . .
Come home: Oh come home!

I wasn't sure if Vincent ever found the home he longed for, but I was hopeful. I was hopeful that in death Vincent was home—that he was in the only place that welcomes the weary, that he finally experienced broken beauty, the shalom of forgiveness that we all need. And I was hopeful that after a long week away from my family, I would be home with them soon, very soon.

seven

GOODNESS HAPPENED THERE

Le Chambon and the Transforming Power of Community

H e had to know. As he stepped into the pulpit on June 23, 1940, he had to know that the words he was about to preach were dangerous—to his congregation and to his family. And his congregation made up of mostly farmers, tradesmen and shopkeepers—a simple but hardy people, descendants of the Protestant Huguenots and people who knew persecution and suffering well—had to know too. They had to realize that their pastor was about to deliver a prophetic message, a sermon that would call them to dangerous action. In fact, they had come to expect it from their young pastor, André Trocmé, who in just a few short years had established himself as a forceful voice and a faithful pastor. A proficient networker and key catalyst in Le Chambon sur Lignon, a small farming village sitting on a wide plateau nestled in the mountains of south central France, Pastor Trocmé had revitalized the neighborhood study groups, faithfully visited them in their homes and challenged them each Sunday to live out their faith in practical ways. Trocmé brought energy and vision to the church and the sleepy village, as if both were waking from a long winter slumber.

He stood in the pulpit, high above the congregation, the air thick with emotion. With his faithful associate pastor, Edouard Theis, next to him, he addressed his congregation, a people deeply discouraged, as if they knew that many bleak years of suffering lay ahead. Just the day before, June 22, 1940, France had signed the armistice with Germany, making official its cowardly capitulation to Hitler. Germany would soon occupy the northern part of France, while the southern part where Le Chambon sat remained under the control of the French, administered by General Marshall Pétain and his puppet Vichy government.

Now, peering down earnestly on his congregation, Pastor Trocmé warned them: "Tremendous pressure will be put on us to submit passively to a totalitarian ideology. If they do not succeed in subjugating our souls, at least they will want to subjugate our bodies." He challenged them to resist. But how? They had no weapons, no military might. "The duty of Christians," he said, "is to use the weapons of the Spirit to resist the violence that will be brought to bear on [our] consciences." He appealed to them to refuse to "cooperate with this violence" and called them to live differently than their oppressors, not with violence but with nonviolence: "Loving, forgiving, and doing good to our adversaries is our duty," he said. Maybe he could read their faces, or maybe he knew how discouraged they already were, or maybe he just knew how hard this road would be. So he added one final exhortation: "We must do this without giving up, and without being cowardly. We shall resist whenever our adversaries demand of us obedience contrary to the orders of the gospel. We shall do so without fear, but also without pride and without hate."

Where would the strength and hope come from to resist the "thousand-year reign" of Hitler's Germany? Where would they look for directions for each new challenge? Despite the bleakness of the situation, all was not lost, he said. "Gospel truths have not been lost. . . . The Word of God has not been lost and that is where we find all the promises and possibilities of recovery for ourselves and our church," as if it were a map to direct their steps, to shape their character and to mold them into a community capable of resisting the Nazi evil. Soon the Nazis would try to divide them, he warned, creating hatred and division, even among Christians; but he exhorted them to stick together. If they did not stay united they would surely fall. If they did not learn how to love one another, they would be powerless to resist the Nazis. With his reference to love, perhaps they thought of the inscription over the door to the church, "Love one another." Soon those words would be more than symbolic and they would be forced to decide if they really believed them. Soon they would face their greatest challenge, one that could lead to their own deaths. It would begin with a knock on their doors.

THE 1:00 P.M. TRAIN

Three thousand feet high in the mountains of south central France, along the Lignon River that cuts through the plateau, surrounded by rolling hills and the distant silhouette of inactive volcanoes, we stood in the small village of Le Chambon. The town appeared not to have changed much since the days of the German occupation, as if it were frozen in time. We had made the three-hour drive from Provence, over half of the trip winding up the mountain through dozens of switchbacks, making clear why this remote area was a good place to harbor Jews.

It was the third week of March, the trees still bare of leaves. Our journey up the mountain had been delayed for two weeks because of bad storms, but now it was sunny and warm, as if spring might come early, the frozen ground already starting to thaw, everywhere turning to mud. Standing in front of the small train station, just a half block from the town square, we were listening to Hélène Crouzet, a lifelong resident of Le Chambon whose family harbored Jews in her childhood home. Though not born during the occupation, she knows the history of the village well, often giving tours. "We start here," said Hélène, "because this is the train that brought so many refugees to Le Chambon, arriving every day at 1:00 p.m., right here in broad daylight." My friend, career French missionary Hugh Wessel, was translating, having driven up from Marseille.

As Hélène described the Jewish refugees arriving on the train, I studied the train station. I imagined Jewish families, sleepless, scared, carrying all they owned in this world, stepping off the train hoping no guards were present to check identification papers. Just then, I heard my girls laugh behind me; I looked over my shoulder and saw them on the swing set near the station, letting off steam after a long car ride. I tried to imagine them getting off the train tired and hungry, a look of fear on their faces. I didn't like the thought.

In front of the Le Chambon train station with Hélène

During the war years, 1940–1944, Jews heard that Le Chambon and the surrounding villages were a safe place—perhaps their last and only hope for staying alive. Since many of the refugees were already in France, perhaps they followed local maps, often hastily sketched on slips of paper stuffed into their pockets. Others came from all over Europe. Thousands made it. The map worked.

In our family's focus on "journey" as a metaphor for pilgrimage and the need for the right kind of map to guide the journey, van Gogh had helped us see the role of beauty. Now we wanted to focus on truth and goodness, the other parts of the ancient triad that have guided people for centuries. We hoped that Le Chambon would be our window into this reality, would be our guide. The people who lived on this plateau were guided by goodness and truth. Making the right decisions, living morally, knowing truth from falsehood—these were not gray areas for them. They were crystal clear, like shimmering diamonds in the warm sunlight. How could we discover this same reality for our family, particularly our children? That is what we were here to find out.

Since the beginning of our pilgrimage, we had been attempting to lay a foundation for our kids that would help them avoid the shallow faith of Moralistic Therapeutic Deism and the lock-box syndrome, to develop a consequential faith that could withstand these challenges to their faith. I knew one of the greatest challenges my kids would face as they went off to college would be in this very area of truth and goodness. Christian Smith and his team, who had been our guides in this area since the start, had documented it, and the results were ringing in my ears as I stood at the train station. After hundreds of lengthy interviews, his team concluded "that moral individualism is widespread among emerging adults and that a sizeable minority professes to believe in moral relativism." Simply put, for these young people the reality of what was right and good was not clear. As I walked around the train station, I wondered how as parents we could avoid this for our kids. I didn't want them to grow up thinking truth, goodness and reality were unclear or up for grabs.

Smith and his team also found something else that was helpful as Michelle and I thought about our children. They discovered that the reason most young people adopt a kind of moral relativism is because they are petrified of any type of fundamentalism and extremism. They have seen its results in the twentieth century through facism, Nazism and Stalinism. They see it now in Arab fundamentalism, and they want nothing to do with fundamentalism of any kind. In order to avoid this, they reject any outside moral or religious authority. To make moral decisions, they rely on themselves or what they glean from the culture around them. It is a kind of ad hoc morality, going with whatever works at the moment, willing to compromise if it benefits them. It just works better this way, they think.

The problem is that this moral pragmatism doesn't work well for them, as the National Study on Youth and Religion discovered. Most emerging adults are having a hard time navigating life, finding that life has not lived up to its promises. In fact, Smith and his team concluded that "a large proportion of emerging adults today are lost, confused, or misled in their thinking about what makes anything morally good or bad—and yet they are generally not aware that this is so." To put it another way, "They are morally at sea in boats that leak water badly."

Michelle and I were determined to help our children avoid being lost at sea, and to achieve this we needed to help them find the right maps to guide them. We were convinced that they existed. That's why we were in Le Chambon. We had come there to continue our map making, and we hoped that the people of this plateau could help us. We had come to experience their guidance and, even more importantly, to find inspiration in their goodness.

She didn't hear the knock. With *la burle* racing down from the north churning the snow in all directions and the frigid cold chilling the granite presbytery, Magda Trocmé was too busy putting fuel on the fire to warm her four young children to hear the visitor at the door. The woman knocked again, this time louder. Finally, Magda heard the pounding and opened the door. "May I come in?" the bedraggled woman asked. A German Jew, she had a look of deep hunger on her face, and her cheeks were reddened by the sharp wind. She was in danger, having fled northern occupied France where the anti-Jewish laws had made it nearly impossible for Jews to live freely. By the winter of 1940–1941, there were already thirty thousand foreign Jews in French concentration camps, and the persecution was growing worse every day.

"Naturally, come in, come in," Magda said, inviting the woman into the house. They sat down at the table. The woman took off her wet shoes and began telling her story of fear and persecution. After hearing it, Magda acted fast. Leaving her guest seated by the warm fire, Magda trudged through the snow to the town hall. She knew if the woman were to stay out of danger—that is, avoid deportation to Germany—she would need identification papers, and the mayor was the one who could provide them. At least that is what she thought. "What?" he said. "Do you dare to endanger this whole village for the sake of one foreigner? Will you save one woman and destroy us all? How dare you suggest such a thing to me? . . . Get her out of Le Chambon tomorrow morning, no later."

Magda hurried home, realizing that she may have done more harm than good. The refugee in her home was now exposed and in mortal danger. Magda needed to get the woman to safety before the authorities deported her back to Germany—and certain death. After arranging for another family to take the woman in and eventually help her escape to Switzerland, the next morning Magda sent the woman on her way, back out into the cold. For the rest of the war, Magda would feel guilty for pushing this woman away, wondering if her actions brought harm to a person seeking help. And yet it was an important learning moment. She realized that to close the door on someone in need of help is to harm them. Never again would she or anyone in the village turn someone away; never again would they reveal to the authorities the location of a Jew in their midst.

Later that bitterly cold winter, in early 1941, André traveled to Marseille, a port city on the Mediterranean coast, to meet with top Quaker leader Burns Chalmers at the offices of the American Friends Service Committee. André had heard about the terrible conditions in the concentration camps—the biting cold, the terrible hunger, the swarming rats and mud, the rampant sickness—and he wanted to help; he was even willing to live in the camp himself if that would make a difference, and he made this proposal to Chalmers. Chalmers loved André's passion, vision and intense desire to help people. He sensed that André was a gifted leader. But Chalmers was so distracted by the constant flow of refugees and relief workers needing his attention that he suggested he and André meet at another time and place to continue the conversation.

A short time later they met in Nimes, a central location, at a nondescript restaurant. Responding to André's offer to volunteer in the camps, Chalmers told him there were already a number of groups working in the camps, so that wouldn't be the best use of his time and talents. But Chalmers had another idea. "You tell me you come from a mountain village," he said, "where one can still enjoy a certain security." André nodded in agreement. Chalmers's mind was racing at the possibilities. He was seeking a safe place to hide refugee children, and he realized that a dozen villages nestled in the mountains of a high plateau, ones difficult to reach, would be the perfect location.

He told André the Quaker strategy in the camps: to provide medical certificates for as many of the fathers as possible, declaring them unfit for labor and thus deportation. If this did not work for the fathers, they would try the mothers—anything to keep the families together. "If the parents are nonetheless deported, we take charge of the children," said Chalmers, "and we arrange that they be boarded outside the camp." But the problem was that the Quakers could not find enough villages to take the children. "We can get people out of the camps," he said, "but nobody wants them. It is dangerous to take them. Is your village prepared to do such a thing? Do you wish to be that community?"

The Presbytery

"The refugees often came here first," Hélène said as she pointed to the solid, dark green wooden door under the austere roof just outside the presbytery. "Here is where they knocked," she added. We were following the journey of the refugees when they first arrived and had walked here from the train station, a short five-minute stroll down the gently sloping hill, past the town square and some shops. My kids recognized the door immediately from the documentary *Weapons of the Spirit,* produced by Pierre Sauvage, a Jew born in the village during the occupation. We had watched the documentary to prepare our children for the pilgrimage to Le Chambon.

Weeks earlier Michelle had also read our kids the engrossing children's book *Greater Than Angels* by Carol Matas, a historical novel

Read

about the journey of seven children who were deported, along with their families, from Germany to Gurs concentration camp in the south of France. After a year in the camp, a Swiss relief organization was able to get them out and relocate them to Le Chambon where they lived in a boarding house, attended Ecole Nouvelle Cévenole and hid in the woods during the frequent roundups. Our kids loved the novel, getting upset every time Michelle suspended reading, eager to find out what was going to happen next to these seven children.

Now that our own children were actually standing in Le Chambon, the book came alive for them. "Dad, this is so exciting to be here," Jonathan said to us. "This is my favorite place."

"You mean of the entire trip so far?" I asked him.

"Yes," he said as his face lit up with a big smile.

His strong reaction surprised me. Jonathan, our quietest child, hardly ever made his opinions known, at least not that strongly. He was polite, easygoing and demure. Finding out what he thought on any given topic was not easy, and often it was like pulling teeth. But over the last month or so I had begun to see a change in him. To say

Presbytery door

he was overcoming his shyness would be too simple, though that was true. No, something more profound was going on, like a metamorphosis. He was not only overcoming his shyness, but his personality was expanding. He was becoming funnier, more lively, more confident in who he was. He exerted his wants and needs with his brother, not just following Jordan's lead or giving in to him. He let us know his opinion more frequently and was learning to tell us more. Little by little, it seemed, Jonathan was discovering his identity. He had always been an amazingly considerate boy, but now he was an engaging boy as well. As a parent it was a joy to watch this change.

After talking to Jonathan, I heard Hélène say something interesting. I swung back to listen, my attention locked on her. She was telling us about Magda and how she and the other women in the village would always open their doors to refugees. "Magda and the other women," Hélène said, "believed that these refugees where God's creatures, created in the image of God. They had dignity and worth because God had made them. For this reason they would never turn them away. They would always find a safe place for them."

At hearing those words *dignity* and *worth,* my mind drifted back to the novel *Greater Than Angels.* In the book, when the Germans come for young Klara (the main character) and her family, her grandmother pleads for permission to talk to a local minister who is a friend, hoping he might save the family: "The guard laughed at her. Then he said, 'Why would a German minister dirty himself by talking to a Jew?' He looked at her with such disgust, as if she were some kind of rat, not a person at all. At that moment I knew how bad the danger was because if you aren't a person anymore, why, they can do anything to you. Anything. And not feel bad about it." How different was the response of the people of Le Chambon. Their map, rooted squarely in the Bible's view of human beings, led them to treat people dramatically differently than the Nazis. And they would treat them differently even if it put the safety of the entire village in jeopardy. Saving one life was worth it.

———————— ✿ ————————

They would do it. The elders of the church agreed to make Le Chambon a place of refuge, primarily for children. Twelve other pastors and their churches on the plateau would make the same decision. Trocmé challenged his congregation, "You must accommodate; you must protect; you must save these refugees." They agreed; after all, as Huguenots, they were accustomed to suffering, to hiding and to sheltering those in need. Yet, they also knew the Bible. As Reformed people who loved the Old Testament, they knew that God had a special place for the Jews in his grand narrative. If the Jews were special to God, they must be special to us, they thought. We must protect them. Understanding the Old Testament, they also knew about the city of refuge where Jews were to protect and shelter the innocent: "I command you [to protect the refugee] lest innocent blood be shed in [your] land . . . thereby bringing the guilt of bloodshed upon you." The members of the church knew the Old Testament instruction "to share [their] bread with the hungry [and] bring the homeless poor into [their] house" (Isaiah 58:7) and the New Testament command to be like the good Samaritan (Luke 10:25-37) meant caring for those Jewish children and anyone else who needed their help.

Once Trocmé's congregation and other surrounding pastors and churches decided that their faith must be lived out in this way, together they made the plateau one of the safest places in Europe for Jews. Dozens of homes, boarding houses and private pensions were turned into places of refuge. When word quietly spread through the Jewish community, many of them made their way to Le Chambon, arriving on the 1:00 p.m. train. For many refugees that arrived, counterfeit IDs were made with false names, giving them new identities. Everyone on the plateau, it seemed, was part of this massive conspiracy of goodness, and if they weren't, amazingly they kept silent.

But in the summer of 1942, things started to get more dangerous. A few months before German troops would take over the southern zone, a response to the Allied invasion of North Africa, Vichy sent Georges Lamirand, the secretary-general in charge of youth affairs, on a formal state visit to Le Chambon. His mission: to find out why none of the youth in Le Chambon had participated in the state-sponsored youth camps and to strongly encourage them to do so—that is, if they knew what was best for the village. "For two years we had tried to escape from the hold of the state on our youth," wrote Trocmé in his journal. "Vichy had first tried to regroup all the young people under the blue shirt of 'Companions of France': Fascist salute to the flag, bugles, file-pasts, social activities, work camps, worship of native land and the marshal." But now a confrontation was brewing.

Lamirand arrived around noon. After a rustic lunch at the YMCA camp and a ceremony at the sports field with official speeches, the festivities moved to the temple (the Protestant church) for a short worship service to conclude the day. André and his associate, Edouard Theis, attended but did not preach, not wanting to give the appearance of support of Lamirand. They had asked another pastor from another village to deliver the sermon. Following the service they walked out to the front court of the church. As the pastors were saying goodbye to Lamirand, twelve students of the Ecole Nouvelle Cévenol (a school that Trocmé and Theis had started in 1938) walked up to the minister of youth and handed him a written document. They asked him to read it immediately. The letter condemned the atrocities that took place three weeks earlier at the Vélodrome d'Hiver (an indoor cycling arena in Paris where almost half of the twenty-eight thousand Jews rounded up on July 16-17 were taken and confined for eight days without water, food, bedding or toilets; hundreds died or committed suicide, while the rest, including over four thousand innocent children, were sent to concentration camps in Germany). Halfway through, the letter became defiant, as if it were throwing down the gauntlet to the Vichy government: "We feel obliged to tell you that there are among us a certain number of Jews. But, we make no distinction between Jews and non-Jews. It is contrary to Gospel teaching." And if you ask us to turn them over, the letter stated, "we would try to hide them as best we could."

Confrontation, not compromise, was the message of the letter. The Christians of the plateau, who up to this point had rebelled in silence and secret, had now gone public and professed their disobedience to Vichy. They had chosen to obey God, not man, chosen to "love their neighbor," even if illegal. Upon finishing the letter, Lamirand hung his head and turned pale. "These questions are not my affair. Speak to the prefect of your department." Then he turned and hurried to his car, undoubtedly angry.

The local prefect was livid. He accused Trocmé of sowing discord on what was supposed to be a day of national harmony. Trocmé responded, "It cannot be a question of national harmony when our brothers are threatened with deportation." Then Prefect Bach issued a threat: in a few days, he said, we will begin rounding up the Jews living in Le Chambon, and you will not be able to stop us. Without hesitation, without concern for his own well-being, André said, "We do not know what a Jew is. We know only men." Prefect Bach responded, "Monsieur Trocmé, you would do well to take care. If you are not prudent, it is you whom I shall be obliged to have deported. To the good listener, warning." And then the prefect walked out.

This was no idle threat. Two weeks after Lamirand's visit, Vichy struck. On a Saturday night, a few cars and some buses surrounded by police motorcycles entered the marketplace of the village. Trocmé was immediately summoned to the town hall, just off the square. Fear was in the air. The chief of police, an important official of the Vichy government, got right to the point: "Pastor, we know in detail the suspect activities to which you are devoted. You are hiding in this commune a certain number of Jews, whose names we know." The chief went on: "You are therefore going to give me the list of these persons and their addresses, and you will advise them to be on their good behavior, so that they should not try to flee." When Trocmé told the chief he did not know the names of these people, he was telling the truth. All the refugees were given false names, so he didn't know their real names. But even if he had, he would not have given them away. "These people have come here seeking aid and protection from the Protestants of this region," Trocmé told the chief of police. "I am their pastor, their shepherd. It is not the role of a shepherd to betray the sheep confided to his keeping." The chief of police became angry and threatened deportation for Trocmé if he continued to flout the laws of the land. "Besides," he laughed villainously, "your resistance is useless." He was determined to find the Jews. The hunt was on.

MEMORIAL PLAQUE

"This is it," Hélène said, motioning to the outer wall of a community building where a large bronze plaque commemorates the heroic deeds of the residents of the plateau, many of whom risked their lives to save over thirty-five hundred Jews. I wanted to come to this spot because it is the only place in the village that tangibly recognizes the rescue effort. But I also wanted to come because it was in the schoolyard nearby that in 2004 French president Jacques Chirac recognized in ceremony and speech what these people had done. It was the first time in fifty years that the French government had officially honored the heroism of this plateau. What took them so long?

Chirac's stated reason for coming was the recent outbreak in France of ugly racist attacks, many against Jews and Muslims. He wanted to make a statement against this outbreak, and he was confident that France had the moral resources to combat it. He began his speech by extolling Le Chambon as the "soul of the nation," "the embodiment of our country's conscience," "a place symbolizing a France true to her principles, faithful to her heritage, true to her genius." In the face of danger, these people, Chirac intoned, "chose the humanist principles that unite our national community and serve as the basis for our collective destiny—the principles that make France what she is."

I had read an editorial that appeared in print five days after Chirac's visit, written by Pierre Sauvage, the producer of the documentary *Weapons of the Spirit* who owes his life to the people of Le Chambon. As pleased as he was that the French government had finally recognized the village, Sauvage took exception to Chirac's words. He wrote,

"In his speech in Le Chambon, Chirac made no reference to the Hebrew Bible or to the New Testament, to faith or the power of religious convictions." He continued: "But had the people of Le Chambon not been motivated to resist the Holocaust by more than mere Frenchness?" Was that their only motivation?

At one time, Sauvage, whose parents never told him he was Jewish until he was an adult, might have agreed with Chirac that tolerance, solidarity and fraternity, common French slogans, were all that was needed to build national harmony and to develop morality and character in children. He was raised to fear religion as divisive and harmful. But everything changed, he said, when he returned to the village to shoot footage for his documentary. "Until then, I had viewed religion as a source of conflict and ignorance, religious people as by definition bigoted and fundamentally stupid." But by listening to what motivated these people, he discovered that religion was the key, that it was the reason that the people of this plateau, out of all the people of France, "have been honored collectively as Righteous Among the Nations by Yad Vashem, the Israel to the Holocaust." Sauvage wondered why in his call to arms against intolerance Chirac could not acknowledge the good that can come "from religious faith and identity."

The reason he didn't is simple: the French, like most of Europe, want to base human rights on secular foundations, eliminating from their memory the religious traditions of the West that, in part, established the concept of human rights in the first place. For Chirac, and many others, secular tolerance is strong enough to undergird human rights. But is it? If secular tolerance was not strong enough to prevent the French from sending ten thousand Jewish children to the gas chambers in Germany, why would secular principles be any help now with anti-Semitism? If these principles were not strong enough to motivate people to rescue Jews then, if these principles were not able to help people articulate the reason why humans are worthy of rescue, if these principles were not robust enough to provide a notion of justice to protect the weak from the strong, why did Chirac think they could do much today to end intolerance?

As a parent I am sad to see so many young people in the West adopting this view, rejecting religious and moral traditions in favor of pragmatism, individualism and relativism. This is better than being intolerant, fundamentalist and oppressive, they say; we don't ever want to be divisive. Much better, they have determined, to morally muddle through life than be intolerant. But are fundamentalism and relativism the only options?

Our family was discovering in our time in Le Chambon that the people of this village—with their strong moral convictions, their well-thought-out social ethic, and their knowledge of right and wrong, of what is bad and what is good—were anything but oppressive, intolerant and divisive. In fact, they were the opposite: kind, generous, tolerant, sacrificial, inclusive, joyful, good—all characteristics of a people motivated by a strong moral and religious tradition. They were not lost at sea, like so many emerging adults in the West, but rather knew exactly where they stood. They had a map and knew their place on that map. And because of that, when the moral struggle came, they acted as if it were second nature to be heroic and good.

It was time to leave the plaque. I thought one more time of Chirac's speech, which he ended by reminding his audience that France has inscribed on all its public buildings the French Revolutionary slogan: Liberty, Equity, Fraternity. "But it was not the motto of the Republic," concluded Sauvage, "that the President could read on the Protestant Temple, across the street, that he declined to visit. It was the religious admonition: 'Love One Another.'" And it was to the temple we went next.

After the confrontation with Lamirand in the front court of the church, the village prepared for a raid. As soon as the meeting with Prefect Bach was over, Trocmé raced back to the presbytery, quickly getting word to the Boy Scouts, his secret messengers, to sound the alarm far and wide, sending the Jews scattering into the forest for safety. The next day, Sunday, Trocmé expected arrest at the church. The temple was packed, and the mood was tense as the service began. André urged his people to obey God rather than man, to disobey the government when its edicts contradict the clear Word of God. He exhorted them to have courage and to trust in God. Finally, he reminded them about their commitment to be a "city of refuge" and how loving God meant loving one's neighbor as well.

When the sermon was over, the mood in the church was thick with emotion, many believing that the pastors had sealed their own fate and would be arrested as soon as they walked out the door. But the front court was empty, devoid of police. They were too busy attempting to round up Jews in the village and the surrounding farms. They had little success though; most Jews were nowhere to be found.

In November 1942, in response to the Allies landing in North Africa, the Germans moved into the southern zone, occupying it along with the north. "From this time on, Vichy police were closely supervised by the Gestapo, the secret police of Hitler, and the danger of giving aid to the Jews became far greater than ever." Throughout the fall of 1942 and the winter of 1943, the "conspiracy of goodness" continued unabated. But now the conspiracy had a new Vichy "convert." Each time there was to be a new raid, a mysterious voice on the other side of the phone would warn them: "Attention! Attention! Tomorrow morning." And then the receiver would go dead. They never knew who made the warning calls, but each time the call was accurate and then the silent alarm would be sounded, alerting the Jews to the raid.

But by the spring of 1943, the Nazis tired of Trocmé, Theis and the "nest of Jews" hiding right under their noses. They were irritated at the waste of resources every time they conducted a raid and it turned up little. Enough was enough. They needed to cut the movement off at the head, and this meant eliminating Trocmé. They had already arrested and imprisoned him once in early 1943 only to find him mysteriously released. Someone high up in the Vichy government was protecting him, but the Nazis could not find out who it was. So they planned to hire a hit man to kill him, an act that they could easily deny or blame on someone else and thus avoid popular unrest and the stirring up of more resistance on the plateau.

In the summer of 1943 a young man who was a member of the French resistance and a double agent walked into André's office and told him his life was in danger: he had learned that the Gestapo had put Trocmé's name on a list for assassination. "You must go into hiding," the young man pleaded. But André was not sure. He wanted to act courageously, to stand against evil even if this meant death, something he had asked his congregation to do many times. How could he flee now in the face of his greatest test? On the other hand, what would happen to the rescue movement if he were not there to help lead it? So much of the effort depended on his leadership, his moral and spiritual authority.

Soon a high official in the Reformed Church in France, who was also a good friend, came to plead with him:

> You know how these executions happen. You go for a ride in a car and your corpse is found at the edge of a forest. Or it could be a break-in at mealtime and your entire family is mowed down by a machine gun fire. Are you willing, because of your stubborn attitude, to be killed and maybe also be responsible for your wife's and your children's wounds or deaths, and maybe even those of others who live under your roof? (There were always refugees in residence at the parsonage.)

André did not want this, of course, but he was still torn. Finally, after nights of agonizing over the decision, he decided for the good of his family and the movement that he had no choice: he had to flee. Magda tracked down a ration card and identification papers for him under the false name of Béguet. With the help of some brave souls he found a safe house in the department of Ardèche, next door to his own department of Haute-Loire. From there he was moved from place to place, ending up in the Drôme. Department across the Rhone River, where no one knew or could identify the well-known pastor.

After many months away, his youngest son, Jacques, missed him so much he was unable to concentrate on school. André arranged for Jacques to come live with him, taking on the duty of teacher, best friend and playmate to his son. Jacques would never be happier; he had his dad all to himself. But something happened that almost killed them both.

André and his son had planned to meet in Lyons and catch a train back to the safe house at 8:30 a.m. Sunday morning. Arriving at the station perilously close to the departure time and nervous about missing the train, André left Jacques and their carry-on luggage at the front of the station, running alone to the baggage room to pick up their stored luggage.

"Stop, stop, stop!" someone kept yelling. André ignored the command, thinking it was for someone else. Out of nowhere an angry German jumped in front of him, blocking his way. Another soldier came up behind André. One of the soldiers placed a gun barrel on André's chest and pushed him through a door. The soldiers then pushed him into a van and slammed the door shut. He had been arrested. Immediately, André thought of his son, shy and sensitive, without money, guile or the wherewithal to know how to find his way home. What would happen to him if his father did not return?

THE TEMPLE: "THE SOUL OF LE CHAMBON"

If the people of the plateau were the heart of the rescue movement, the temple was its soul. It was there that the Word was preached, a word that called them to be God's people and that reminded them of their salvation in Christ, their adoption into his family, and the gift of the Holy Spirit that empowered them to love and serve others. It was there that these Christians learned about the "city of rescue," about the good Samaritan, about the Ten Commandments. It was there they were told that if their faith was real it would result in good works. It was there that they internalized the message that in God's service is perfect peace and freedom. And it was there that they became a community.

When we walked into the temple, my kids scattered in every direction, excited for a new place to explore. I stopped and looked around, pondering what had taken place here seventy years ago. In my mind, I envisioned this place filled to capacity each week, with people desperate for the presence and protection of God, knowing that at any moment a raid could take place and that they, along with those they were harboring, could end up in concentration camps. I thought about how often I just go through the motions in church. But I imagined they didn't have that problem. Fear has a way of focusing the mind.

We walked to the front of the church and sat down in a pew. I recalled what Gérard Bollon said to us earlier in the day. Bollon, a local expert on the history of the plateau, told us that "these people did what they did because of their faith. It was the core of who they were and why they acted." But he also stressed that it was not a theologically liberal, do-goodism kind of faith that believes if you perform good works you will be saved or that the whole goal of religion is to make moral people. Trocmé had seen this kind of faith up close when he was a graduate student at Union Seminary in New York City and had rejected it as too secular, too rational, too Americanized. This kind of faith, one that only cares about making people good, was not strong enough to transform human hearts, Bollon contended; it was not strong enough to override humans' innate desire for self-protection in order to heroically resist the Nazis and possibly sacrifice their lives for total strangers who needed help. "Only a Christianity that has a cross, forgiveness, redemption and resurrection," he stressed, "could produce this kind of person." I felt that as I sat in the pew.

My thoughts were broken when Hugh climbed into the pulpit and invited my boys to join him. He wanted to show them how his voice, sans microphone, could travel the whole length of the building because of the sound board right over his head that projected the voice. I ran to the back of the church to confirm his contention. He was right—I could easily hear him. The boys found that fascinating. Then Hugh stepped aside and let Jordan have a try. He pretended he was preaching. When I said I could hear him in the back, he smiled. I appreciated Hugh making this long day fun for my boys.

I returned to my seat near the front of the church. Hélène told us more about Trocmé's sermons and how energized he got when talking in the pulpit; "he would come alive," she said. "He was a strong preacher, able to captivate his audience." His passion won them over.

Once again my mind returned to *Greater Than Angels*. In the book, Klara is arguing with a friend about who was happier, the Nazi soldiers in the village or Pastor Trocmé. Klara's friend Peter, who does not believe in God, says, "Those Gestapo goons looked *perfectly* happy to me."

"They *think* they are," Klara counters. "But they don't know the real happiness of behaving with goodness. Theirs is a little world. Look at Pastor Trocmé. His soul is huge. He is connected with the goodness of the universe."

Although fiction, that description seems to fit his life. Trocmé did believe he was connected to the goodness of the universe, and he wanted his parishioners to experience that same connection every week in worship. He knew that God's law, summarized in the Ten Commandments, was not a killjoy to steal their freedom and fun, but the road map to perfect peace and freedom. It was a detailed picture of the fullest life, *not* a recipe for unhappiness.

Years later Trocmé would write that he and Magda had never been "happier than during those years of rescue in Le Chambon-sur-Lignon." During those years they were fully alive, living out their faith in the face of profound danger and suffering. Life was exciting; it had meaning. They knew that true liberty, equity and fraternity were produced by the gospel. The best community would come about as a result of God's Word breaking down barriers and creating real fellowship, and it was this community that would produce one of the greatest rescue movements in the war. It is a shame that President Chirac missed this reality on his visit. At the time, France could have benefited from this message.

"Look, it is getting dark and cold, and the kids are going to be hungry soon," said Hélène as she finished talking about André. "Maybe this is a good time to suspend our travels for the day." With glee in their voices, the kids shouted their agreement. I agreed; it was time to take a break.

"Tomorrow," Hélène informed us, "we will visit Cévenole School, some farmhouses that harbored Jews and the House of the Rocks, the boarding school led by Trocmé's cousin Daniel Trocmé, who in the closing months of the occupation sacrificed his life for the rescue effort."

It was going to be another good day.

Despite our hunger and tiredness, I wanted to do one more thing before we ended our day: locate a farmhouse on the outskirts of Le Chambon where a man recuperating from tuberculosis found himself trapped when the Germans occupied the free zone on November 11. Over those eighteen months he had written one of the most famous novels of the twentieth century: *The Plague*.

André's mind raced. Why had he been arrested? Was it for running in the station, or did they know who he was? He had to think fast to save himself and his son. "Listen for a moment!" he yelled out in German through the barred window of the rear door of the van. But the guard did not move. Trocmé yelled it again. Finally the guard came over to the window. "Look," André said in the fluent German he had learned from his cousins, "my son, a tall, blond twelve year old boy, is waiting for me to bring the luggage. He is at the top of the stairs in the railroad station. Could you please have someone get hold of him? I need to tell him where he should go because I have been *verhaftet* [arrested]."

Skeptical, the guard went to get his supervisor. He too was incredulous and called over the captain to hear André's story. "You are telling me stories," the captain barked back. "Why were you running?"

"I was late," André pleaded, "and I ran to get the suitcase in a hurry so that we wouldn't miss the train. Here is the baggage check. You can verify it."

"You were not trying to flee from the police roundup?"

"What roundup?" André asked.

"Haven't you noticed the station is surrounded by troops?"

"I didn't, I was in a hurry!"

After thinking for a while, the captain decided to test André's story. He ordered the guard to take him to find his son. He warned André not to attempt escape or "you'll be a dead man."

Soon André and the guard found Jacques waiting at the top of the stairs. "Jacot," André said calmly to his son, "the Germans have arrested me. Come along, we must see a German officer in front of whom I will explain what you should do and where you should go."

His son, seeing the rifle pointed into his father's back, cried out, "Daddy, Daddy, what is going to become of us?"

The three returned to the captain, who took one look at the tall blonde boy crying in despair and was visibly moved. "You have told the truth. I understand," he said to André.

André and his son were taken by the guard to the control booth. If their identification papers passed inspection, they would be free to catch a train to Valence. The guard at the control booth was comparing photo IDs with a special directory containing pictures of people wanted by the Gestapo. Would André's new photo, showing him without a mustache and with glasses, fool the guard? Even if it did, his papers identified his last name as Béguet, but Jacques, whom André had claimed as his son, had the name Trocmé. He knew they would be caught. He had to find a way to avoid the control point. Carefully he leaned over and whispered to his son, "Jacot, do exactly what I do, and slowly without running. Get ready."

THE PLAGUE

"Is that it?" Hugh asked as he pointed to an outcropping of farmhouses beyond a large granite farmhouse.

"That's it, that's it," I answered, recognizing it from the photos I had seen online. From August 1942 until late 1943, Camus lived in this hamlet called Panelier. It was here that he wrote most of *The Plague*, a novel about a plague brought on by rats in the city of Oran, on the coast of Algiers. As I stood in front of the farmhouse, I imagined Camus sitting in his third-floor room, the fire burning in the hearth, his scarf wrapped around his neck for warmth, a hat on his head, writing about his heroic characters as they bravely fight the plague. Though he struggled to get it right, having to rework the novel many times over, when it was finally published it was an instant bestseller.

Yet despite the acclaim it has received over the years, religious critics have focused on one area they say weakens the entire story: the area of motivation. Without God, they ask, what motivation was there to oppose the evil of the plague? Without God, why were people worth saving? The novel never answers that question, at least not in a way that satisfies the critics.

Camus's farmhouse

As I stood there looking at the window, imagining him writing up there alone day after day, another thought came into my mind though, a thought sparked by the story of this plateau: what was most striking about the novel was *not* the rejection of God, as shocking and existential as that was meant to be, but the fact that Rieux begins to fight

the plague alone, apart from any involvement in a community. Why
was this important? Well, if there was anything we were learning
from Trocmé and the people of the plateau it was that individuals
acting alone don't often become rescuers. Le Chambon had taught us
that individuals who become rescuers are almost always part of a
strong ethical or religious community. Their community so shapes
them that when they are faced with the challenge of rescuing it is
"ordinary to them, for it [is] their normal way of relating to others." If
there is a flaw in Camus's engaging book, it is that.

I turned from the house and headed back to the minivan where my
family was sitting, not wanting to encourage my exploration any
longer than necessary. Before getting in, I looked at my kids sitting in
the back. If they were faced with a similar situation as the people of
Le Chambon, I wondered, would they be rescuers? I knew the answer
to that question: Not unless they grew up in the kind of community
that would make that kind of action second nature, as it was for the
people of Le Chambon and the surrounding villages.

The community of Le Chambon formed people to be rescuers, to
stand for truth even in the face of danger. The convictions, the history
of persecution and the strong religious foundation of Le Chambon
shaped, motivated and guided many people into doing the right
thing. As parents trying to morally shape our kids into people who
know right and wrong, who care for and respect the other, and who
seek out the good in life, Michelle and I were anxious for our family
to be part of this kind of a community. Harvard sociologist Robert
Coles has written that "the most persuasive moral teaching we adults
do is by example: The witness of our lives." If this is true, then our
children needed to learn it from Michelle and me, as well as other
adults in the community that surrounds them.

But finding or developing this kind of supporting community
would not be easy. As Christian Smith found out, because of our twin
commitments in the West to individualism and soft relativism, schools,
parents, sports teams and civic organizations have stopped teaching
our kids how to think, reason and act morally. Is it any wonder they

fail the moral test when acting morally would jeopardize their own happiness? And when the next major crisis hits, such as another holocaust, should we be surprised when a whole generation acts more like the 99 percent in Europe who did nothing to rescue Jews than the 1 percent on the plateau who responded morally? I desperately wanted my kids to be part of that 1 percent. But I knew that if this was going to happen, Michelle and I needed to model it better.

The identification checkpoint line moved slowly. Bored, the guard that was overseeing André and his son started talking to some of the other guards nearby, and as the line moved forward, he neglected to stay alongside them. Another few steps and they would be next to a large stone pillar. André thought to himself, if I can just put the stone pillar between the guard and us, we can slip away without him noticing. He whispered to his son to do as he did. "Yes, Papa," the boy said.

André and Magda Trocmé

Just then the guard stopped looking at them. André got out of line and walked five steps and stood behind the pillar, out of view of the guard. Jacques followed his father, and the guard didn't react. From there, they could see the exit from the station, just a few more steps away. Keeping the stone pillar between them and the guard, they slowly walked toward the exit. They merged into a stream of arriving passengers heading out the exit. Just as they exited the station, a tram opened its doors, and they jumped aboard. The tram pulled away. Later, the Gestapo realized who had just escaped: André Trocmé, someone they had been after for months.

Fifteen minutes later, André and his son were in a local church, worshiping God on the Sabbath, deeply grateful for their escape. The following day they went back into hiding.

Months passed, and on June 6, 1944, the Allies invaded France, signaling the end of the war. André and Jacques returned home to Le Chambon that very evening, welcomed back by their family, the church and the entire village. The next day, he had a chance to survey the rescue movement, and what he found astonished him: Magda and the other pastors on the plateau had turned the area into the most successful station in the entire underground railroad, perhaps the safest place in the world for Jews.

EMPTY SCHOOL BUSES

Early afternoon on our last day in Le Chambon, I was sitting on a bench in the main square, facing the train station, deep in thought. I was trying to process all that we had learned and experienced in Le Chambon. I looked around the edge of the square, imagining those school buses, waiting to take captured Jews to concentration camps. But in my mind I saw empty buses. There were no Jews in them. In most other small towns in France, I saw in my mind buses packed with terrified human beings on their way to the camps, and ultimately their deaths. But here the buses were empty. Why?

Earlier that morning, we had visited some surrounding farms that had harbored Jews. I asked Hélène if we might see some of their hiding places—a trap door in a barn, a fake wall in the house, a dugout in the woods.

"They won't show you them," she said.

"Why?" I asked.

"Because they might need them again someday," she said.

Might need them again? Always ready to rescue people.

Those buses were empty because the people of Le Chambon and the surrounding villages had a moral horizon; they possesed a moral map to lead them. They believed in the dignity of all human beings, the image of God in people. They called evil, evil, and stood up to it even though it put themselves in harm's way. They were people of strong convictions. And yet their convictions never made them intolerant; rather, they were more tolerant of people different from themselves—the Jews. They did not budge in the face of moral challenges, but they were never fundamentalists. In fact, the stronger their convictions, the more civil they acted toward everyone, including the Nazis. They were deeply loving people, filled with compassion for people different from themselves.

Richard Mouw, former president of Fuller Seminary in Pasadena, once said that the problem today is that the most civil people have the least conviction, and the most convicted people have the least civility. But the goal, he said, is convicted civility. The people of Le Chambon had convicted civility—they had strong convictions and expressed them with civility. We had come to Le Chambon to learn how to be like them. We wanted our kids to see this, to be shaped by it. Michelle and I wanted to be inspired to parent our children the way the people of Le Chambon raised their children. Because someone's future might depend on it.

Empty school buses.

Goodness happened here.

eight

SUFFERING

The Case of Corrie ten Boom

Corrie heard the buzzer. Then she heard it again, this time wishing someone, anyone, would stop pushing it and quit interrupting her flu-induced sleep. She rolled over, in and out of consciousness, fever wracking her head and body with intense pain. She noticed people quickly but quietly passing her bed in her small, top-floor bedroom. Was she dreaming? She wasn't sure. "Hurry, hurry," they were whispering as they disappeared into the small opening below the lowest shelf in the bookcase. She bolted up in bed. She suddenly realized this wasn't a dream, and it wasn't a practice drill either. It was real—a Gestapo raid.

There were already five people in the secret room, and when the last person, a member of the Dutch underground, crawled in, the trap door was lowered. Tumbling out of bed, panicked, Corrie shoved her emergency prison bag, filled with a collection of warm clothes, vitamins, some sewing needles and a Bible, onto the bottom shelf, directly in front of the trap door. She collapsed back into her bed, feigning sleep. Immediately, the door slammed open.

"What is your name?" the officer screamed, as if he was ready to strike her if she did not answer.

"What?" she said hesitantly.

"Your name!"

"Cornelia ten Boom," she replied.

"Get up! Get dressed!" he yelled.

She looked for her clothes. This was the moment that Corrie ten Boom, fifty-four years old—who, along with her eighty-four-year-old father, Casper, and her older sister, Betsie, ran the family watch business—had rehearsed for months. For almost a year and a half the ten Booms' home had been the center of the underground resistance in Haarlem, a small city twenty miles west of Amsterdam. Helping any Jew who asked for assistance, the underground forged identification papers, provided ration cards, which had been stolen from a governmental office, and secretly, often by dressing the men in women's clothing, moved the Jews to farms or small villages far from the eyes of the Gestapo. The ten Booms also sheltered other permanent "guests" (whose ethnic features were too hard to disguise) in their own home, constructing a secret room and installing an alarm system throughout the house to alert the Jews of a Gestapo raid. It was these other guests that were now hiding behind the secret brick wall on that fateful day, February 28, 1944.

"So you are the ringleader?" he asked as she got dressed, not bothering to remove her pajamas first, trying to avoid the leering eyes of the agent. "Where are you hiding the Jews?"

"I don't know what you are talking about," she responded.

She finished dressing, anxious to get out of her room before someone in the hiding place made a noise that would give them away. Out of the corner of her eye she saw her prison bag. How could she get it without drawing attention to the trap door? Reluctantly, she turned and headed down the stairs, stumbling at each step, her legs weak, her head throbbing, her mind anxious. When she arrived in the dining room, Betsie and her father were sitting in chairs against the wall. Beside them sat three underground workers.

On the floor beneath the large picture window that overlooked the main street rested the Alpina sign, broken in three places. One of the Gestapo agents, wondering if it might be a signal that it was safe to enter the shop or the house, put it back in the window. His hunch was correct. The doorbell started ringing, members of the underground coming to warn the ten Booms of an impending raid. The house had become a trap, luring resistance workers inside to their doom.

By now, Gestapo agents were all through the Beje, the name the ten Booms had given to their home, breaking through walls, rifling through drawers, pounding on floors looking for clandestine radios or secret rooms hiding Jews. One agent came running in; he had found the massive stack of food ration cards, vital to the rescue operation, hidden in a secret compartment under a step at the top of the stairs.

At that moment, one of the agents grabbed Corrie by the arm and pushed her down the remaining five steps into the workroom of the watch shop. He shoved her up against the wall.

"Where are the Jews?" he demanded, losing his patience.

"There aren't any Jews here."

The agent slapped her hard across the face. "Where is your secret room?"

"There is no secret . . ." He hit her again. She staggered under the blows as if her feverish head was about to explode like a watermelon hitting the hard pavement. She could taste blood in her mouth. She was losing consciousness.

"Lord Jesus," she cried out, "protect me!" The agent, hand raised to strike again, suddenly paused.

THE HIDING PLACE

"Mr. Belcher, I need some volunteers. Would your children like to help me?" asked Marijke, one of the guides, as she stood next to the secret room. We, along with a dozen or so other English-speaking guests, none of whom we knew, were having a tour of the Beje.

"I think so," I said hesitantly as I looked over at them. They moved further into the hallway.

"When I push the secret buzzer, they need to take off their shoes, carry them with them, and crawl through the trap door into the hiding place and then pull the gate shut."

She pushed the alarm. "Hurry, hurry," we whispered to our kids. "This is a Gestapo raid."

We had arrived in Holland four days earlier and were staying as guests at the Dutch L'Abri, a Christian study center and live-in community in the countryside, about an hour from Haarlem. After leaving Provence a week ago, we had driven to Frankfurt, Germany, to pick up a large RV that would be our home for three weeks. As a family, we were still learning about journey, the second pillar of pilgrimage. With van Gogh we had explored beauty, and with André Trocmé we had investigated truth and goodness. All three are part of the map that guides us on our journey. But as we had discovered in our exploration of broken beauty, the moral and the real, you can't talk about

The ten Boom watch shop and house (the Beje), Haarlem, Holland

any of these without understanding suffering. When we live morally, when we stand up for truth, when we resist evil in our lives and in the world around us, when we seek broken beauty, when we pursue shalom, there is no doubt we will face suffering, either in our own lives or in the lives of others. Suffering can't be avoided. And yet.

Like so many Americans, I try to avoid suffering in order to make my life easier, more secure and more comfortable. I also try to avoid others who are suffering, lest this trouble rubs off on me, like a bad omen. But to ignore the suffering of others is to turn a blind eye to injustice, to evil, to the image of God in others. It is selfish and individualistic. And to live this way is to live a life devoid of courage. We learned this in Le Chambon.

So we were at the Beje to learn and experience what Corrie and her sister could teach us about how to face suffering head-on, to understand it, to prepare for it and even to welcome it. We were there to train our children. If we wanted them to stand up for justice, to work for shalom, to love others, to be makers and lovers of beauty, to live heroic lives, then we needed to teach them about suffering, because to live heroically is to invite suffering. "All who desire to live a godly life . . . will be persecuted," said the apostle Paul (2 Timothy 3:12).

There was also another reason we wanted to learn about suffering. Put simply, nothing can derail our journey faster and more profoundly than the trials of life. They have the power to knock us off course, to discourage us to the point of giving up, to trick us into relieving our pain through counterfeit idols, to cause us to doubt God's goodness. If we did not want this to happen to us, then we needed to learn from suffering. Suffering would come. Were we prepared?

"Forty-five seconds," said Marijke as my children crawled into the hiding place and pulled the trap door shut. "Well done."

The agent's hand had stopped in mid-air.

"If you repeat that name again I will kill you!" he yelled, his hand inches from her face. Then, putting his hand down, he grabbed her and shoved her back up the stairs. She stumbled across the room to a chair next to her father.

Two men bounded into the room carrying an old radio they had found under the stairs. "And you claim to be law-abiding citizens."

"I see you believe in the Bible," said Wilmese, the lead agent, jabbing his finger at the well-worn Bible on the dining room table that Casper read to the family at every meal and before bed every night. "Tell me," he asked Casper, "what does it say in the Bible about obeying the government?"

"Fear God, and honor the queen."

"It does not say that; the Bible does not say that!" he screamed at Casper.

"No, that is right," Casper admitted calmly. "It says, 'Fear God and honor the king,' but in our case that is the queen."

The doorbell continued to ring. With the sign in the window signaling it was safe to enter, underground workers, who came and went often throughout the day, walked into the trap. Each one was questioned and then arrested. The house began to fill up.

Then, hearing a new sound, Corrie jumped. It was the secret telephone ringing. Her heart pounded. Wilmese glared at Corrie. He grabbed her by the arm and led her over to it. "Answer!" he said, gruffly.

"This is the ten Boom residence and shop," she said stiffly, hoping to send a message. But the caller did not get it. As the agent listened in, the woman on the other end of the line blurted out, "Miss ten Boom, you are in terrible danger! They are on to everything." On and on the voice continued with the agent hearing everything. When that call ended, the phone rang again. Another warning. And again. This time when she repeated the greeting, the phone went dead. The agent grabbed the receiver. "Hello, hello," he said. Nothing. The phone never rang again; the underground had finally gotten the message.

For the next five hours the Gestapo continued to interrogate people in the house. They also continued their frantic search for the secret hiding place and the Jews, but they could not find them. "If there is a secret room here," one agent said, "the devil himself built it." By now the doorbell had stopped ringing. Word had gotten out— no one else would walk into the trap.

At 11:00 p.m. about thirty people, including Corrie and her family, were marched out of the house into the back of a large truck. They were taken to the police station for the night; the next morning they were herded like cattle back into the flatbed truck. Many who knew the ten Booms gathered to say goodbye.

Before Casper was helped into the truck, one of the officers took pity on him. "Old man, if you promise to behave yourself from now on, we may leave you here."

Without hesitating Casper replied, "Young man, if you leave me here today, tomorrow I will open my door to anyone who needs help." The agent walked away in disgust.

The truck's tailgate was slammed shut, and the truck began to move. As Corrie sat on the cold, hard steel of the truck bed, she must have thought that she might never see Haarlem again. She must have wondered what would happen to her family. How could they survive the hardships of a concentration camp? Perhaps she recalled her father's evening prayers the night before as they sat on the hard floor of the police station: "Thou art my hiding place and my shield: I hope in thy word. . . . Hold thou me up, and I shall be safe." She must have wondered why God had not kept them safe from the Gestapo. How did this fit into his plans? She was about to find out.

LESSONS AT THE BEJE

"Why is this happening to me?" asked Marijke, a woman a little younger than Corrie was at the time of her arrest, repeating Corrie's question to herself those first few days in prison.

The tour was over but we had remained in the house to ask Marijke more questions. As I sat with Marijke, Michelle and three of our children (Jordan was back at L'Abri, sick in bed) lingered in the gift section, looking for mementos and postcards. I was sad Jordan had to miss this experience, but I was glad he was safely asleep back at L'Abri. He was happy there. Over the four days we had been their guests, our kids had bonded with the young children of the community directors, who had introduced them to country life—feeding the animals, chopping wood and racing around on the go-cart. Lindsay and Meghan loved playing with the baby goats, carrying them around like dolls. On more than one occasion my kids told me they didn't want to leave Holland. I had never seen them happier, enjoying life and reveling in the fun. I was pleased my kids had the chance to experience L'Abri, to taste a wonderful community in action. Michelle and I appreciated it too, especially the tea breaks every two hours that fostered conversations and new friends.

Back at the Beje, after the kids got to buy some keepsakes, we listened to Marijke talk about Corrie's and Betsie's initial responses to the arrest.

"Weren't they angry with God?" I interjected.

"Ah, good question," she said. "When they were first arrested and taken to the local prison, Corrie didn't understand why this was happening. After all, wasn't their favorite family Bible verse 'My times are in your hands; rescue me from the hand of my enemies and from my persecutors' (Psalm 31:15)? Didn't he promise to keep them safe from their enemies? He had protected them so many times before, why not this time? Was he no longer their hiding place?"

Michelle wanted to know what happened next.

"Well," Marijke continued, "this is where it got interesting. Once Corrie obtained a Bible, smuggled to her by another prisoner, she aggressively started looking in it for examples of suffering. And to her surprise, everywhere she looked in the Bible, good seemed to come out of the bad, particularly in the life of Joseph, who was sold into slavery by his brothers and by the end of the story was saving his brothers from the famine. So as she read the Bible in prison, she began asking a different set of questions. Instead of asking why she was suffering or how a good God could allow it, she began asking what good could come out of this situation, what purpose did God have in putting her in prison, and did he still have a plan for them?"

I asked Marijke what they thought that plan might be, and she didn't hesitate: "Corrie started to see more clearly; she believed that God had allowed the Germans to arrest them so that they could tell people in prison about Jesus. She could see that every day they had a divine assignment—to tell people about what Jesus had done for them on the cross. And this included telling guards, orderlies and even a high-ranking German officer who, many years later, became a Christian through their witness." But then Marijke stopped herself.

She looked pensive, as if she needed to add something to what she had been telling us.

"What is it?" I asked.

"I think it is important to point out," she continued cautiously, "that seeing reality differently didn't mean that they no longer saw evil, as if they had become a Pollyanna. They still saw it; how couldn't they? It was all around them. Yet although suffering was all around them, they refused to give in to despair. Although there were many questions they did not have answers for, they refused to stop trusting God's providential care. *Corrie and Betsie still believed that God had their times in his hands.*"

Our conversation with Marijke now over, it was time to leave the Beje. We had learned a lot about the ten Booms' profound faith—a faith that sustained them over the first six months while they were in a Holland prison and then a Dutch concentration camp. But eventually it would be pushed to the breaking point. For Corrie in particular, suffering would rip at her core, threatening her trust in God and forcing her to make an important decision.

The name filled all who heard it with dread. As the train approached a small, remote town surrounded by forest and sitting on a picturesque lake, a tourist destination deep in the heart of Germany, a prisoner peered through a tiny slot in the side of the car and screamed out the name, a name synonymous with death, sending shivers down the spines of hundreds of women: Ravensbrück. They were being taken to the infamous women's death camp, which by war's end had been the site of the murder of over ninety-six thousand innocent women.

For Corrie and Betsie, hell was about to get hotter. They had survived three months separated from each other in a Dutch prison, cold, hungry and sick, followed by three more months at Vught concentration camp where they were worked to the bone and where, on their last day, they heard the summary execution of seven hundred male prisoners, all husbands, fathers and sons. They were now on the final leg of a three-day, nonstop train trip from Holland to Germany, where they had been stuffed on cattle cars like sacks of fertilizer, devoid of proper food, water and space to stretch or sleep, and nothing but a bucket in which to relieve oneself. Now they were about to enter the inner ring of hell, and there was no way of escaping it.

After being marched from the train station through town, spit on by some locals, ignored by others, they were taken to an open field directly outside the gates of the camp with a large canopy tent standing in the middle. Clinging to one another, Corrie and Betsie settled down to rest under the tent. No sooner had they collapsed in exhaustion than they were ordered out from under the shelter to sit in an open field. Petty evil. It was there they would sleep. When night came, so did the rain, pouring down. They awoke covered in mud, drenched and dejected. For most of the next day they were forced to stand at attention, given little food. They spent another night outside, the blankets still damp, making it hard to sleep. Betsie's cough, a problem for months, was getting worse. By the third night, they were finally marched into the camp and assigned to barrack number eight, built for four hundred women but stuffed with fourteen hundred. With six women sharing a bunk constructed for two, they were asleep in minutes, exhausted from the ordeal of the previous six days.

But they did not sleep long. Awakened by roll call sometime around 3:30 a.m., they had to stand in the predawn cold without jackets, in blocks of one hundred women, ten rows deep and ten rows wide. Not allowed to avoid puddles, many women stood for hours in ankle-deep, freezing water. But they could not move. If they collapsed, they would be beaten, and they were told by other prisoners that if they were unable to get up, they would be "sent to the infirmary," which meant one thing: the gas chamber.

Not far from roll call stood the punishment barracks, named the Cell Building, from which they could hear rhythmic screams following the blows of the whip, the sounds of systematic torture. Corrie and Betsie wanted to cover their ears, but this would invite their own punishment. So they had to endure the harsh sounds.

Days later, with little food or rest, they stood in the penetrating cold of another endless roll call when a young girl in front of them accidently soiled herself. The guards descended on her like vultures on a dead carcass, brutally beating her as she screamed out in pain. Then an elderly woman next to them collapsed to the ground, dead. The faces of some of the women around Corrie and Betsie were filled with horror and hate; others looked on with stoic resignation, too numb inside to care. At that moment Betsie leaned over to her sister and whispered, "Oh Corrie, this is hell."

A month later, in mid-October, they were transferred to another barrack, toward the back of the camp. They hoped that their circumstances would improve, but upon entering they realized life had just gotten worse: instead of individual bunks they saw "great square piers stacked three high, and wedged side by side and end to end with only an occasional narrow aisle slicing through." Fighting back claustrophobia and the stench of rotting straw and human feces, they climbed to their assigned pier, having to crawl over numerous "beds" to get to their space. They laid down, then immediately sat up, banging their heads on the pier above them.

"Fleas!" cried Corrie. They were everywhere in the straw. At that point she lost hope: "How can we live in such a place?"

"Show us. Show us how," Betsie prayed.

Betsie asked Corrie to turn in their little Bible, which they had smuggled in the first day in the camp, to 1 Thessalonians 5:16-18: "Rejoice always, pray constantly, give thanks in all circumstances; for this is the will of God in Christ Jesus."

"That's it Corrie! That's his answer. 'Give thanks in all circumstances!'" Betsie said. She started to thank God for everything—for knowing Christ, for having a Bible, for being together, for the overcrowding, for the conditions in the barracks and even for the fleas. That was too much for Corrie. She could not thank God for the fleas. No way. She argued with Betsie, but Betsie countered. "Give thanks in *all* circumstances." Betsie reminded her that the *all* does not mean just the pleasant circumstances. "But this time," wrote Corrie some time later, "I was sure Betsie was wrong."

Ravensbrück Concentration Camp

"Why was this place so huge?" Jordan asked as he looked from one end of the camp to the other, amazed at its size.

"This camp imprisoned tens of thousands of women," I said. "At one point more than thirty thousand women were crammed in here. This is where they lived, where they were forced to work and where ninety-six thousand of them died."

We were standing in Roll Call Square, just inside the main entrance that at one time had the ironic motto of the camp—"Freedom through Labor"—emblazoned on the gate. Three days had passed since our visit to the Beje, and after a long drive to Berlin on April 6, my birthday, and a couple of nights' stay at a campground in the city, we had driven ninety minutes north to Ravensbrück. Our kids knew about Ravensbrück because Michelle had read them *The Hiding Place* in preparation for our visit.

Roll Call Square, Ravensbrück Concentration Camp, Germany

As we stood there, black volcanic stones under our feet to reduce the dirt and dust but also to give the camp a feeling of darkness and death, Michelle explained to the kids the purpose of Roll Call Square, refreshing their memory from the book. She reminded them of how long the ten Boom sisters had to stand in formation and how painful it was.

"Can you imagine standing in this square at 4:30 a.m. in the cold with nothing but flimsy prison clothes on?" she asked as the icy wind of the lake cut right through our own spring jackets, making her question starkly relevant to the moment. The kids jumped up and down to stay warm.

As we walked down the main camp road, the *Lagerstrasse* as Corrie called it, we noticed the six-inch indentations carved in the volcanic stones to mark the spot of each barrack. There were dozens of them, stretching more than a couple football fields in length. Each indentation had a sign in front of it. I paused at one that read "Sick Bay Huts (Blocks 8-11) 1944–45." I called over my family, mentioning to them that this might be where Corrie and Betsie lived those first few weeks in camp. Corrie mentioned that they were in barrack number 8 in the quarantine huts. She also said that they were next to the "Penal Block."

"From our map that is right across the road," I said as I pointed to the indentation that marked the spot. I reminded them of Corrie's description of the screams and how hard it was to listen to them. We kept walking. The boys got quieter. I was not trying to give my kids nightmares, but I wanted them, especially the boys, to realize how bad the suffering was in this camp and what a challenge it was for the sisters to keep believing in God. I kept asking my boys how they thought they would have done here. Would they have trusted God? Would they have still believed he cared for them? Would they have still believed that God was in control?

As we continued to walk, my kids running ahead, I tried to imagine life in the camp. I tried to imagine the suffering that went on here. I tried to imagine Corrie's sense of calling, to tell everyone she could about God. Would I have done the same? At that moment, the cold freezing my bones and starkness oppressing my mind, I was not so sure.

Days before I had been reading *The Sunflower* by Simon Wiesenthal, a concentration camp survivor who was an avowed atheist. He described his cousin, who was in the camp with him, as a person of strong faith—that is, until he was sent to a concentration camp. One day, after 280 children were gassed in their camp, his cousin, a practicing Jew, abandoned his faith, never to regain it again. "We lived in a world that God had abandoned," said Wiesenthal. "Very few of us prayed." Wiesenthal continues, "He who is incessantly tortured in spite of his innocence soon loses his faith." As I passed hut after hut, I thought about this. Had God abandoned these people? These camps? This world? If I had been there, would I have prayed after seeing so much evil and torture? Would I have told others about my faith? Was my faith deep enough to have withstood the suffering of Ravensbrück? I couldn't answer my own question.

Evil was all around them. They saw it, they felt it, they tasted it, they smelled it. Each day seemed worse than the previous one. Women died all around them, some in their bunks at night, others at roll call and still others by the gas chamber. One day, the entire sick bay was emptied onto flatbed trucks and taken to the gas chamber. The crematorium worked nonstop. Death and disease were everywhere—constant companions. Dejection and despair tore away at their souls.

Corrie struggled to understand the senseless suffering and evil around her. She fought the temptation to be consumed with hatred toward the mean guards who killed so cruelly and forced them to live in such lousy conditions. She fought the temptation to lash out at God, recalling her sister's admonition to give thanks in all things, to bear up under suffering. Remarkably, most days she was able to succeed. But one particular morning tested her resolve.

As she walked along the barracks, she saw, through a half-broken window, a small, concrete-walled room. Against one wall was a small child, barefoot, almost naked, horribly emaciated, a vacant look in her eyes. The little girl, an orphan, had been living in that room for weeks, on half rations, sleeping on the cold concrete floor without a mattress or blanket. Corrie turned away, a shudder going through her. Was this reality she was looking at or just a bad dream? There was nothing she could do; she walked on, wondering, *Why must there be so much pointless suffering?* She thought of the hundreds of concentration camps, the bombed-out cities across Europe, the war and civilian deaths. Limitless suffering. For her this child represented the insanity of the world. She struggled to make sense of it.

She did not know the why of the suffering child in the cinderblock room or of the masses all around her. She knew that senseless suffering seemed to contradict the reality of a good God. But what was the alternative—to stop believing in God? To contend that we are utterly alone in this world of sorrows? To contend that there is no plan for this life? For Corrie, to turn her back on God was a dead end. She had seen what had happened to women who took that position, giving in to despair, losing all hope and easily succumbing to death. She could not go down that road. It seemed a prison worse than Ravensbrück. She was convinced God did not make mistakes.

By mid-December, freezing cold temperatures had descended on the camp. Typhoid was rampant, killing hundreds every day. The gas chambers were working overtime. Betsie—emaciated from lack of food and covered with infectious sores and scars—was dying. She was deathly weak, her sixty-year-old body unable to fight off the disease of the overcrowded and vermin-infested camp. She began coughing up blood, her legs became painfully swollen, and soon she was too weak to walk.

One morning she found herself unable to get out of bed. Corrie and a friend carried her to roll call and afterward to the hospital, but she could not be admitted until her 102-degree fever reached 104. For a number of days she was so weak she had to sit on a stool at roll call. But eventually she was too weak to even sit up. Finally, her temperature reached 104 and they called for the stretcher and took her to the hospital. Yet without proper medicine, food and rest—three things in short supply in the camp—she would die. And Corrie would lose her best friend, her constant companion, her best encourager.

BIBLE STUDIES AND FLEAS

"What was this building?" Jonathan asked as he pointed to an abandoned yet intact building at the back of the camp.

I looked down at the brochure given to us when we arrived. The building, it said, was a workshop owned by the SS, where prisoners spent ten-hour days making SS uniforms. There was also a section of workshops for weaving and making leather belts.

As we walked around the building looking in the windows, I explained that following the war, the Soviets liberated the camp and used it for a military base and to house German prisoners of war. When this area became East Germany, the Soviets continued to use it for military purposes, knocking down the barracks and most of the buildings. It made sense that the large factory building had been kept, most likely as a storage facility.

Jonathan asked another question, the camp clearly sparking his imagination: "Is this the place Corrie and Betsie worked? I remember in the book that they worked in a factory each day."

I told him that according to Corrie's account, she and her sister worked at the Siemens Production Facility. I mentioned that I thought it was about a ten-minute walk outside of the camp.

We walked around the back of the factory and stood in the corner of the camp, where the twenty-foot wall and barbed wire was still intact, the only section of wall not destroyed by the Soviets. I thought of Corrie lying on her overcrowded pier each night looking out at the wall and following the searchlight that scanned the camp, listening to the guards patrolling.

We stopped to rest, all of us getting tired of tramping in three inches of volcanic stone. The powerful wind coming off the lake, some gusts reaching thirty miles per hour, made it hard to walk, as if we were trying to walk in water up to our necks. The girls sat down on the sooty stones, out of energy. They pulled their hoods up over their heads and picked up some of the rocks.

Original camp wall and barracks at Ravensbrück Concentration Camp

As they rested, I told them I thought this might be where the sisters' barrack, number 28, had been located, the place they held their daily Bible studies. They would meet twice a day, sometimes more, in the back of the barrack, where a single light bulb dangled from the ceiling, and read and discuss the Bible. Women would gather around them, packed into the bunks three levels high, to listen to Betsie read the Scriptures and Corrie explain them. They would tell the women that the reality of the Nazis was false and that there was a different way of looking at life—one even more real than the dreadful camp around them. It was here that they told them about the reality of God's presence, that they had dignity, that they were important to God, that he sent his son to die for them. They would tell them that he had their times in his hands and that he was still in control, in spite of the outward circumstances.

To drive home this point, Michelle mentioned the story of the fleas, reminding our kids of Corrie's struggle to follow Betsie's counsel to thank

God for *all* things. At the time, Corrie could not see how fleas fit into God's plan. *They must be a mistake. I can't give thanks for them,* she had said. As I looked over at Michelle, the wind blowing so hard it was difficult to hear, she was energetically retelling the story of the day, many weeks later, of Corrie returning to the barracks to find Betsie smiling.

"I have found out why our clandestine Bible studies have never been discovered by the guards," said Betsie.

"Why?" asked Corrie.

"Earlier that afternoon," said Betsie, "there was a dispute among some women in the barracks and they went to get the guard to settle it. But she refused to step through the door. Do you know why?"

With an "I told you so" tone to her voice, Betsie said triumphantly, "Because of the fleas! The guard said the barracks were crawling with fleas. That is why they never discovered the Bible studies. So you see, Corrie," said Betsie, "God is really in control after all."

Walking back to the camp's entrance, I imagined Corrie and Betsie teaching the women that God was still in control, even in a hellhole like this camp. But I had to wonder: was this explanation enough to hold on to hope, to overcome despair, to put their faith in God? For many, myself included, knowing that God is sovereign, while deeply comforting, is often not enough to sustain us on our hardest days, which, for the women of Ravensbrück, were every day. Sovereignty is often a doctrine for the head—important but not the whole picture. The women at Ravensbrück also needed a teaching of the heart.

By now, we were almost back to the front of the camp and had located the hospital where Betsie had been taken when her fever reached the required level. This was the place where Corrie would learn her greatest lesson on suffering.

She had to see her sister, but she could not get permission to visit the hospital. Finally, after roll call on the second day of Betsie's hospitalization, without authority, Corrie slipped out of her barrack, risking a beating if caught, and hurried to the hospital, trying to avoid guards along the way. Wiping away the frost on the glass, she peered through the window. At first, two nurses blocked her view; then she looked again. This time she saw two nurses wrapping up the emaciated body of a dead patient. It took her a second to realize it was Betsie. "She is dead," Corrie moaned.

Corrie walked back to her barracks, suddenly all alone. One minute her best friend was alive, the next, gone. What thoughts must have raged through her mind. On the day that Betsie had been admitted to the hospital, Corrie had yelled at God. "Oh, why do you leave us in this prison so long? Why must Betsie suffer so? Will you never rescue us?" Now, heading back to her barrack, her sister gone, perhaps she wondered what she would tell the women. She had taught them to give thanks in all things. Could she give thanks now? She had taught them that God had their times in his hands. Did she still believe this? "My soul was a battleground," she would write years later, "of a struggle between light and darkness. Would joy for Betsie's release, or grief for my own loss, win the battle." She prayed:

> Teach me, Lord, to bear the burden,
> In this dark and weary day.
> Let me not complain to others
> Of a hard and lonely way.
>
> Every storm to Thee is subject,
> Storms of earth, or mind and heart.
> Only to Thy will submitting
> Can to me Thy peace impart.
>
> So to suffer, so keep silence,
> So be yielded to Thy will.
> So in weakness learn Thy power—
> Teach me, Father, teach me still.

THE CREMATORIUM

"Do you think we should let the kids see it?" Michelle whispered to me as we walked in the direction of the crematorium.

"No," I said, shaking my head.

Not wanting our kids to have nightmares, Michelle took them back to the RV, leaving me to explore on my own. After they were gone, I strolled between the indentations marking the hospital buildings and made a sharp right in front of the Cell Building (still standing), which contained seventy-eight cells and was used to house and punish prisoners who broke camp rules. From these cells, the sounds of torture were heard each morning during roll call. I turned left between the Cell Building and the crematorium and walked down a small alley called Execution Passage, the place where the SS carried out daily murder. With my back to the empty space

Ravensbrück Crematorium

that had been the gas chamber, I now faced the door of the crematorium. Every afternoon, after a ten-hour day of physical labor, Corrie walked past this crematorium, seeing and smelling the smoke coming from its chimneys. I hesitated to enter, not sure I was ready for what might be inside.

I had been reading Tim Keller's book *The Reason for God*. In it he quotes one skeptic who says about God, "He might be either all-powerful but not good enough to end evil and suffering, or else he might be all-good but not powerful enough to end evil and suffering. Either way the all-good, all-powerful God of the Bible couldn't exist." Undoubtedly, Corrie not only faced this objection from skeptics in the camp but also must have felt it deep in her gut. How could she not, every day passing the smokestacks, wonder why God would let this evil continue. She faced it when Betsie died and God seemed unable or unwilling to save her and liberate them both from the camp. Everyone who goes through suffering at one time or another, if they are honest, asks this question; I certainly have. But I also wondered if there was a third way, one that transcends the question. I had to believe there was, for one thing was sure: if God could not be all-powerful and all-good at the same time, the only alternative was complete despair. Corrie saw this despair on the faces of other women all day long, and she knew she could not go down this path. She also realized that to hold this view of God took away any incentive to resist evil or to help others. Without the biblical God, it would be pointless, a waste of time.

As I stood at the door of the crematorium, I understood her struggle, for at that moment it was my struggle too. Taking a deep breath, I plunged through the doorway.

On the day of Betsie's death, around bedtime, Corrie sat on her bunk watching a Russian woman, a panicked look on her face. Each time she approached a bunk, she was mercilessly turned away, the selfishness of human beings on display. Corrie kept watching. She looked down at her bunk. With Betsie gone, she now had space. But would she share it, or would darkness win out in the battleground of her heart? Since Betsie had been dead less than twelve hours, Corrie had every reason to be protective of her space, to guard her heart, to push away the world and to grieve alone. Who would have blamed her?

But as she looked at the lonely Russian woman, perhaps she thought of what had happened the day that Betsie was admitted to the hospital. After Corrie yelled at God, she heard a voice speak three words: "Rempli de tendresse" (Dutch for "Filled with tenderness"). She stopped in her tracks and looked around. There was no one in sight. Was her mind playing tricks on her? Suddenly she was overcome with deep shame. She felt bad that she had yelled at God and given in to despair. Tears filled her eyes. She felt that she deserved to be cast away from God for her profound doubt, but instead he was giving her grace, one more time, and enough to sustain her. She was not alone, God was with her, she felt his tenderness.

At that moment, she realized that no matter what happened to Betsie or to her, she was convinced that God would work all things out for her good. What she needed to learn, she thought, was the secret of contentment. She remembered Paul's account of his "thorn in the flesh" and how he prayed three times for God to take it away. Each time God said, "My grace is sufficient for you." Corrie wanted to learn what it meant to be content in the midst of suffering and loneliness. She had much to learn. But God was using the suffering to break her pride, her selfishness and her ego, and to teach her to rely on his strength, wisdom and grace.

Back at the barracks, Corrie was still watching the Russian woman. At that moment, she had a choice to make: to be angry at God, to doubt his goodness and his power, or to move forward, without Betsie, in trust and love. She invited the Russian woman up to share her bunk. Within moments they realized they were both Christians and they embraced. The Russian woman kissed Corrie on her cheek.

Over the next few days, Corrie continued to teach the Bible twice daily to large groups of women in her barracks. She would remind the women that despite their horrible suffering, nothing—even the death of her beloved sister—happened outside of God's plan. But comfort extended beyond this fact of God's sovereignty, which often spoke only to their heads. Corrie had a message for them that spoke to their hearts as well. *Filled with tenderness.* Corrie now knew what this meant.

Perhaps she thought back to several weeks ago, during one of the

Friday medical exams in which the women had to strip naked. On that particular Friday, standing naked in line, never feeling more wretched, cold or humiliated, she recalled something from the Gospels—Jesus hung naked on the cross. They took his clothes too. They beat him, spit on him and mocked him. She had known this before, but now it meant something.

She recited a hymn:

> O Jesus, can the pain I bear
> Compare with what You bore for me?
> And can I not in my despair
> Find courage as I look on Thee?
>
> Was it for me You bore the cross
> To set me free and cleanse my stain?
> And shall I murmur at my loss
> When Thou art here, my lasting gain?

What makes suffering bearable, she undoubtedly told the women, was not just that God is in control—for he is—but that he is a suffering God. He suffered, through Jesus, like we are suffering right now. God understands your pain; he knows what it is like to feel abandoned, to be alone in a hopeless situation, because he experienced it on the cross. He knows what you are going through. He is with you in your pain and suffering and anguish, and he is your only hope. Run, run to the arms of this suffering servant, she told them, before it is too late. There is no pit so deep that Jesus is not deeper still. God is both sovereign and suffering, and he loves you.

On the morning of the third day after Betsie's death, something unexpected happened. With thirty thousand women standing at attention on Roll Call Square, the loudspeaker blared, "Ten Boom, Cornelia." She hesitated. She had been prisoner 66730 for so long that she almost forgot her real name. She walked forward. Stand aside, she was ordered. As she stood at the front of the roll call she could look back and see tens of thousands of women standing erect, their breath rising in the cold morning air. But she was worried. What did this mean? Had someone reported her Bible and her secret studies? Did this mean the gas chamber?

Finally the siren blew, signaling roll call was over, and the women were dismissed back to their barracks. The guard motioned for her to follow him and led her into the administration building. She approached the counter, steadying her badly swollen legs. The man took a slip of paper, wrote something on it, signed it and then stamped it: *Entlassen.* Released. At the top of the certificate it said, "CERTIFICATE OF DISCHARGE."

Before she was released, however, she had to pay one last visit to the doctor, who, ironically, had to agree she was healthy enough to travel. After taking one look at her edema-swollen legs, a result of poor nutrition and lack of vitamins, he ordered her to the sick bay, delaying her release until the swelling went down. Her heart sank.

But after a week in the sick bay, though her edema was not markedly improved, the doctor unexpectedly stamped her paper: released. She was taken to the administration building, where her watch, her Dutch money and her mother's ring were returned to her. She was given new clothes, a day's bread ration, food coupons for three additional days and a train pass, good for travel anywhere in Germany.

She left the administration building and walked toward the train station. It was New Year's Day, 1945. Betsie was right. They were both out of prison before the New Year.

The train system in Germany was so badly damaged by the ongoing war that it took a number of days for her to get back to Holland, but eventually she made it, exhausted. Once over the Dutch boarder, she stumbled into a hospital to ask for help and they spent the next two weeks nursing her back to health.

Soon she was home at the Beje where she settled back into her life and began working at the watch shop again. But after about a month, she found herself daydreaming at her workbench, unable to concentrate. Hours would pass without her doing anything. Something was missing. She knew what the problem was. It was Betsie. Without her, the Beje was no longer home. Even though

Holland wouldn't be liberated from the Nazis for another five months, making any moves dangerous, she realized she couldn't stay in the Beje.

At that moment, her mind drifted back to something Betsie had said a few days before she died. She said God revealed to her that they would turn a former concentration camp in Germany into a place of healing for those scarred emotionally, physically and spiritually by the war, and also that they would start a home in Holland for former camp inmates. Confused at the time, Corrie bent over her dying sister and asked softly: "Must we stay in that camp which we will open for the people here in Germany, or will we be able to stay in the house for the ex-prisoners, at home in Holland?"

"Neither," Betsie said, laboring to speak. "You must travel all over the world and tell everybody who will listen what we have learned here—that Jesus is a reality and that he is stronger than all the powers of darkness. Tell them. Tell everyone who will listen!"

As Corrie sat at her workbench she knew her calling was to begin working on Betsie's vision. Within a year she had opened a former camp in Germany to minister to war-torn people and established a home in Holland to care for former prisoners. Her suffering was not in vain. That same year she went to America and began her speaking ministry, telling the world about what God did in Ravensbrück. For the next thirty-two years, until she was eighty-five years old, she traveled to over sixty countries telling people about God's amazing love. No pit is so deep that Jesus is not deeper still.

Over the years, when she was tired or discouraged, when her health began to fail or when she needed hope, she would remind herself of something her father said to her right after they were arrested, just ten days before he died: "Corrie, the best is yet to be."

OUTSIDE THE CAMP: A NEW HEAVEN AND NEW EARTH

I exited the crematorium, my mind filled with images of gas ovens and death, and headed to the memorial garden, outside the walls of the camp. To my left was the camp wall, covered with memorial plaques for the dead, their bodies buried in one large mass grave running along the foot of the wall. I turned to my right to look out over the lake, the wind nearly tearing off my jacket.

In front of me was a huge statue of a woman, dressed in prison garb, holding a sick prisoner in her arms, peering out over the water. She looked forlorn but at the same time strong, a look of determination on her face. In the distance, I could see the steeple of a church in the heart of Ravensbrück. Corrie had mentioned seeing the steeple every day as she walked to and from the Siemens Factory. Was the church calling her or mocking her? I wondered as I looked out across the lake. Was the God of that steeple silent the whole time? Or was that a sign that he was still there?

Memorial Statue overlooking lake, Ravensbrück, Germany

At the time of Betsie's death, Corrie realized that, although she could not explain it, she believed God was all-powerful and all-good at the same time. He had her "times in his hands"; he was in control despite outward circumstances, and at the same time he knew what it was like to suffer because Jesus, his Son, had suffered. Sovereign God, suffering Redeemer—only this belief provided hope, only this belief impelled her to resist evil, only this belief motivated her to help others.

Perhaps the view of that beautiful steeple may have given her something she desperately needed: the hope that one day all evil and suffering will be judged and eliminated. Revelation 21:4 says that a day is coming when "he will wipe away every tear from their eyes, and death shall be no more, neither shall there be mourning, nor crying, nor pain anymore, for the former things have passed away." Why didn't Corrie succumb to despair? She held on to the promise of Revelation that a better day was coming, a promise that is for all of us.

I spun around and looked again at the camp, imagining it teeming with thousands of tortured souls, suffering beyond imagination. I tried to imagine what a place like Ravensbrück would look like in the face of God's new future. Revelation 21 says there will be a new heaven and a new earth and that the holy city, Jerusalem, will come down from heaven, cleansing, renewing and perfecting this broken and sinful material world. Ravensbrück and all broken things will be made right. I then thought of the camp without that vision, and the thought was overwhelmingly depressing. Without hope of a day when all things will be made new, all we are left with is complete despair. As Tim Keller contends rightly:

> The secular view of things, of course, sees no future restoration after death or history. And Eastern religions believe we lose our individuality and return to the great All-soul, so our material lives in this world are gone forever. . . . The Biblical view of things is resurrection—not a future that is just a *consolation* for the life we never had but a *restoration* of the life you always wanted. This means that every horrible thing that ever happened will not only be undone and repaired but will in some way make the eventual glory and joy even greater.

It was this truth that sustained Corrie every time she walked back into the camp each night. It was this vision that empowered her to trust God in suffering and continue to serve him. It was this grand view of the future that I wanted my family to embrace now, giving us all a new perspective on suffering. The ten Booms had given us a great gift—the gift of knowing that in the midst of suffering God was always with us.

These last moments outside the camp turned my mind to the importance of knowing what would happen at the end of time but also the importance of understanding the impact that knowledge has on our lives right now, in this world. If knowing our true destination is so important, as Corrie recognized, I realized right then that this topic had to be my family's next theme of exploration.

But for now I had to return to my family and start the long drive back to Berlin. I looked for the way back to the RV. The path would take me between the lake and the crematorium, walking directly over a former mass grave. As I crossed it, Corrie's words echoed in my mind. *No pit is so deep that he is not deeper still.*

Part Three

SEEING
OUR DESTINATION

nine

CONFIDENT HOPE

Learning to Die with Dietrich Bonhoeffer

The conspiracy was dead. On the morning of July 21, 1944, Dietrich Bonhoeffer, along with other prisoners in the Tegel Prison sick bay, was listening to the radio when he heard that the plot to assassinate Adolf Hitler (code named Operation Valkyrie) had failed the previous day. Perhaps he sighed and closed his eyes in prayer, having developed an unusual calmness in the midst of storms. But he knew what this meant.

Although the briefcase bomb had exploded in the secret Wolf Lair in East Prussia, killing a number of high-ranking officials, amazingly the strange design of the thick wooden table blocked most of the blast, sparing Hitler. He was stunned but ecstatic, crediting divine providence. No sooner was he done celebrating than he began rounding up, torturing for information and executing those involved. A devout Catholic motivated to kill Hitler by his faith, Colonel Von Stauffenberg, the man who planted the bomb, shouted just before he was executed, "Long live sacred Germany!"

While Bonhoeffer was not involved in the July 20 plot, he had known about it and waited anxiously for its success and his freedom. Its failure was bad news, not only for Germany but also for his sixteen-month-old case that was awaiting trial. Now everyone who had protected him in prison was either in a prison themselves or dead. But it got worse. In September, the Gestapo discovered the secret "Chronicles of Shame" (the Zossen Files), kept by his brother-in-law Hans von Dohnanyi, detailing the history of Nazi atrocities and the two failed assassination plots in March 1943. The files contained Bonhoeffer's name, proving for the first time his direct involvement in the plots. He could no longer deny his role. The discovery dashed any hope of a release from prison. "Grim impressions" and his deep fear of torture must have returned. He may have even considered suicide. At night, waves of anxiety would grip his heart. He worried about his young fiancé, Maria, his aging parents and the others involved in the conspiracy. He worried about torture and whether

Dietrich Bonhoeffer in Tegel Prison

he could stand up under it, both physically and spiritually. He worried that he would betray his friends. More than anything, he worried that he would deny Christ in a moment of weakness.

The only way out, he thought, was to escape. Corporal Knoblauch, his favorite guard, agreed to help. The plan was for Dietrich to dress in a mechanic's suit and simply walk out of the prison with Knoblauch at the end of the day. From there he would go into hiding and then leave the country as soon as possible. On September 24, Bonhoeffer's sister Ursula and her husband delivered to Knoblauch's home a package with the mechanic's suit and some money. They arranged a false passport and a flight to Switzerland. The plan was now in motion. But then something unexpected happened, an event that would force him deeper into the moral crucible than he had ever been before.

BONHOEFFER HOUSE

On a drizzly and cold morning on April 7, 2011, we arrived at Marienburger Allee 43, located in the leafy Charlottenburg section of Berlin, an upper-middle-class neighborhood of two-story, well-manicured homes. The house, built by Karl and Paula Bonhoeffer in 1935 for retirement, contained an attic room, built for Dietrich whenever he was in Berlin.

We were in Berlin to tour the Bonhoeffer House and learn about the life of Dietrich Bonhoeffer. Our time with Corrie ten Boom had sparked our interest in the importance of destination and knowing where we are heading in life. At this point in our pilgrimage, we had spent six months in Oxford rediscovering our roots, we had taken a number of months in Europe to focus on the theme of journey and our need for maps, and we were now ready to experience our destination, the third pillar of pilgrimage. We had seen how important knowing the true end of life was for people like Thomas Cranmer, C. S. Lewis and Corrie ten Boom, and over the next two months we would dig deep into the topic of destination and its implications for our own lives. We started with Bonhoeffer, a person who longed for the eternal, thought about the end of life often and found profound hope in heaven.

One of my kids rang the doorbell and stepped back. They were expecting us, and the door opened momentarily. "Please, please, come in," said Knut Hämmerling, a graduate student living at the house, as he greeted us at the door. "Welcome to the Bonhoeffer House," he said warmly in fluent English with a strong German accent.

After some time of introductions, Knut began telling us about that fateful day on April 5, 1943, when Bonhoeffer returned home around noon. With the two failed assassination attempts from the previous month on his mind, he must have been anxious for word of whether the plots had been discovered. Would he be implicated? He needed to talk with his brother-in-law Hans to get an update.

Hans, who was married to Dietrich's sister Christine, was well connected, Knut told us, to the anti-Hitler elements in the military intel-

ligence and had kept the Bonhoeffer family informed of Nazi atrocities from the early thirties. For many years Bonhoeffer did not get
involved, acting only as a sounding board and conscience for those in
the resistance. But by the time of the "Night of Broken Glass" in 1938

Bonhoeffer House, Berlin, Germany

when close to a hundred Jews were murdered and thirty thousand
deported to concentration camps, he had thrown his lot in with the
conspirators. In early 1940 Hans informed him that war with Europe
was imminent. In August of 1940 when he was looking for a way to
avoid the draft, he met at the house with Hans and a few key men in
the conspiracy. They suggested he join military intelligence (as a
double agent) and become a more active part of the resistance. This
would keep him out of the war but at the same time give him the
chance to act on his strong convictions. He decided to take their offer.
They had to stop Hitler; it was a matter of justice and saving lives.

Returning to the afternoon of the arrest, Knut said, "Dietrich called
the von Dohnanyi residence. A strange voice answered, and right
away he knew that von Dohnanyi had been arrested and that they
were searching his home." They would come for him next.

Not wanting to wake his elderly parents from their afternoon nap, Bonhoeffer went next door to his sister Ursula Schleicher's to explain what had happened. While she began preparing him a large meal, he returned to his attic room to destroy key papers and planted a letter, backdated to provide plausible deniability.

"Let me show you Bonhoeffer's room," said Knut as he moved toward the stairs and led us up to the attic. The room was sparsely decorated, containing just a bed, a desk, a striped rug and some bookcases. Jonathan sat down at the desk. "Dietrich wrote parts of his *Ethics* at that desk," said Knut, as well as his essay "After Ten Years," which provided the theological justification for his involvement in the conspiracy. After finishing it, he gave it to a few key friends and then hid a copy in the rafters to prevent the Nazis from finding it.

Motioning to the area in front of the bookcases, Knut said, "Right there a cot was set up for his best friend, Eberhard Bethge, who was a frequent guest at the house." Dietrich and Eberhard would spend hours each day reading and talking about theology, the church and what needed to be done to rid Germany of Hitler. Years later, Bethge, who would become Dietrich's official biographer, summarized what he and Dietrich were thinking just before they joined the resistance. "We were approaching the borderline between confession and resistance," he wrote, "and if we did not cross this border, our confession was going to be no better than cooperation with the criminals. And so it became clear where the problem lay. . . . We were resisting by way of confession, but we were not confessing by way of resisting." They realized that if they wanted to avoid "cheap grace," that is, a counterfeit faith that does not produce discipleship, they needed to act. It was now time for "confessing by way of resistance."

I took my turn in the chair and looked out the window at Ursula's house next door. "There used to be a garden path connecting the two homes," said Knut. "The owners of number 42 put up a fence years ago."

After he had gotten his papers in order, Bonhoeffer walked across the garden path to his sister's to eat his last big meal and to wait. Over those few hours they must have discussed all the possibilities—where he would be taken, what charges would be brought against him and whether the Gestapo would discover the conspiracy. Around 4:00 p.m., his father came over to tell him that two men were there to see him. He returned to his attic room. The Gestapo found the paper he had planted. Then they searched his room.

As I got up from his desk and walked around the attic, I wondered if Dietrich worried about them finding his essay in the rafters. "Who

Bonhoeffer's writing desk, Bonhoeffer House, Berlin Germany

stands fast?" he asked in the essay. Only the man "who is ready to sacrifice all . . . when he is called to obedient and responsible action in faith and in exclusive allegiance to God—the responsible man, who tries to make his whole life an answer to the questions and call of God." Providentially, the Gestapo did not find it. Nevertheless, they arrested him, cuffed him and took him away.

As we descended the stairs, I realized that he had made his courageous decision to act, to resist the Nazi evil, in the comfort of his home while surrounded by family and friends. Once on his way to prison, with the ever-present threat of torture and execution hanging over him, would he be so courageous?

———————— ✿ ————————

After the black Mercedes arrived at Tegel Prison, located in the northwest section of Berlin, Bonhoeffer was taken to the reception area, processed and then placed in the admission cell for the night. The cell was bitter cold, and the blankets smelled so foul he refused to use them, making the first night of sleep fitful as he tried to stay warm. He could hear prisoners being tortured, their screams penetrating his cell throughout the night.

The next day he was moved to another cell on the top floor of the prison where those on death row were held. His door opened only for food. No one spoke to him. Separated from family and friends, he was completely alone. "A few times in my life I have come to know what homesickness means," he would write later. "There is nothing more painful." He missed his family, his friends and his fiancé, Maria.

Finally, two weeks later, when the prison officials discovered he was the cousin of Berlin's military commander, Paul von Hase, his conditions improved. He was moved to a new cell on the first floor, a seven-by-ten room with a plank bed, a bench against the wall and a chamber pot. His food rations improved slightly. But the isolation continued, long days left alone in his cell to ponder and think about his life.

But he did not just sit around. As soon as the authorities returned his Bible, which they had confiscated on the first day, he began rising early each day to pray, sing the psalms and read Scripture. He meditated on a verse of the Bible for thirty minutes. He interceded for others, lifting up his friends and relatives, as well as his former students, some of whom were in prison or in concentration camps. He prayed for the Jews, who were suffering so much. And he prayed for his new friends, both prisoners and guards, at Tegel. His daily liturgy gave him strength. In spite of the isolation, the dark thoughts at night, the constant homesickness, and the fear of torture and execution, Bonhoeffer began to build a life in prison. For hours each day he studied, wrote letters and continued his scholarship.

His strong, optimistic outlook began to win over many guards. Impressed by his strength through trial and his good cheer to all, the guards started to bring their own problems to him, looking for advice or wisdom from this well-connected prisoner. In return for his counsel, they, at great danger to themselves, smuggled out his letters to Bethge, which years later would bring him great fame. Prisoners also sought his counsel, knowing that he was someone they could talk to, a person who would understand them. As one of the few people that truly cared for others and not just for himself, fellow prisoners wanted to be close to him.

In those early days at Tegel, he survived in prison but also thrived. What was his secret? According to Paul Busing, one of Bonhoeffer's former seminary students, the secret was Finkenwalde.

"LEARNING TO DIE"

As gale-force winds attempted to knock us off the road and dust and dirt pelted the side of our RV, we passed through a dense forest of pine trees, piles of freshly cut logs stacked on the side of the road. Michelle was in the back making sandwiches for the kids as they sat quietly reading their books. An hour outside of Berlin, the forest opened up, revealing miles of wide-open countryside, the horizon broken only by an occasional outcropping of trees, a barn, and the ever-present post and beam fences. It was the day after our visit to the Bonhoeffer House and we were in search of Finkenwalde, a small town 135 kilometers northeast of Berlin, where the illegal seminary Bonhoeffer led was located from 1935 to 1937.

Before we could go to Finkenwalde, however, we needed to travel to Stettin, located eight kilometers north of the seminary, to visit the Bonhoeffer Study Center. For the past six months I had been trying to track down the address of the seminary, demolished long ago after the war. No one, not even the director of the Bonhoeffer House in Berlin, could tell me the exact location. This was not a good sign. I had emailed the Study Center numerous times asking for the seminary address but never got a response. I thought maybe

I could get it if I went in person. It was my last shot.

My mind drifted to Bonhoeffer and what he might have been thinking when he first made this same trip. In early 1935, Bonhoeffer had accepted an invitation to lead an illegal seminary. For the past year he had been pastoring a German church in London, keeping abreast of the church struggle in Germany. Eventually he knew he had to return; he could not stay at a safe distance for long. "He was beginning to understand that he was God's prisoner, that like the prophets of old, he was called to suffer and to be oppressed—and in that defeat and the acceptance of that defeat, there was victory." He understood that the German church had compromised with Hitler, selling its birthright for survival. The only hope was to train new pastors strong enough to withstand the pressure, the indoctrination and the false promises of the Nazis. In a letter to his eldest brother, Karl Friedrich, explaining why he wanted to lead an illegal seminary, Bonhoeffer wrote, "The restoration of the church must surely depend on a new kind of monasticism, which has nothing in common with the old but a life of uncompromising discipleship, following Christ according to the Sermon on the Mount. I believe the time has come to gather people together for this."

In the spring, he began the seminary in the temporary location of Zingst, a seaside community on the Baltic. By that summer, they had moved into a more permanent location in Finkenwalde, taking over a defunct school that at one time had been a large manor house. The live-in training course would run six months and would include lectures, reading, service, morning and nightly prayer, meditation and singing.

He began the training on an optimistic note. In a sermon preached that first June, he called his students to long for a better day, to long for a deeper faith: "Lord, awake in my soul that great longing for you. . . . Help me to seek and to find you." He continued, "My thoughts turn toward my spiritual homeland where there will be peace and joy, where the soul finds refuge with God. When shall I see it again?" He seemed to know that real trouble was brewing and that things were going to get much worse before they got better, if ever. He was calling his students to join him on a dangerous road. "Father, when you send me into foreign lands, preserve in me that wholesome longing for my spiritual homeland, and direct my thoughts to the eternal homeland, where you will comfort us," he preached. Bonhoeffer was teaching them theology and worship but also something more: how to suffer and die.

That fall, things did get worse. In September 1935, Hitler announced the Nuremberg Laws, a series of laws that discriminated against the Jews, officially taking away their citizenship and other legal rights. The Confessing Church was slow to act. But Bonhoeffer believed the church must speak up for the Jews. "Only he who cries out for the Jews may sing Gregorian chants," he said. But the church was too afraid and did nothing.

For Bonhoeffer, there was no question about the kind of evil that had been loosed upon Germany, and he knew that if he and his ordinands stood up to this evil, they would likely die. He was ready to be a martyr. But he also knew that to have the courage to be a martyr would require a new strength, an ability to die daily.

In November 1935 he responded to the worsening conditions in Germany by preaching a chapel sermon titled "Learning to Die," based on John's vision in Revelation 14. In a not-so-subtle reference to the Nazis, Bonhoeffer talked about the second angel, who said, "Fallen, fallen is Babylon the great, who made all nations drink the wine of its impure passion." Babylon was the enemy of God, "the city which does not cease building its tower up into the heavens" and which opposes God at every turn, enticing people with "heavy wine," "godless splendor," and "all their hearts and wild desires crave." But as powerful as Babylon has become, it will not last. In fact, it has already been defeated, said Bonhoeffer. God has defeated it in Christ on the cross, and with the reality of his second coming. So you have nothing to fear, he told his listeners.

How did he know? Because John also tells us that the first angel preached the everlasting gospel, the good news that has triumphed over all false gods, ideologies, liturgies of desire and rulers. Therefore we should not fear anything. Bonhoeffer said: "Do not fear the coming day, do not fear other people, do not fear power or might, even if they are able to deprive you of property and life; do not fear the great ones of this world; do not even fear yourselves." God is greater than all these fears and thus we are to stand in awe of him, his power, his glory. When the angel says "blessed are the dead, which die in the Lord," he is referring to their freedom from all earthly worry, strife or trouble. They have "kept the faith," "clung to Jesus up to the last hour." This should be our goal, Bonhoeffer said. In his closing remarks, words that were a harbinger of things to come, he said, "To die in Christ—that this be granted us, that our last hour not be a weak hour, that we die as confessors of Christ, whether old or young, whether quickly or after long suffering, whether seized and laid hold of by the lord of Babylon. . . . That is our prayer today, that our last word might only be: Christ."

By the middle of 1937, the Nazis had thrown aside any attempt to hide their true intentions toward the Confessing Church. They arrested and imprisoned over eight hundred pastors and lay leaders, including Martin Niemoller, the leader of the Confessing Church and the most outspoken member. In his final sermon Niemoller was defiant: "No more are we ready to keep silent at man's behest when God commands us to speak. For it is, and must remain, the case that we must obey God rather than man."

Four days later, on July 1, he was arrested. Bonhoeffer and Bethge showed up at Niemoller's house to discuss the grave situation of the church in Germany, but Niemoller was already gone, arrested moments earlier. While Bonhoeffer and Bethge were there, the Gestapo arrived. Bonhoeffer and Bethge tried to escape by the back door but were stopped, placed under house arrest and detained for seven hours. After lengthy questioning, they were released. Niemoller would remain in prison for seven years, enslaved in Dachau. The Allies would free him in 1945.

During the summer of 1937, while the Gestapo scrutinized everything he did, Bonhoeffer continued to teach his students. He taught

them about discipleship, the costliness of the Christian life and how
to avoid a life of cheap grace. His lectures covered the Sermon on the
Mount, the best summary of the Christian life: "Only those who obey
can believe, and only those who believe can obey." Each day he taught
them how to die to themselves, to experience deep grace and to
prepare for the ultimate sacrifice. In November of 1937 these lectures
were published as *The Cost of Discipleship*, a book that would become
one of the most influential books of the century. For Bonhoeffer, the
message of the book would be put to the ultimate test in his own life.

Searching for Finkenwalde

After two and a half hours of driving, we finally crossed the Polish
border, moving deeper into the countryside of Pomerania, far removed from Berlin. I kept looking for Stettin. I still had not seen a
house in miles, and I wondered if anyone lived out there. I guess if
you are doing something illegal or treasonous, this would be a good
place to do it, far from the watchful eyes of the SS.

About twenty minutes inside the Polish border, we finally spotted

Kids reading in the back of the RV on the way to Stettin, Poland

signs for the city of Stettin. As we approached the edge of the city, it felt as though we were entering a dustbowl. The landscape was devoid of trees and greenery, and people along the street struggled to walk, bent over from the wind, sheltering their eyes from the dust. Once a striking German city, Stettin now seemed old and run down, the buildings not having been renovated since before the war. We stopped at a traffic signal. People looked up from inside their small cars, eyeing our large RV, as conspicuous as a tank driving down a suburban neighborhood.

After winding through city streets for another five minutes, we arrived in front of a large, three-story home—the Bonhoeffer Study Center. As I walked toward the house, it looked freshly painted and rehabbed, in stark contrast to the run-down homes around it. Years earlier, a wealthy donor gave the house for the study of Bonhoeffer's work in Finkenwalde. I climbed the front steps to the entrance and rang the bell. No answer. I rang it again. Nothing. It was Friday afternoon; it must have closed early, and with it, my last chance to find the location of the seminary. That was a low point for me, shaming myself for missing the opportunity to take my family to such hallowed ground.

Reluctantly, after weighing the dangers of being in Poland one minute longer than needed, we began our drive back to Berlin. As we got outside the city, the countryside once again opened up. With storm clouds forming on the horizon, I wistfully looked south in the direction of Finkenwalde. I longed to find the memorial that marks the spot of the illegal seminary and walk around that sacred space. Once there, I had hoped to talk to my children about the radical experiment in Christian community that occurred there and that Bonhoeffer would later describe in his book *Life Together*. During those crucial years at the seminary, Bonhoeffer had learned a great deal about suffering, hope and destination, three realities I desperately wanted my family to understand. But, alas, it wasn't meant to be. That lesson would have to wait until another day.

As I drove toward Germany, I saw an outcropping of trees hiding a farmhouse. I pointed it out to Michelle and the kids, who were playing a board game in the back. They moved quickly to the windows to look. "Perhaps that's what Finkenwalde seminary looked like," I yelled to them over the sound of the RV's engine.

My thoughts drifted back to that fateful day in October of 1937. With the term over and the students gone home, Bonhoeffer and Bethge went on vacation in the mountains for some much-needed rest. Unannounced, the Gestapo arrived at the house and shut down the seminary. The doors were sealed forever. Bonhoeffer's experiment in Christian community and pastoral training was over. It was a profoundly troubling moment for him. All his life, in whatever he set his hand to—academics, teaching, pastoring—he had experienced success. The closing of Finkenwalde was a new experience for him. Finkenwalde, wrote Edwin H. Robertson, was "both the scene of his greatest achievements and the scene of his first real failures. It is with the closing of Finkenwalde that Bonhoeffer begins to learn the meaning of Suffering as a station on the way to freedom."

Over the next few months, the reality of suffering must have been on his mind. In March 1938, he preached a sermon titled "The Secret of Suffering" based on Romans 1:1-5. After the events of 1937, he saw suffering not as something to avoid but as a gift. He did not believe that suffering was ultimately a good. But he saw that God could use it for good. Bonhoeffer told his audience that God often uses suffering to try and test our faith, making sure it will be strong enough to stand on the last day.

For Bonhoeffer, this topic was personal; he was constantly concerned about remaining faithful to the end. For that reason, "the sufferings, which appear so hard and objectionable to us in our lives," he said, "are in reality full of the greatest treasures a Christian can find. They are like the shell in which a pearl rests." And what is the pearl, the end result of the sufferings? Hope. Suffering produces hope. "'And hope does not disappoint us.' Where there is still hope," Bonhoeffer continued, "there is no defeat; there may be every kind of weakness, much clamor and complaining, much anxious shouting; nevertheless, because hope is present, the victory has already been won." In his sermon, he seemed to be not only trying to convince his listeners about suffering and the need for hope but, more importantly, trying to persuade himself. He was preparing himself to die in the service of God.

Six months after he preached "The Secret of Suffering," the "Night of Broken Glass" took place. By that point Bonhoeffer had joined the resistance movement. Two years later he would become a double agent. Dark days remained ahead, but he was ready. What he had discovered during those Finkenwalde years—about suffering, dying daily, eternal hope—would be the rock on which he would lean. And at no time did he need the power of this hope more than those last months in prison, awaiting the end.

As Bonhoeffer sat in his Tegel cell in July 1944, seven years after the Gestapo closed the seminary, he pondered his escape. The plan was set in motion, and all the systems were go. But then something unexpected happened. The Gestapo arrested his brother, Klaus. If Dietrich escaped now, the Nazis would assume Klaus was guilty, and they would round up the entire family, including Maria. The Nazis would have no qualms about enslaving them all in concentration camps. But if he didn't escape now, he would be tortured for what he knew. And his greatest fears of betraying his friends and, even worse, denying his God might be realized. More than anything, he feared not dying well, turning his back on God in a moment of weakness.

But in the end, what should have been a difficult decision was easy. He would not put his family into that kind of jeopardy. He knew what he had to do—sacrifice his life for those he loved. So the escape plan was called off. He knew what this meant—facing death head-on— and he welcomed the challenge. Alone in his cell, he must have thought of the words he wrote years earlier:

> Death is only dreadful for those who live in dread and fear of it. Death
> is not wild and terrible, if only we can be still and hold fast to God's

Word. Death is not bitter, if we have not become bitter ourselves. Death is grace, the greatest gift of grace that God gives people who believe in him. . . . It beckons to us with heavenly power, if only we realize that it is the gateway to our homeland, the tabernacle of joy, the everlasting kingdom of peace.

Three months after the failed Valkyrie assassination attempt, on Sunday, October 8, 1944, Bonhoeffer's year and a half at Tegel came to an abrupt end. He was moved across town to the Gestapo house prison. No longer under the watchful eye of his uncle, who had been hanged for his role in the conspiracy, he was now in the grips of the Gestapo, and his life was about to become much more difficult.

GESTAPO PRISON: THE TOPOGRAPHY OF TERROR

"Do you know which cell was Bonhoeffer's?" Jordan asked, as we looked down into the bombed-out basement of the Gestapo prison known by the name Prinz-Albrecht-Strasse.

"There is no way to tell," I said. "But we know for sure it was in the basement somewhere."

It was the day after Finkenwalde, and we were spending the afternoon touring the Berlin Wall and the Topography of Terror, the outdoor museum built on the site of the former Gestapo headquarters, a building that had housed the SS from 1933 to 1945 and from which it ran the entire concentration camp system throughout the Nazi empire. When Bonhoeffer arrived at Prinz-Albrecht-Strasse, he discovered that almost the entire leadership of the conspiracy was in this prison. But he also learned that conditions were much worse than Tegel.

"It's hell in here," said Admiral Canaris, the former head of military intelligence and Bonhoeffer's friend.

"Look down there," I said to my boys as I pointed into the cell blocks. I did my best to describe the prisoners' conditions: small cells, no outside light, poor food and unsanitary conditions. "Pretty depressing, don't you think?"

I wanted my boys to see how hard these last days were for Bonhoeffer, how he could have easily cursed God or claimed that the universe was devoid of God, meaning and purpose. At times it must have felt that way for him. But he never took this tack. Why? Because he knew his destination, his *telos*. I wanted my children to have a clear destination.

According to Smith and Denton, most teenagers live in a "morally insignificant universe" where "moral commitments, decisions, obligations, and actions have little if any larger meaning, purpose, significance, or consequence; that universe is, in short, a morally empty reality." The problem is that most young people have no "telos," no "end, goal, and standard, by which one knows where one is and to where one is headed." They have no "big script of a very real drama . . . within which the living out of one's life really means something significant." Bonhoeffer had this "big script" and he knew he was living in a real drama. I wanted my children to understand this and to want it for their own lives. Standing at the Gestapo prison, I hoped that his story would shape their imaginations, would inspire them to see the world differently as God's big Story and their part in it.

Bonhoeffer himself saw the world differently from most of those around him in the cells. But it wasn't because he ran from reality. Day in and day out for months, reality looked Bonhoeffer in the face. He couldn't ignore it or run away to creature comforts like so many of us can when life gets hard. He had to either deal with the reality or be crushed by it. Yet, amazingly, he never threw up his hands and sat around and complained or turned his attention to his own self-preservation, which is what most young people do when hard times and anxiety arrive. As he had said in his sermon "Learning to Die," "So much is clear at once: that world [that is, the world after death] is anything but dead; it is alive to the highest degree, full of action, full of visions, full of words . . . and full of bliss—the world after death is life in the highest degree."

Even in his small, dark and damp cell, Bonhoeffer believed that this life was pregnant with meaning because he knew this life had an important destination. His eschatology (view of the end times) shaped his thinking and his imagination in the present. He had the ability, unlike so many of us today, to envision a different world. He didn't just think about hope; he lived it. In spite of the reality that was all around him, a reality profoundly marked by evil and decay, he saw the world differently—he had an *eschatological imagination*. And

Basement of the Gestapo Prison, Berlin

this allowed him to live courageously and hopefully in the midst of the darkness.

He was able to look out for the interest of others, to make the right moral choices because he knew the end of the story: God triumphs in Christ over evil. Unlike so many young people today who are depressed, fearful and committed to self-preservation, he didn't need to be anxious about life; he didn't need to be afraid of others; he didn't need to strike back; he didn't need to preserve himself, because Christ had secured his future.

As we continued to walk around the grounds of the Topography of Terror, I thought of a way to drive home for my family the importance of destination in our lives. Imagine, I said, that you can't be present to watch your favorite team on TV in the Super Bowl. So you DVR it. On the way home to watch it, you stop at the 7-Eleven for some chips and salsa and overhear, to your chagrin, the final score of the game. Your team has won, but you are ticked at the spoiler. You go home and start watching the game anyway. Right away your team falls behind by two and then three touchdowns. Normally, you would be losing your mind and your temper, throwing things at the TV, full of anxiety and anger. But this time you aren't. Why? Because you know the end of the story, and your team wins. This knowledge transforms how you see the sporting world on that day. You are not anxious or angry; in fact, you are fine. You sit back, eat your chips and salsa, and enjoy the game, fueled by confident hope. The end is secure; your team wins. And when the end of the game comes, the feeling is fantastic. Knowing the end beforehand changes everything.

On February 7, 1945, Bonhoeffer's stay at the Gestapo prison came to an end. He and twenty other high-ranking prisoners, most involved in the conspiracy, were moved to Buchenwald, out of the reach of Allied bombs hitting Berlin. He had not seen daylight in four months. When they tried to cuff him and fellow prisoner Dr. Joseph Muller, Bonhoeffer protested. For Muller, who had been badly mistreated in prison for years, this was his chance to repay the favor and encourage Bonhoeffer: "Let us go calmly to the gallows as Christians," he said to Bonhoeffer.

By late March 1945, the end of the war seemed near. American guns could be heard in the distance. It was only a matter of time before Germany surrendered. Food in Buchenwald was scarce, and Bonhoeffer and the other sixteen prisoners fought off hunger and cold. Then on April 3, the chief guard informed the prisoners that it was time to go. The Gestapo wanted to move them further south, out of the liberating reach of the Americans.

After thirteen hours of travel, they reached Weiden, a small town in Bavaria, just ten miles from Flossenburg. Just outside of town, a police car pulled them over. Two policemen opened the doors of the van and called two prisoners; Bonhoeffer was one of them. One prisoner jumped out. Bonhoeffer leaned back so as not to be seen. At that moment another prisoner, who was friends with the one called first, jumped out of the van. The doors were shut and they continued south.

It took four days for the Gestapo and Hitler's judge to realize the mistake. They sent two guards back to find Bonhoeffer. By now the prisoners from Buchenwald were in Shönburg. It was Sunday morning, a week after Easter. Another prisoner had asked Bonhoeffer to lead a service. He opened in prayer and read the Scripture for the day: Isaiah 53:5 ("With his stripes we are healed") and 1 Peter 1:3 ("Blessed be the God and Father of our Lord Jesus Christ! By his great mercy we have been born anew to a living hope through the resurrection of Jesus Christ from the dead" RSV). He then gave a short homily on these verses. No record exists for what he said, but based on his past sermons, we can guess that he addressed those scared, tired and beleaguered prisoners with an eschatological imagination, telling them to look to Christ for hope. It is their hope in him, he would have told them, that will help them overcome their fear and live heroically and justly in the face of despair. "Fear not," he might have said, "for 'by his great mercy we have been born anew to a living hope through the resurrection of Jesus Christ from the dead.'" We know the end of the story, and it makes all the difference. His words that morning must have hit home. Payne Best, an Englishman who shared a cell close to Bonhoeffer, recalled that he "spoke to us in a manner which reached the hearts of all, finding just the right words to express the spirit of our imprisonment."

Just as he finished the last prayer, the door slammed open and two men came in, their boots clopping on the ground as they walked. "Prisoner Bonhoeffer. Get ready to come with us." Everyone present knew what this meant—the scaffold. They all said their goodbyes. Bonhoeffer pulled Best aside and said: "This is the end. For me the beginning of life."

Buchenwald Concentration Camp

The next morning we left Berlin and drove five hours south to Weimer and the Buchenwald concentration camp, nestled in the tree-covered hills overlooking the city. While the kids rested in the RV, Michelle and I went to the information desk, located in part of the former Gestapo camp headquarters outside the barbed-wire fence, and asked the man behind the counter where Bonhoeffer's cell was located. He knew right away. Taking out a map he said, "Right here, in the basement of the Gestapo barracks."

After a quick tour of Buchenwald, we went in search of his cell. We found it just outside of the camp. All that remained was the basement. For seven weeks this was Bonhoeffer's home. Seventeen members of the conspiracy shared twelve cells in the dank basement, which formerly housed disobedient SS guards.

Starting down the steps, we immediately saw at the bottom a silver plaque on the wall, testimony that Bonhoeffer and others in the con-

Basement prison in the SS Barracks, Buchenwald Concentration camp

spiracy had been here. It was a powerful moment. Light in the midst of darkness. After reading the inscription on the plaque, we turned right and walked down the narrow hallway. It could not have been more than thirty feet long. On each side were six cells. When they were let out of their cells each day for exercise, the hallway was the only place the prisoners were allowed to go. Six at a time could pace up and down the corridor to stretch their legs. During this time, they were able to talk and share information. Best later wrote that Bonhoeffer was "all humanity and sweetness; he always seemed to diffuse an atmosphere of happiness, of joy in every smallest event in life, and of deep gratitude for the mere fact that he was alive. . . . He was one of the very few men that I have ever met to whom his God was real and ever close to him." Best continues, "[His] soul really shone in the dark desperation of our prison. . . . [He] had always been afraid that he would not be strong enough to stand such a test but now he knew there was nothing in life of which one need ever be afraid." He chose each day to be hopeful because he knew the end of the story. His view of the end, his knowledge of his destination, fueled him to live heroically, kindly and joyfully.

It was now late afternoon and time to leave. We still had a three-hour drive ahead of us to get to Flossenbürg concentration camp before dark. Michelle started to prepare dinner for the kids, who by now were hungry. As we drove south into the Bavarian Mountains, the late afternoon sun streamed into the driver's compartment, keeping me warm and putting me in a reflective mood. I began thinking about Bonhoeffer's last six days of life, after he left Buchenwald. His true *telos*, his true homeland was calling him. I clicked on a radio station that played American music. I was startled when a familiar song began to play: Bob Dylan's "Knockin' on Heaven's Door." Somehow it seemed appropriate.

It was late Sunday afternoon when they walked through the main gates of Flossenbürg concentration camp. Spring had not arrived in the mountains of east-central Germany, and a late-afternoon chill had descended on the camp. Two guards led Bonhoeffer through Roll

Call Square. They turned and walked past three barracks on the right and the sick bay on the left. At the far southern end of the camp, just inside the barbed-wire fence, sat a long building called the detention barracks, comprised of a single row of cells. Special prisoners, mostly Russian and Polish officers, were executed here. In the final year of the war, fifteen hundred special prisoners were brutally murdered, their bodies burned on a massive funeral pyre.

As they entered the barracks, Bonhoeffer was escorted down the hall. Watching faces appeared in the six-by-nine hole in the doors. Among others he recognized Admiral Wilhelm Canaris and General Hans Oster, who, along with Bonhoeffer, were part of the failed plots to assassinate Adolf Hitler. The guards shoved Bonhoeffer into an open cell and locked the door. He was tired and hungry. He sat down on the edge of the bed and prayed for strength—for himself and for the other prisoners awaiting death. Just then his train of thought was broken. A door down the hall swung open and the guards removed General Oster. Thirty minutes later they brought him back. Then it was Admiral Canaris's turn. Over the course of the evening, guards removed each of the conspirators one by one. Hitler had sent a judge to quickly set up a summary court to try the conspirators. But it was a mock court, the verdicts already handed down by Hitler, the final arbiter of justice in the Third Reich. Bonhoeffer was tried last. When he got back to his cell around 2:00 a.m. he fell asleep quickly.

He did not sleep long. At 5:00 a.m., a guard unlocked his door and kicked it open. "Get up and undress."

"Where am I being taken?" Bonhoeffer asked.

"To hear the verdict," the guard said. The guard walked to the next cell, leaving Bonhoeffer to undress. Before doing so, he kneeled down in front of his bed, bowed his head and began to pray.

FLOSSENBÜRG

We stood just outside the barracks near the spot where the judge, on April 9, 1945, would have read the verdicts and pronounced the sentence—death by hanging. Herbert Soergel, a local pastor and our

Flossenbürg guide, turned to look at the plaque on the wall and the newly placed flowers marking the anniversary two days earlier of Bonhoeffer's death. Soergel had led the memorial service himself. I asked him what Dietrich might have prayed that last time as he kneeled before the place of his execution.

Slightly hesitating, he said, "I can't be sure. Maybe he was thanking God, grateful that he had given him the strength to make it to the end, you know, to die well."

Bonhoeffer's barracks and place of execution, Flossenbürg Concentration Camp

Herbert's countenance then brightened as he asked me, "Do you remember his last letter to Maria?"

"I do not," I said.

"Well, it contains a clue to how Dietrich managed to survive faithfully to the end. It may also be a clue to what he prayed that last time before he went to his death. In it he says, 'I have not felt lonely or abandoned for one moment. You, your parents, all of you, the friends and students of mine at the front, all are constantly present to me. It is a great invisible sphere in which one lives and in whose reality there is no doubt. It says in the old children's song about angels:

"Two, to cover me, two, to wake me.""

"For Bonhoeffer," said Soergel, "the people in his life were angels who were constantly with him, even at the moment of death, reminding him of the true end of life. They pointed him to hope."

As I turned to look at the spot of the execution, I imagined Bonhoeffer slowly climbing the steps to the gallows. Did he think of his words from his prison poem "Stations on the Road to Freedom"?

> Come now, O supreme moment on the way to freedom eternal.
> Death, lay down the burdensome chains, break down the walls of our
>   transient bodies,
> the barriers of our deluded souls, that we might gaze at last on what
>   here we are impeded from seeing.

He could now see clearly, as if he were seeing a vision in broad daylight. As he said years ago in a sermon at Finkenwalde, "It is not a nothing, not an extinction that awaits us when we close our eyes for the last time; rather, we go to meet undreamed of events."

The noose was put around his neck. The trapdoor swung open. He died in seconds. He was finally free. He had died well, with only one word in his mouth: Christ. "Undreamed of events" awaited him, the same reality that gave him hope while he was alive and had empowered him to live in a morally significant universe. Now he was seeing his true end.

Years later the Flossenbürg camp physician said of Bonhoeffer, "In almost fifty years that I worked as a doctor, I have hardly ever seen a man die so entirely submissive to the will of God."

THE VALLEY OF THE DEAD

From the place of the scaffold, past the special prisoner barracks that held the conspirators, we walked to the back corner of the camp, now shrouded in green pine trees and dense undergrowth. Standing on a precipice, the crematorium just below us, we noticed the old gates of the camp had been placed here. Strange. What were they doing here, so far from the entrance?

Herbert said, "A few years after World War II a Romanian group decided to make the camp into a memorial for the dead. The reconstruction of these gates was part of this remembering." Waving his hand toward the crematorium and then over the entire "Valley of the Dead," he pointed to a large green pyramid-like mound in the center. "Dietrich's body," he said, "was piled there and then burned, along with all the other conspirators." That grassy mound was put there by the Romanians as part of the memorial. "But that funeral pyre does not have the last word," Herbert said.

"Look," he said, as he pointed across the valley, "do you see that chapel on the hill? That small chapel was built using the stones from one of the four massive guard towers. It now stands as testimony over the valley: death does not have the last word—resurrection does."

As we stood there gazing at the chapel in the distance, shimmering in the morning sun, its meaning for my family was clear. To see the chapel we had to look past a crematorium, a funeral pyre and mass graves. If we only looked down at the symbols of death below us, we would lose all hope. We would be overcome with bitterness. We would see Dietrich's death, just two weeks before the American army liberated the camp, as a tragic waste. But when we looked up, we saw a symbol and the reality of hope.

This is what we came to Flossenbürg for. This is why we had studied Bonhoeffer's life. To learn this lesson about eschatological hope. Like Bonhoeffer, we did not have to fear pain or suffering or death, though they are powerful. We believe and hope in something greater. Bonhoeffer once preached, "There may be every kind of weakness, much clamor and complaining, much anxious shouting; nevertheless, because hope is present, the victory has already been won." Victory has already been won. We wanted our kids to understand that the kind of life Bonhoeffer lived—a life of joy in the midst of suffering, a courageous life of obedience—only happens when we know our true *telos*, our destination. We wanted them to realize that, like Bonhoeffer, they are part of a huge drama and that they know how it ends. And because they know how it ends, and because they are part of this big script, they are able to live lives of meaning and significance. They can live in confidence, with boldness, with joy in suffering, with peace, in service to others, and with a sense of expectation and hope. Knowing their end makes all the difference; knowing their destination provides the hope they need.

Walking back through Flossenbürg concentration camp that warm April morning, the sky speckled with cumulous clouds, I knew we needed to figure out how to make this eschatological hope a reality in their lives every day, not just this one time in Germany. Looking to their *telos* had to be a daily habit. But how?

As we got back into our RV, my attention was immediately turned to our next destination: Berchtesgaden and Salzburg. Right then I had a hunch that the person we would study next, a young lady from Nonnberg Abbey, would give us the insights we needed.

ten

CONFIDENCE

Searching for the
Real Maria von Trapp

It was mid-April and we were traveling through the Bavarian mountains on our way from Flossenbürg to Berchtesgaden, a small, historic town of nine thousand people in the southeast part of Germany, surrounded on three sides by the Austrian border, some thirty kilometers from Salzburg. The last forty-five minutes of our drive we had an unobstructed view of the Alps soaring above us, the vagaries of the light and the hour changing the hues of the snow-scarred mountains. As we continued to ascend, the mountains seemed to pull us in, as if they were offering us sanctuary and much-needed rest.

We were in Berchtesgaden to slow down, enjoy some camping and reflect on the past month of travel through France, Holland, Poland and Germany. We had moved so fast that we had not taken much time to process what we had experienced emotionally. We also had a sense that our pilgrimage was nearing its end, that the lessons we had focused on—roots, journey and destination—were almost complete, and we wanted some time to reflect on and pull these experiences together. We needed this time or we would miss one of the most important elements of travel—extended reflection. But we also wanted some space for gratitude, to count our blessings and to celebrate how God had cared for us on this long journey.

As Michelle prepared dinner in the small kitchenette, a challenging feat given the limited space and sparse ingredients, I threw on my coat and stepped out of the RV to prowl around. Over by the main lodge I looked for my children, who earlier had been playing with a go-cart around the drained pool. When I couldn't find them, I discovered that they were climbing the hill above our campsite, slowly traveling in the direction of Obersalzberg, the mountain retreat made famous by Hitler's vacation home, the Berghof, his southern command during World War II. He spent more time there than any other location, and toward the end of the war much of the Nazi leadership was stationed there, having built deep underground bunkers and tunnels to survive Allied bombing.

"Hey Jordan and Jonathan," I yelled, cupping my hands around my mouth to project my voice, "be careful. Remember, Meghan is only four."

As I watched their ascent, proud of their adventurous spirit yet worried about Meghan, I turned my eyes higher up the mountain, almost directly above my head, looking for Hitler's "Eagle's Nest," the mountain retreat that was built on the mountain peak for his fiftieth birthday. At first I couldn't see it, but then the clouds shifted slightly and it appeared, covered in snow. Seconds later it was gone, once again engulfed in clouds. A chill ran down my spine, as if I were looking at Mount Doom.

For the past month, with Jordan reading *The Lord of the Rings* and Jonathan listening to the audio version, we had been discussing Tolkien's grand epic. We had also watched parts of the movies. Like the best fantasy and myth, Tolkien's tale had fired our imaginations. Through the quest of the ring, the tale helped us see new worlds and alternate realities that we hadn't seen earlier, inspiring us to pursue goodness and beauty, to live lives of meaning. Having read Tolkien's thoughts on myth and fantasy, this was undoubtedly what he wanted; his goal was to reshape our imaginations through his story. Tolkien wanted readers to see that things not visible to the senses may indeed be real, in their own way, regardless of what others might say. But this new sight required a new imagination, and it was Tolkien's goal to foster that. At least for our family, he succeeded.

Since our time in Oxford, we had been on a pilgrimage, and our guides had been some of my heroes of the faith. Studying them was an immersion into stories that have the power to reshape our minds and hearts and imaginations. Our goal had been to experience their lives—the false realities they faced and the true narratives they relied on. We wanted their stories to become our stories and, in the process, to engender in us the correct emotional responses for each challenge we would face. Each of the heroes had (through their stories) become part of us, helping us see reality in new and profound ways. And for this I was grateful.

I paused from my thoughts to shout another word of caution to my sons. They assured me Meghan was fine and was having fun, and they continued to climb higher. I thought of Sam and Frodo, with the ring in their possession, climbing ever higher toward Mount Doom. In *The Lord of the Rings*, Tolkien paints a vivid picture of two contrasting visions of reality. He wants one to repulse us and one to create a holy longing in us. In Mordor's dark and desolate wasteland, devoid of the good, Tolkien shows us a picture of evil's destruction and inhumanity. In Hobbiton, on the other hand, we see warmth and generosity, the beauty and charm of a people who laugh readily, celebrate easily, and drink and eat cheerily. Through Hobbiton's bucolic beauty, charming homes and winsome people, Tolkien hopes to stir our hearts for what it represents: the essence of a life lived well. By dramatically contrasting these two different realities, Tolkien activates our imaginations in ways that logical, reasoned arguments couldn't. He wants us to envision a world that can't always be explained with cold, hard reason.

In essence, that was what we hoped for on our pilgrimage—that the stories and myths and metaphors we were experiencing, the places and people we were encountering, would activate our imaginations and illuminate for us the different realities competing for our affections; that through these stories and encounters we would learn about our roots, understand the journey we are on and recognize the importance of knowing our destination. Michelle and I wanted our pilgrimage to shape and guide our family's desires, what we love and what we long for, and ultimately, what we worship. After nine months, we believed this process had begun.

I finally yelled up to my kids that they had climbed far enough; it was time to come down for dinner. They stopped climbing, turned around and began their descent. At that moment, I swung around

Nonnberg Abbey viewed from Kapuziner Hill, Salzburg, Austria

and looked at the mountain behind me—the majestic Untersberg. I later read somewhere that Hitler loved this mountain so much that he installed a huge plate-glass window in his home to view it. Each morning at breakfast he looked out on the Alpine grandeur and, as if he were the all-seeing eye of Sauron, schemed ways to spin his web of deceit and destruction over the imaginations of millions of his countrymen.

Hitler wasn't the only person stirred by the beauty of that mountain. For Maria Kutschera, known better as Maria von Trapp, the mountain was a place to nurture her imagination as well. But her imagination was captivated by a completely different reality than Hitler's. Having encountered Hitler many times over the past three months (and being slightly depressed because of it), we were now ready to experience Maria's story.

A Family Divided and Without Direction

"Why does the captain not look happy with those precious children, this wonderful home of his and everything that money can buy?" Maria asked the housekeeper, Baroness Matilda.

"Everything money can buy," responded Matilda, "is very little. Oh, the poor man has lost so much." For the next couple of hours, Maria sat spellbound as Matilda told her Captain von Trapp's story: how at a young age he was already a decorated naval hero; how he met a nineteen-year-old beauty, heiress to a great fortune, at a public ceremony; how they were married in a fairytale wedding; and how, after the subsequent birth of seven children, scarlet fever attacked their home and eventually took the life of his beloved wife at the age of thirty-two.

By the time his wife died, Austria had lost the war, losing its navy and forcing the captain to retire. "Half his life had died with the navy," Matilda said, and the other half was buried with his wife. "The shining hero of Austria's youth became a silent man with an empty look in his eyes." He was a man without direction, without a calling.

"He is never happy," the Baroness continued. "He has tried different jobs, but nothing worked out. He doesn't stay home long, always going away on hunting trips or to visit family in Hungary. He loves his family and showers them with gifts when he is home. But for some reason he is shy with his children. They seem to remind him too much of their mother," she said.

It was only Maria's third day on the job, and what she was hearing was a lot to digest. The story explained a great deal and she now had some sympathy for the captain. But she still wondered how her time with the von Trapps would go. Would she survive her nine months? As a nineteen-year-old novice at Nonnberg Abbey, Maria Kutschera was on loan in 1926 to the captain, assigned to tutor his young daughter, also named Maria, who had been weakened by scarlet fever at the same time her mother had died from the disease. On her first day on the job, the captain informed Maria that she was twenty-sixth in a long line of nurses, governesses and teachers that had passed through the home in the three years since his wife died. Whether it was a warning or not, she wondered at the cause of the turnover.

Maria soon found out. Over the next few weeks, she learned that the children had been divided into three groups—the two boys, the older girls and the younger girls—and each group was assigned their own area of the house. They were forbidden to mingle except at dinner when the whole family came together. The three groups fought each other continually, and the adults assigned to each group participated in this rivalry, leading to a hostile work environment.

When Maria first met the children, she was struck by how pale they were. She soon discovered the cause of that as well: the children never went outside to play. Since they had to remain in their formal school uniforms, which looked like little navy suits, they were not able to get dirty. Hence, they never saw the sun. For Maria, a child of the mountains, this broke her heart. Each night when she went to bed she prayed, "Let the children be happy from now on."

THE SOUND OF MUSIC TOUR

"Welcome to the Original Sound of Music Tour," our ebullient tour guide said as the red bus pulled away from Mirabellplatz, one of the most picturesque squares in the world. Other than the red double-decker bus tour in London, we hadn't signed up for anything this touristy on our pilgrimage. But because we adored the movie, we were willing to make an exception for this. Lindsay and Meghan, who had seen *The Sound of Music* dozens of times and listened to the soundtrack even more, were so excited they could not sit still.

As the bus wove through Salzburg's medieval streets, I remembered reading somewhere that Bob Wise, the director of *The Sound of Music*, wanted to make Salzburg and the Alps major characters in the movie. He filmed dozens of scenes around the city, highlighting the beauty of the city in every shot and cutting in many panoramic views of the mountains. As a result, viewers fall in love with the city as much as with the von Trapp family. Salzburg never seems dated in the movie, allowing each new generation to claim the movie as its own and long to experience the city. It's a magical combination.

The bus wound its way along the Salzach River, which runs through the city. Pointing across the river, the tour guide showed us where Maria and the kids ran along the river singing. Next we passed the Mozart footbridge, featured in the movie on the day the kids first wore their new play clothes, sewn by Maria out of old drapes. Five minutes later we were let out near Schloss Leopoldskron, an eighteenth-century rococo palace built on the edge of a small lake, the same lake where Maria and the kids tumbled out of their capsized rowboat. Many think this was the house in the movie, but it wasn't. Instead, Wise had a replica of the palace's terrace built at the home next door and used that for all the lake shots.

But other than for movie trivia, that fact really didn't matter. The real von Trapp house, which was never used in the movie, was fifteen minutes outside the city in Aigen. It was in that home that Maria, from the first day of her arrival, began influencing the captain's family. Even though Maria was hired to tutor only one child, and many of the older ones had no interest in getting to know her, she began befriending them all. Because she was only six years older than the eldest child, she had no trouble relating to them as friends, almost peers. A naturally gifted conversationalist with a warm heart, big smile and easy laugh, Maria had won them over within weeks. She brought the three groups of children together, spending time laughing and telling jokes. When one of the children saw her guitar, they asked her to play and sing. She asked them to join her. Though all the children already knew how to sing and play instruments (something the movie portrays wrongly), they had not sung together since their mother died. Maria started teaching them Austrian folk songs, and they sang together for hours.

It was this singing together that the movie dramatizes so well and that brings so much emotion to the film. Just a few weeks ago, we had watched the film in our RV in preparation for the tour. Even though I had seen the movie dozens of times over the years, I was surprised at my emotional reaction to the scene where the captain hears the children singing "the hills are alive with the sound of music," and he goes into the house and joins in with them. It is touching, tender, beautiful, and it moved me deeply. I thought of my dad, who died many years ago and whom I loved deeply, and how I had always wished we had more moments of reconciliation like that. I had read somewhere that for many viewers this was their favorite scene. It was for me as well.

We were now back on the bus heading toward Nonnberg Abbey, where Maria was a candidate for the novitiate. In the distance I could

The Original Sound of Music Tour bus

; baroque red dome, one of the most famous landmarks
, ... guide was busy telling us all kinds of interesting trivia
about the movie. As he talked I wondered about Maria's faith and
why he didn't bring it up.

Earlier in the trip, Michelle had begun reading the kids *The Story of
the Trapp Family Singers*, written by Maria. In the book she writes that
in her teen years, years marked by rebelliousness and lack of direction,
she went to hear a Christian evangelist and was deeply affected by his
message. Soon after that she experienced a powerful conversion to
Christ and this led her to join the nunnery, although she would admit
years later that she had joined for the wrong reasons. Yet from the
time of her conversion, her faith was extremely important to her,
touching every aspect of her life. So, soon after her arrival at the von
Trapp home, when she realized that the children were only nominal
believers, she was determined to lead them back to God.

During her first Advent with the family, she infused the holiday
with so much spiritual significance that when she was heading out
the door to attend Christmas Eve midnight mass at the abbey, the
captain pulled her aside and said, "I always feared Christmas more
than any other day. But this year you have made it very beautiful for
us. Thank you." On the way to the abbey she said a grateful prayer to
God: "I thank You so much for sending me there. Please help me to
draw them all closer to You."

Over the next few months, the family gathered each night in the
great room. As the girls made crafts or the boys whittled sticks, Maria
read to them from the Bible. "Protestants read their Bibles and Catholics don't," she said. "We need to change that." So each night she in-
structed them from God's Word. After reading from the Bible, she read
them great books of literature, bathing their imaginations in stories
and providing them with strong role models. Soon they added to the
reading an hour of singing each night and learning new sacred music.
Slowly Maria was shaping them into a family who loved God and one
another more each day. By the end of the nine months, they had fallen
in love with her too and needed to find a way to keep her around.

Family Liturgy

Along with family evenings filled with Scripture, stories and song, Maria brought something else to the von Trapps that shaped them into a family: the liturgy of celebration. Whether it was elaborate birthday celebrations for each child or the festivities around national holidays, Maria taught her family to celebrate and enjoy life. Although you only see a small portion of it in the movie, the scene with the "Lonely Goatherd" puppet show captures this sense of celebration well.

I was thinking about celebration when I looked over at Michelle, who was listening to the tour guide, and it dawned on me that Michelle has brought the same quality to our family. I did a quick review of our family's history. From the start of having children, Michelle has been the master of the celebration. For hours the night before our kids' birthdays, she decorates the entire house in streamers, balloons and signs. She wraps the gifts, pens a loving birthday card, bakes a cake and plans our child's favorite meal. She attempts to make the entire day a special one for the birthday child. I once asked her why she did so much work and she said, "I want them each to know how special they are and how much they are loved by their heavenly Father and by us." For my kids, birthdays are amazingly special times in our house.

As I sat there on the bus, now gazing pensively out the window, I realized that Michelle is like Maria in other ways as well. For years she has read aloud to our kids at night, introducing them to dozens of powerful stories and inspiring role models. Though the singing time was never as formal as the von Trapps', Michelle has taught our children dozens of songs, many based on Scripture and others from the various musicals she saw growing up. Yet it wasn't until I read Maria's book that I realized that what Michelle was doing in our family was actually liturgical; through these rituals, celebrations and stories she was helping to order our children's desires, that is, what they love and worship. Like the liturgy in a worship service, her liturgy was shaping our children and our family to imagine and act differently. Her liturgy has taught our children new habits, virtues and ways of being in the world, and these habits have steered their desires in the right direction.

I don't think Michelle has ever thought of what she does this way; she just does it instinctively. But like the impact of Maria's family liturgy on the von Trapp children, powerfully pulling together a divided and unfocused family, Michelle's family liturgy has been shaping our children and our family for years. Like Lewis's and Tolkien's fantasy stories, Trocmé's sermons and Bonhoeffer's underground seminary, Michelle has been giving our family "sensations we never had before," and has been enlarging "our conception of the range of possible experiences" with a "fresh, childlike wonder." Without even realizing it, in many ways the pilgrimage in our family had started years ago.

I scanned the tourists on the bus, many of them listening attentively to the guide, others looking out the large windows. Why were they here? Some of them had flown all the way from the States to be here, others from Japan. What had drawn them? After seeing the movie multiple times, even hundreds of times for some of them, I believe they have come to see the movie, even though they wouldn't say it this way, as a liturgy, something that orders their desires, their moods and the way they see the world. Even if they are unaware of it or have no idea what is behind it, the movie inspires them to be better people, to hope for a better day.

Bankrupt. That was the word Maria heard through the telephone. The bank that held most of the family fortune had gone under, taking all the von Trapp money with it. September 1929, three years after Maria had first become the tutor and two years after she and Georg had been married, and they were now nearly broke, no longer part of the rich upper class. When they got over the shock, they told the children, whose response shocked them. Every one of them took the news with joy, as if God was taking them on a new, grand adventure, which he was. They were prepared to live without a car, maids, servants, groundskeepers and other luxuries. They rolled up their sleeves and were ready to work. "In those days," wrote Maria years later, "we reaped the first harvest of that blessed custom we had started long ago of reading the Gospel together with the children. At every crossroad, in every tribulation" they were ready to do whatever God asked them. Their family liturgy had shaped them.

They began praying for ways to financially support the family. One answer came right away: they would rent out their extra rooms to seminary students and professors. At that time, they also got permission from their church to convert one of their rooms into a chapel. The first boarder, a seminary professor, was also clergy, and he began

The castle of Leopoldskon, used for several scenes in *The Sound of Music*

leading worship every morning for the family and the boarders. What began as a discouraging trial, the bankruptcy, had now been turned into good.

A year later, their large house was filled with young people, professors and seminary students. Maria writes, "Seldom before had there been so much laughter, so many spirited discussions, so many worth-while people to meet. . . . What richness that brought into our lives, especially to the growing children." During that time the family continued to sing, often entertaining their guests and sometimes having them join in the fun.

In the spring of 1935 a young minister, Father Wasner, was asked to lead worship in the family chapel. When he discovered they could sing, he said, "You really sang quite well this morning" but went on to tell them how they could improve, actually making them re-sing correctly the songs from morning worship. Right then and there, the Trapp Family Singers was born, within a year winning first prize in their first Salzburg Music Festival competition.

For the next two decades Father Wasner would be their vocal coach, manager, pastor and dear friend. Once again, the von Trapps recognized the hand of God providentially taking care of them, even in the midst of hard times. Through it all, they were learning to trust him more, and it was their family liturgy of reading, song and prayer that helped guide them.

FROHNBURG ESTATE: "I HAVE CONFIDENCE"

"That is Frohnburg estate," our guide said, "the house used for shots of the front of the house in the movie. This is the spot where Maria shows up right after singing 'I Have Confidence,' and later, when she and the captain return from their honeymoon, where he rips up the Nazi flag."

As we looked at the house, images of Maria's secondhand clothes and leather bowl hat flooding our minds, I mentioned under my breath (so as not to be tarred and feathered by the other fans on the bus) that this was my least favorite song in the movie. And it's not because it isn't a catchy number or isn't well done by Julie Andrews. It is my least favorite song because it doesn't fit the real Maria. Undoubtedly she was a woman of confidence and being confident was important to her. Certainly she needed courage to meet all the tests she would face ahead. And she did trust that all things would work out. The song gets all that right. But she would never have sung the words "I have confidence *in me!*"

These are not Maria's words. When faced with daunting challenges and serious trials she would never have said that her confidence and trust was in herself, let alone the subjective feeling of "confidence in confidence." From her conversion as a young woman, her confidence was in God, never herself. To put confidence in herself was a recipe for disaster. She had lived that way before her conversion, and it almost ruined her life. That is why she spent each day lovingly teaching her family to put their ultimate trust in God. Every time they were faced with trials or suffering they prayed to him for strength and guidance, not relying on themselves.

We see this most vividly years later when the captain dies, and that same year her daughter Martina (Gretl) and her baby die during childbirth. Maria does not put her confidence in herself to overcome her broken heart; rather, she places it in the strong hands of her loving heavenly Father. Only by doing this does she have the confidence to carry on with life.

Pondering this point with Michelle, I suddenly thought of something I had not seen before. Was it possible, I thought, that there is a connection between the order of our desires and the reality of our confidence and trust? In other words, was what we had been teaching our kids about roots, journey and destination in reality a lesson about ultimate trust? Is to desire God and his kingdom really to trust him?

At the moment I wasn't sure, but as I looked back at our trip I realized that we had had many conversations with our kids about whether they trusted God enough to put their lives in his hands and willingly obey him. Did they doubt his goodness and, as a consequence, struggle to obey him? Desire and trust are intermingled, and we tried to help them see that until they trusted him they wouldn't desire him or worship him or obey him.

Michelle and I faced this question ourselves each day as well. Did we trust God and put our confidence in him, that is, desire to serve and obey him fully? Sometimes we did. But I think there were plenty of days we ignored him and sang in our own hearts, "I have confidence in me." That is when we got ourselves into trouble.

MONDSEE CATHEDRAL

After a forty-five minute drive through the lake district outside of Salzburg, we were standing inside St. Michael's Cathedral in Mondsee, the church used to film the wedding scene in the movie. As we stood in the back of the church, I envisioned Julie Andrews walking down the aisle with her long train behind her, the organ belting out the processional, and her meeting Christopher Plummer at the front altar. In real life, they were married in the Nonnberg Abbey chapel. But undoubtedly Robert Wise wanted a much grander church, and he got it with St. Michael's.

As I wandered around the magnificently beautiful church, I thought about how important daily worship was for the von Trapps.

Maria and Captain von Trapp leading the wedding party outside Nonnberg Abbey in 1927

Their music was first an expression of worship for them. Many of the songs they sang in concert they first sang together in worship. And their worship shaped their desire; it made them who they were. I wondered, did worship play the same role in our family?

After leaving St. Michael's, Michelle and I went to collect our children, who were wandering around outside the cathedral, in order to eat some apple strudel and talk more about the movie. After we found them, I stood one last moment outside the church, looking up to the great bell towers. In *The Sound of Music*, after the camera pans the countryside of Mondsee, it then cuts to Salzburg, slowly descending down onto the old town's main square, dramatically showing Nazi flags pinned on buildings and German soldiers

At the von Trapp wedding

marching through the square. It was a signal that the von Trapps were about to face one of their greatest challenges. Would their family meet the challenge? Where would they put their confidence? Whom would they worship?

"I am yielding to force," intoned the Austrian chancellor. "My Austria—God bless you!" Then the Austrian national anthem played. It was March 11, 1938, eleven years after their wedding, and Maria and her family sat stunned around the radio in their library. Moments later, their blank stares were interrupted when the door opened and in came Hans the butler.

"Captain," he said, "Austria has been invaded by Germany, and I want to inform you that I am a member of the Party. I have been for quite some time."

Right then, the anthem finished, and a harsh Prussian voice sounded over the radio: "Austria is dead: Long live the Third Reich!"

The family filed silently out of the library and into the chapel. In the darkness, some of the children sobbed; others sighed deeply as if a member of the family had suddenly died. The captain broke the silence. "Austria," he said, tears slowing his speech, "you are not dead. You will live in our hearts."

Werner ran over to the window and flung it open. "Listen," he said. "All the bells in Salzburg are ringing. What does it mean?"

Recognizing that the bells were announcing the invasion of the Germans, the captain told him to shut the window. It made him sick that the bells would be used for this occasion.

The next day the town was covered in red and black flags, the swastika on almost every house. For the first time, the family had to be careful what they said around Hans the butler and, for that matter, anyone in Salzburg. An innocent remark, a slip of the tongue could and did land people in concentration camps.

Just before summer break, the children came home one day and told Maria that some of their teachers had disappeared and new ones had taken their place. At an assembly these new teachers told the children that they were the hope of the future, the hope of the whole world, and that their parents were old fashioned and didn't understand the new party. They taught the children that Jesus was a bad little Jewish boy and should not be worshiped. In the end, they warned them: don't speak of anything you are learning at school to your parents at home.

The next day, Maria was summoned to the school regarding Lorli, her first grader.

"You must do something about your little girl," the teacher warned, "or you will get into serious trouble. She refuses to sing the Nazi anthem. When I asked her why, she announced to the whole class that her father had said he'd put ground glass in his tea or finish his life on a dung heap before he would ever sing that song." The teacher coldly looked at Maria and said, "Next time I will have to report this."

Soon after the warning at school, the captain received a telegram asking him to take over a new submarine that would eventually be launched in the Adriatic Sea and then in the Mediterranean. This could only mean one thing: the Germans were preparing for war. He knew he had to reject the offer.

That same day, coming back from an outing, Maria and the captain ran into their son Rupert, who had just become a doctor. He handed them a letter from a big hospital in Vienna offering him a job.

"Will you take it?" they must have asked him.

"I don't think so," he said. "I know the reason they need doctors. The Nazis have imprisoned, tortured and killed so many Jewish doctors that there is now a shortage in the hospitals. I will not help, and I could never conduct the kind of experiments on human beings they would require of me."

A few days later they received a call from Munich informing them they had been chosen to sing at Adolf Hitler's birthday party, a prospect that could bring the family fame and fortune. The Captain called the family together for a meeting. "Our family is faced with a huge choice," he told the children. "On the one hand we are being offered jobs, prosperity and great fame. But to get it we would have to give up our faith, our convictions, our honor. We can't have both. Do you agree?"

In one resounding voice the children said, "Yes, Father."

"Then let's get out of here soon. You can't say no to Hitler three times—it's getting dangerous."

In September, just six months after the German invasion, the von Trapps walked out of their house accompanied by Father Wasner, leaving behind all their property and furniture, taking only what they could carry. They walked through their yard, across some tracks and into a train station and boarded a train for Italy. Once safely in Italy, they would take a boat to America. They didn't know it at the time, but the next day the Germans would close Austria's borders, trapping wanted to leave. As the von Trapps waited for their boat, Maria thought, "We have now the precious opportunity to find out for ourselves whether the words we have heard and read so often can be taken literally: 'Seek ye first the Kingdom of God and His justice: and all these things shall be added unto you.'"

MIRABELL GARDENS

On the way back from Mondsee to Salzburg, the tour guide popped in *The Sound of Music* sing-along DVD. I sang for a while but then dozed, leaning against the window. My kids fell asleep too, worn out from the long day. When we got back to Mirabellplatz, slightly groggy from our naps, our guide handed us a map with all the locations used for the filming of the "Do Re Mi" song in Mirabell Gardens and told us we were on our own, saying a warm goodbye.

Entering the garden, we spilled down the steps that the children and Maria climb at the end of the song. My girls jumped on the giant bronze lions, one on each side of the steps. As soon as I pulled out the map to start finding the other sites, my kids were gone. They had spotted a playground next to the gardens.

"Let 'em go," Michelle said. "It's been a long day and they just need to play."

I found a number of spots from the movie, including the ivy-covered tunnel that they ran through, with the Untersberg mountain providing the perfect backdrop for the scene. I walked the length of the gardens, sleuthing for other scenes in the movie and humming one of the songs. But I wasn't humming "Do Re Mi," which would have fit the moment, but instead the song "My Favorite Things." In her charming book *Forever Liesl*, Charmian Carr talks affectionately about that song and when it was performed the first day on the set. She was mortified, but Julie Andrews put her at ease by telling jokes. And the song helped too. Throughout the book, Charmian shares some of the difficult things she has gone through over the past five decades since the movie debuted, and "My Favorite Things" has encouraged her to get through those hard times. The song has undoubtedly encouraged millions of others going through hard times to do the same. It has encouraged me at times as well.

But as I strolled the gardens I now thought about the song a little differently. After all we had learned about what made Maria tick, where she found her confidence and how quick she was to go to prayer, I now doubted that simply thinking about our "favorite things" was strong enough to sustain any of us in times of trouble and suffering. Counting our blessings is important; thinking positive thoughts is crucial. Recalling our favorite things helps. But, I had to

Beautiful Mirabell Gardens, with the Fortress in the background.

wonder, can "my favorite things" bear the weight of profound depression, for instance? Can they sustain us when someone we love dies? Can they teach our children to push back against false liturgies, like Lorli did when she refused to sing the Nazi anthem? I wasn't so sure they could.

I thought of the children in the movie, sitting on Maria's bed, some hiding under the covers shielding their ears from the loud thunder outside, joyously singing about their favorite things. It is a wonderful moment. But I still wondered, can thinking about our favorite things truly reshape our imaginations to see the world differently? Can they inspire us to love the beautiful, true and good when the temptations of the world are so strong? Can they help my kids avoid the "lock box" syndrome? After learning more about the real Maria, I had my doubts.

As I read Charmian's winsome book, I wondered if the solution to our suffering is found less in Julie Andrews's song and more in the message that the real Maria clung to when suffering hit. In other words, was the key to getting through suffering less about the blessings in our life and more about the one who blesses? Was the key to persevering not in the gifts but in God? If he is the giver of all good gifts, wasn't it important that our favorite things be linked to him?

I walked over to a bench and sat down. I was in a reflective mood, the kind of feeling one gets when an event is over and it has stirred some deep emotions. I knew I needed to find my family, but I lingered for a moment longer, enjoying the serenity of the gardens. I lifted my eyes from the grand fountain to the Salzburg Castle in the distance, sitting high atop a mountain peak, and my mind drifted to a different castle in another charming medieval city. In that city, a young man, commissioned by the Prince Elector, wrote a document to shape the theological imagination of young people (and adults) in the new churches of the Reformation. It was a document that contained a message, one that I thought might be strong enough to help my family through even the most trying times, a message that would inspire us to worship, powerful enough to shape our imaginations and direct our affections to our ultimate destination. It held a message that included "my favorite things" but at the same time looked beyond them to something much greater. I was convinced we needed to go to that city. It would be the last stop on our pilgrimage.

eleven

HEIDELBERG
AND NORMANDY

Lessons from Castle and the Cliff

Heidelberg Castle

It was the end of April, three days before Easter, and we were in Heidelberg. I thought back over the two days since we had arrived, and my mind was a blaze of images: our RV encamped outside of the old city twenty feet from the Neckar River; Jonathan cooking bacon the next morning; returning the RV to Frankfurt; our wonderful Christian host family, the Dreyers, who live in the Rhine Valley, stuffing us each morning with an assortment of breads, meats and cheeses; and my girls spending every free moment with the Dreyers' massive Newfoundland dog, Baloo, leading him around their home as if he were a giant but tame bear.

Driving through the medieval and Renaissance streets of the city, students bustling to class, others standing on corners enjoying the warm Neckar Valley sun cascading off buildings and trees and flowers, we passed the magnificent Church of the Holy Spirit, whose spires dominate the skyline. Then we started our slow, winding ascent up the side of the mountain toward our destination: the Heidelberg Castle. As we wound our way up the mountain, a famous document written in this city gripped my mind: the Heidelberg Catechism. It is the most famous and beloved catechism to come out of the Reformation, still used by parents worldwide to teach their children the basics of the faith. The writing of the document was overseen by Zacharias Ursinus, a professor at the Heidelberg University, the pastor of the Church of the Holy Spirit and the leading Reformed theologian of the region.

After parking our minivan just above the castle, Rolf Dreyer, his wife and their teenage daughter led us down some serpentine steps to

The Heidelberg Castle

the castle grounds. "It stands upon a commanding elevation," Mark Twain wrote after visiting the castle. "It is buried in green woods, there is no level ground about it, but, on the contrary, there are wooded terraces upon terraces, and one looks down through shining leaves into profound chasms and abysses where twilight reigns and the sun cannot intrude."

When we approached the castle, we paused and Rolf pointed to the collapsed tower and destroyed walls. "It was the French," he said with a slight condescension in his voice. "They blew up the tower with massive amounts of gunpowder."

My boys were amazed at the size of the blown-up
leaned against the castle right where it fell 250 years a
to believe. "Why haven't they rebuilt the tower?" Jonathan asked,
always in the habit of asking good questions.

I wasn't sure. Some say they have not done so on purpose. It is
thought that in the nineteenth century, the Romantics celebrated
"the beauty of the ruin" as a metaphor for life and made this a great
tourist destination. Mark Twain, whose description of the ruins did
much to make the castle popular with American tourists, wrote:

> Nature knows how to garnish a ruin to get the best effect. One of these
> old towers is split down the middle, and one half has tumbled aside. It
> tumbled in such a way as to establish itself in a picturesque attitude.
> Then all it lacked was a fitting drapery, and Nature has furnished that;
> she has robed the rugged mass in flowers and verdure, and made it a
> charm to the eye. Misfortune has done for this old tower what it has
> done for the human character sometimes—improved it.

Having learned earlier in our trip about van Gogh's "broken beauty,"
I thought of this broken tower as a metaphor for the city that has
seen its share of religious division between Catholics and Protestants
and for our lives that are so often rent asunder by brokenness. When
I looked at the tower laying there broken, it made me slightly anxious;
it gave me the unsteady feeling of needing to fix it, to set it right. I
wondered if that is why they left it unrepaired—to remind us of our
own brokenness and to make us anxious over our incompleteness.
An interesting sentiment for romantics to have, I thought.

As I looked at the tower and the missing walls of the castle, rooms
exposed to the outside "like open, toothless mouths," I thought of
the main concern behind the Heidelberg Catechism, written down
below the castle in the halls of the great university. At the time, the
catechism was written for a people who were worried about religious
wars but also about the vagaries of life. The aim of it was to get to the
heart of the human condition: What calms your anxiety? Where do
you put your ultimate confidence? What gives you hope each day?

What do you desire? These were questions the people of that day had, but they are questions we all still have today.

My mind raced back to Costa Mesa. I thought of Jordan as a little boy, his blond hair slightly disheveled, sitting next to Michelle as she quizzed him. "What is your only comfort in life and in death?" Michelle asked tenderly.

"That I am not my own," Jordan said confidently, "but belong, body and soul, to my faithful savior, Jesus Christ."

Michelle prompted Jordan to finish the answer. He had only recited the first part.

"I don't remember it, Mom," he said.

Michelle prompted him again.

"He has fully paid for all my sins with his precious blood," Jordan said haltingly, trying to remember the words. "And has set me free from the tyranny of the devil." Jordan stopped.

"Keep going," Michelle said. "It gets better."

"He also watches over me in such a way that not a hair can fall from my head without the will of my Father in heaven. In fact, all things must work together for my salvation."

Michelle explained to him what that meant: that God loved him so much that nothing escapes his concern or fatherly care, even suffering. God is looking out for him all the time. "Isn't that the kind of God you can trust and obey?" she asked him.

I looked over at my girls sitting on the wall, Michelle carefully holding them so they wouldn't tumble down into the moat that contained the broken tower. I read somewhere that the word "comfort" in the first question is another word for trust: "What is your trust in life and in death?" In other words, where is your ultimate security and hope? Where do you put your confidence—in yourself or in God? As I said, we asked our kids this question many times over our travels. We knew that if they could answer it correctly and live it out, they would possess a calm and comfort that the world could never provide.

Rolf motioned to me that it was time to move to the next part of the tour. As we entered the castle, the crowd thickened, and I r̲e̲a̲c̲h̲e̲d̲ ̲f̲o̲r̲ my girls' hands, wanting to protect them from the onrush of people.

The catechism summarizes so well what we had been learning through Maria's life but also through the other historic heroes we had been studying. The reason we are "wholeheartedly willing and ready from now on to live for him," that is, to desire his kingdom, is because we trust him, we find our confidence in him, and we realize that all good gifts come from him. This piety, this love of God is at the heart of our desire. We want to live for him because he has set us free. We want to obey him and trust in him because he is our loving heavenly father. This was the story we wanted our kids to be part of—to be pilgrims of comfort, hope and obedience.

We made our way through the crowds into the castle, walking through an arched gate onto the grand terrace. Bursting in front of us was the most glorious view of Heidelberg, the Neckar River and the valley below. Even with sunglasses on, I had to shade my eyes from the brilliant sun. One can't stand on that terrace and not be reminded of the holy, eternal city; the image is that overwhelming.

City of Heidelberg, Germany

In *Pilgrim's Progress*, as Christian nears the end of his journey, he comes to a spot where he has a clear view of the eternal city: "It was built of Pearls and precious Stones; also the streets thereof were paved with Gold." With "the natural glory of the City, and the reflection of the Sun-beams upon it," Christian falls down, sick with desire for the eternal city. Standing there with my family gazing over Heidelberg, a pang of longing for the day when the heavenly city, Jerusalem, comes down from heaven, filled me with a terrible ache. Mingled with feelings of comfort, confidence and trust was a profound desire to know God better, to see him more clearly, to be with him. I longed for my true home. And I wanted it for my family.

From the sprawling terrace we headed back through the massive castle gardens, lingering for a moment, knowing that our pilgrimage was coming to an end. Three of the kids ran ahead to throw coins in a shimmering pool, while I carried Meghan on my back, something I had done many times over the past year.

When Christian in *Pilgrim's Progress* regains his strength after being overcome with the sickness of longing, he also enters a garden. "Whose goodly vineyards and Gardens are these?" he asks.

"They are the King's," says the gardener, "and are planted here for his own delight, and also for the solace of Pilgrims."

Christian flops down on the grass and rests in the gardens, steadying himself for the last leg of the journey to the city. I wanted to do the same. For our family, the stories we have bathed in for the year, ones that shaped our identity, helped us push back on false liturgies, provided maps and taught us about our destination, have been like a vineyard to us, not only inspiring our imaginations and guiding our actions but providing amazing solace and comfort— nourishment for the soul.

Like Christian we had more challenges ahead; that was true. But our last few days in Heidelberg had taught us much and had provided just the solace we needed to keep going. Because we knew whom we belonged to, body and soul, we had the courage and strength to move forward. "The pilgrim goes on," said van Gogh, "sorrowful yet always rejoicing."

The next day the Dreyers loaded our bags with two dozen boxes of German chocolate, prayed for us and sent us on our way, pilgrims keeping our eyes on our ultimate destination, a family reveling in God's comfort and now more than willing to serve him with grateful obedience. We had hoped God would break into our lives during this pilgrimage and teach us new things about him. And now, through the many twists and turns, happy times and sad moments of our journey, we knew one thing: he had.

NORMANDY: SEVEN WEEKS LATER

The warm June sun was glimmering through the trees, their long branches waving in the breeze, the immaculate flower beds providing punctuation, the blue seas a dramatic glassy backdrop to nine thousand white crosses, perfectly arranged, stretching as far as the eye could see. Tears came to my eyes, catching me off guard. I had seen the American Cemetery on TV, but nothing prepared me for walking on this hallowed ground.

It was June 9, and we were in Normandy. Seven weeks had passed since Heidelberg. Over those weeks, with our formal pilgrimage over, our kids enjoyed the start of their summer vacation. We traveled through Italy, showing them Roman ruins and Christian churches while at the same time I worked on another writing project—this one on architecture and how buildings shape us. We visited Rome, Pompeii, Florence and Venice, to name a handful of places we went. After that, we made our way back toward France, stopping to see friends in Nice and then spending two weeks snorkeling in the Mediterranean, north of Barcelona, compliments of an American businessman living in Switzerland who owns a tiny cottage overlooking the sea. I recalled watching the sun rise each morning over the sea, nothing stirring but some fishing vessels going out for the day's catch.

Now in Normandy, we had two days before we boarded our flight home. By God's grace we had accomplished so much. But one goal wasn t met: Finkenwalde. We had never found the site of Bonhoeffer's illegal seminary, and it was still nagging at me after all this time. I had desperately wanted to show my family the place where Bonhoeffer had developed a radical community of pastors strong enough to resist the lure of Hitler's false ideology.

But standing there in Normandy among so many lives cut short, so many dreams unrealized, I now understood that in some ways not getting to Finkenwalde might be one last metaphor for our pilgrimage. For all pilgrimages—and all earthly lives—are never com-

The American Cemetery, Normandy, France

plete until we, like Christian in *Pilgrim's Progress*, cross over the dark river and tumble into the Celestial City. Until the last day, our pilgrimage will be filled with a sense of incompleteness, a holy longing. It is true, we never made it to Finkenwalde. But that didn't invalidate our pilgrimage; in fact, in some ways it made it more realistic, more true to our lives.

After ninety minutes in the cemetery, we strolled toward the cliffs. As I walked past more white crosses and flower beds I realized that although it is a profoundly sad place, it is not a depressing place, which it easily could have been. Instead, it was a deeply hopeful place, as if the eschatological, the hope of the resurrected life, were breaking into the present, reminding us of a new day. "Solid joys and lasting treasures," John Newton, the hymn writer, once wrote.

We walked over to the wall overlooking the D-Day beaches below. Images of young men bloodied by bullets, falling dead into the sea, rushed into my mind. So many young boys died down there, I thought. I imagined dozens of boys emerging from the sea, running to seek cover under the cliffs, German mortars and gunfire raining down on them as they ran. Taking a deep breath, I raised my eyes from the beach and looked across the wave-capped channel, trying to see England. I thought of Lewis in Oxford. I thought of Narnia. I thought of Lucy and Eustace and Edmund and Reepicheep at the end of the *Dawn Treader*, "seeing beyond the End of the World into Aslan's country." I could almost see it; I longed to see it.

"This," said Reepicheep, "is where I go on alone." The children helped him lower his little boat into the water and "then he took off his sword ('I shall need it no more,' he said) and flung it far away across the lilied sea. . . . Then he bade them good-bye, trying to be sad for their sakes; but he was quivering with happiness." As Reepicheep's boat moved out from shore, it was caught by a large wave, pulling it higher onto the wave's crest, as if it were on a post where the mouse could see Aslan's country on one side and the children on the other. Then suddenly, with a rush, he tumbled over the wave, cascading down into Aslan's country. The children saw him no more.

As I looked out over the English Channel to England, I was not sure what I wanted more—to begin our pilgrimage over again in England, our "Narnia," or to travel to the real Narnia, the Celestial City. I was overwhelmed with sadness, knowing our pilgrimage was over yet still longing for a new day.

Soon after Reepicheep leaves, Aslan shows up. The children beg him to let them stay; they don't want to be sent back to England. They don't want the journey to end. But it is no use; they have to go home. "This was the very reason why you were brought to Narnia,"

Aslan tells them tenderly, "that by knowing me here for a little while, you may know me better there."

The same was true for us. We had gone, like so many pilgrims before us, to "Narnia" to get to know God better. We had gone on this pilgrimage to encounter him in new ways, and we had. We had hoped this adventure would help us desire him and his kingdom more, and it did. We had sought, on this quest, to be shaped by our roots, our journey and our destination, and we had been. But now it was over. And as sad as we were to leave, it was time to go home to our own country. And there we would get to know him even better.

PILGRIMS IN
SOUTH FLORIDA

For the past two years that is what we have been doing: getting to know Jesus better.

In the summer of 2011, when we returned to the States, I interviewed for a professorship at Knox Theological Seminary in Fort Lauderdale. We were sad to leave Southern California, having to part with Michelle's family, Redeemer Church and decades of dear friendships. But in our gut we knew the move was a perfect fit for our family at this stage of life, so we accepted the job and moved to South Florida that November. The kids started school a week after we arrived—quite a shock.

All four of our children attend Westminster Academy, across the street from Knox and next to Coral Ridge Presbyterian Church. They are all doing well, having caught up to grade level in their first three months thanks to Michelle tutoring the kids each night.

Like many families we struggle each morning to get six people out the door on time, and fail more often than not. After long days of school we return home to hours of homework, dinners interrupted by baseball, ice hockey or gymnastics practices, and piles of dirty dishes and laundry. We fall into bed at night wondering how we are going to do it all again the next day, trying to remain grateful for all the blessings in our life.

Invariably, in the most pressure-filled moments each week someone in our family will bring up Oxford or Provence or Salzburg, and we will talk about all the memories. Reliving the stories makes us nostalgic for a time long gone, a time we wish we could have back. But the other day when this happened, I had to stop and remind myself of something. Yes, we had come home; we had to. But we were still on the pilgrimage. Even though we have returned, the pilgrimage has not ended, and it will not end until the new heaven and the new earth arrive.

Like Christian in *The Pilgrim's Progress* we are still journeying toward the Celestial City, and our journey in the past can help us. Although daily life is filled with myriad challenges, ones that we often don't seem up to meeting, they reveal opportunities for us to remember and relearn what we experienced on our journey, and they provide us with yet another opportunity to trust our heavenly father— to realign our passions, renew our desire for his kingdom and learn to serve him even when life is hard. This is the journey of deep faith that we have begun to live out. It is the pilgrimage we are on every day. We just have to remember that.

Looking back, each of our children grew in different ways. Jordan learned much on the pilgrimage about identity and seeing himself in the light of God's forgiveness and his glory. He continues to learn not to shame himself and to view himself as God sees him, a person adopted, forgiven and called to God's kingdom. He still struggles with his identity and knowing deep down he is loved. He has a hard time being content, grumbling far too often when he is bored, unchallenged or simply does not want to obey. But he is growing in these areas, and as parents we pray and hope he grows up to trust God more, learning that God knows best what he needs, even if this means suffering.

Jonathan flourished on the journey. He began it as an insecure and quiet boy and ended it more confident and secure, as if during the year his personality came alive. I remember at the end of our time in Oxford Jordan saying how funny and engaging Jonathan had become. None of us had seen this side of him. We also saw his emotional intelligence blossom. Spending hours each day with him, we witnessed his ability to read a social situation correctly and take care of the people around him, particularly his sisters. He has wonderful gifts of friendship and hospitality. As admirable as his character and personality are, we sometimes worry about his faith. We wonder whether he obeys just to keep the peace or because he truly believes. We hope that one day he will have an articulate faith, one that he can not only explain but also desires more than anything in life. But we worry. And we pray.

Our girls, Lindsay and Meghan, were just six and four when we began the pilgrimage. We often said they were along for the ride, but we have been surprised by how much they remember and how deeply our experience changed them. Granted, they don't recall much of my heroes or the stories we told them (in part, this book is a written record for them when they get older), but they do fondly recall our house in Oxford, traveling in the RV and laughing together as a family. From the trip they gained a sense of security, confidence in life, and the knowledge that they are loved by God and their parents deeply. All the travel opened the world to them and has given them an amazing confidence. They are still learning about their faith, but I am encouraged each night when they beg me, even when I am weary, to read from *The Jesus Storybook Bible* by Sally Lloyd-Jones or to sing to them some hymn or say a blessing to them before they go to sleep.

Michelle began the pilgrimage tired. After a decade and a half of supporting me as a pastor she was worn out and often lost sight of her own calling. For her the journey was a time to unearth her heart, to rekindle her desires and stoke her passion for the kingdom and her calling as a child of God, a wife, a mother and a teacher. Over the months in England and Europe she experienced again her love for learning, teaching and mothering in ways that she didn't know were possible. Whether it was taking the kids on a field trip or reading to them for hours each night or making them sandwiches from the front seat of the minivan, she rediscovered her sense of self, calling and purpose in life. The journey was not always easy for her—living in thirty-six different places wouldn't be easy for anyone—but in the end it strengthened her as a person and gave her a deeper trust in the providential care of her heavenly Father.

Now as a teacher's assistant and the main tutor of our children each afternoon, she draws from our trip every day as she inspires our kids in their learning. The other day she was helping Jonathan review for a history test, and she said to me later how much she just loves to teach our kids and how deeply it satisfies her soul. Our pilgrimage rejuvenated her love of learning and helped her to see that she is a lifelong learner. And she wants our kids to be lifelong learners too.

There are still days where she struggles with trust, especially regarding two of our children with learning difficulties; sometimes she comes home in a panic, fearing that they are falling too far behind in reading. Yet I have seen her go down this road of panic only to catch and remind herself that God is in control, even in the midst of suffering and trials. Just yesterday she was helping Jonathan memorize Romans 8:28: "And we know that for those who love God all things work together for good, for those who are called according to his purpose." She is learning that even in the midst of scary times her only comfort in life is that she belongs body and soul to her faithful Savior, Jesus Christ.

Since our return, as a family we have pursued a liturgy of worship and growth, some days better than others. We read Scripture, memorize the Heidelberg Catechism, sing hymns and sometimes use the evening prayer service from the *Book of Common Prayer*. We are never as consistent in these areas as we would like, but we continue to pursue them, asking God to help us all develop an articulate faith strong enough to resist the false liturgies of desire around us and the ill-fated identity lock box for our kids. We are grateful that we have found a solid, gospel-centered church in which to nurture our family. Last week as we went up for the Lord's Supper, taking the meal together, I was overwhelmed with gratitude for the church and for God's faithfulness to our family.

As for me, since our return from the pilgrimage, Knox Seminary has been my academic home, the place where I pursue my calling of teaching and writing. The fit has been miraculous. The other day I told my colleague Michael Allen how grateful I am to be at a place that allows me to pursue my calling and actually encourages me to close my door and bury myself in my writing.

For the past year, I have spent three to four days a week telling the tale of our journey. I have spent so much time with my heroes that they have become dear friends to me; their impact on my life as a teacher, writer, husband and father has been incalculable. No doubt the year changed me. My roots are deeper, my maps are better, and my destination is clearer. My desire, so weak at the start of the journey, has been reignited. My calling, once buried, has been reaffirmed. My understanding of life as a journey, once forgotten under the day-to-day struggles of life, has been reawakened. My realization of the importance of my destination, once lost in the spell of the world, has been rediscovered. Life is not always easy, and like the children in the Narnia Chronicles who have to return home, I long in the hard moments to go back in time. I can't, so sometimes I grumble. Yet I realize that it is here in south Florida that I have to learn to get to know God better, to trust him more, to keep moving forward.

At times, the pilgrimage seems like a lifetime ago. We are sad that we can't recall all the emotions we had or all the experiences we went through. Sometimes the memories seem to fade like an old photograph that yellows. But even as they fade, one thing does not: we will never see the world or God the same way again; we have been changed. How could we not be? We saw and experienced too much to remain unchanged. Our pilgrimage taught us to trust God more and to find our ultimate comfort in him. And it has taught us that the last chapter of our adventure has not been written for any of us, that "the best is yet to come," as Casper ten Boom would say.

Before I close, I want to thank you, my reader, for letting me tell you the tale of our journey and for sharing it with us. Even if we haven't met, I feel as if we've been on this journey together, and even become, in a way, friends. I pray for you, as I do for my family, the following:

That wherever you live or whatever stage of life you are in you will see life as a pilgrimage. That starting today you will begin the quest to redis-cover your roots, understand that life is a journey, and passionately em-brace your destination.

That as you embark on this pilgrimage you will learn to trust God more than you have ever done and to take some risks, to step out in faith, leave your comfort zone and open yourself (and maybe your family) to meeting God in new and exciting ways. That you will come to see that your heavenly Father has your best in mind at all times.

That you will have the courage to begin today. It may be scary, but not as scary as doing nothing. It may be risky, but not as risky as a lifetime of regrets. Step out your door. And may the words of Frodo in The Lord of the Rings *be your song:*

The Road goes ever on and on
Down from the door where it began.
Now far ahead the Road has gone,
And I must follow, if I can.

Finally, that as you start this grand adventure, the pilgrimage of your life, I pray you will know, in the words of Jeremiah, where the good way is, how to walk in it, and, in the process, find rest for your soul.

ACKNOWLEDGMENTS

I am grateful to many people who contributed to our pilgrimage. From the start, a number of people believed deeply in this project, and without their support we couldn't have made the journey: Mark Roberts and Foundations for Laity Renewal, Dr. Richard and June Lee, Michael and Betty Carroll, Mark and Shelly Ensio, David and Joleen Bahnsen, and Redeemer Presbyterian Church—all contributed to the project financially and prayerfully over the year.

When we arrived in Oxford in August 2010, our possessions were still on a boat somewhere over the Atlantic, our house was unfurnished, and the kitchen was bare. Within two weeks we had outfitted the kitchen, adequately furnished the house with secondhand furniture, wired the house for Internet and bought six bikes for transportation. We couldn't have accomplished all of this without the help of our new friends Bill and Ky Prevette, who as veteran missionaries had set up house in a myriad of countries over the years and knew how to help us do it. And for the six months we were there, Ky took Michelle grocery shopping, providing not only transportation but her friendship. Christian Hofreiter, one of my study mates at Wycliffe, helped us gather free furniture from all over Oxford and was always available to help when needed.

Wycliffe Hall provided me the perfect academic home. My colleagues Simon Vibert, Peter Walker, Richard Turnbull, Benno Van den Toren, Andrew Atherstone and Justin Hardin encouraged the project by steering me to the right sources and contacts time and time again.

I want to thank our tour guides and those we dialogued with along the way. Tim Keller, Will Vaus, Michael Ward, Debbie Higgens, Ross Kuehne, Steve Turner, Stephen Tomkins, Peter Hitchens, David Mayernik, David Aitken, Os Guinness, Hélène Crouzet, Gérard Bollon, Rolf Dreyer, Rev. Burckhard Scheffler, Knut Hämmerling, Herbert Soergel, Hugh Wessel and The Original Sound of Music Tour—all of you enriched the book and my family in more ways than I could say.

Over the course of the year many people generously gave us free places to stay and showered us with hospitality. I want to thank the Rev. Andrew and Rachel Baughen (London), Rev. Scott Herr (Paris), Willem Strauss (Loumarin, France), Rob and Crista Ludwick of the Dutch L'Abri (Eck en Wiel, Holland), Greg Laughery of the Swiss L'Abri (Huemoz, Switzerland), Scott Harris and family (Nice, France), Ralph McCall (Llanca, Spain), and Justin and Jill Hardin (Oxford).

I also want to thank the people who provided lodging for us before we arrived in Oxford and after we returned to the States as I was finishing the book: John D'Elia (London), Christian Hofreiter (Oxford), Bill and Annie Mahr (Maryland), John and Laurie Truschel (Beverly Farms, Massachusetts), Carolyn Belcher, my mom (Charlestown, Rhode Island), Dave and Andrea Reinkensmeyer (Irvine, California), Nancy and Diego Ruiz (Vienna, Virginia), Fred and Marna Miller (Big Bear Lake, California), the Fuller Theological Seminary Guest House (Pasadena, California), Grant and Francis Delgatty (Pasadena, California), and Bruce and Kristen Abbink (Camarillo, California).

So many people helped us connect with the right people for lodging, interviews, speaking opportunities and tour guides. I am grateful to Gideon Strauss, Steve Garber, Bruno Roche, Scott Harris, Hugh Wessel, Doug Birdsall, Bruce Terrell, Luder Whitlock, Kelly Christelle, John D'Elia, Mark Carver and Vinay Samuel. If I have forgotten anyone, please forgive me.

As with my first book, *Deep Church*, I want to thank InterVarsity Press, particularly my editor, Al Hsu, and the publisher, Bob Fryling, for believing in this project. To the editorial staff, marketing team, marketing manager Deborah Gonzalez, and cover design team, led by Cindy Kiple, I owe you my appreciation. Thanks to my copy editor, Allison Rieck, for smoothing out my prose. It has been a joy to work with you all. I am grateful to my student Sean Molloy for producing the index.

Along with the team at IVP, I received wonderful editorial advice from David Jacobson, a freelance writer and editor living in Bend, Oregon, and Thomas Lake, a senior writer at *Sports Illustrated.* Both have made the book better, improving the flow and style of my paragraphs and sentences. Any weaknesses that remain are my fault, not theirs.

I want to thank my beta readers, who made the book better with their comments and insights: Laurie Truschel, Matt Redmond, Rick Hunter, Will Vaus, Michelle Belcher and Jordan Belcher. I am grateful to Nelly Trocmé Hewett, the daughter of André and Magda Trocmé, for reading the chapter on her parents and making sure that I credit not only her parents but also the dozen other villages that participated in the heroic rescue operation. She also saved me from some historical mistakes. But as is the case, all remaining errors are attributed to me.

Like most writers, I have been influenced and inspired by other writers and coaches. Robert D. Kaplan (*Balkan Ghost* and *Mediterranean Winter*), one of the finest travel writers alive, and Bruce Feiler (*Walking the Bible* and *Where God Was Born*) both inspired me to pursue travel writing, and I read their books continuously throughout my own writing, trying to emulate their craft. Jack Hart (*StoryCraft*), Jon Franklin (*Writing for Story*), Annie Dillard (*The Writing Life*), William Zinsser (*On Writing Well*), and Stephen King (*On Writing*) have been my coaches and inspiration from afar. I owe a special word of thanks to David Grann of *The New Yorker* (*The Lost City of Z*), whose style influenced the way I structured *In Search of Deep Faith*.

I want to thank the president of Knox Seminary, Luder Whitlock, for supporting this project every step of the way and hiring me to teach at the school. The fit couldn't be better. I am grateful to my colleagues at Knox for their constant encouragement to see this project to the end.

Finally, I want to thank my children, Jordan, Jonathan, Lindsay and Meghan, for their adventurous spirits and for allowing me to lead them on this amazing pilgrimage. We learned more than we could have imagined, and we have memories for a lifetime. I couldn't have done this without Michelle, who was a full partner in this expedition, mentoring our kids, taking care of us on the road, being our navigator, providing wisdom and insight at every step, and being my best friend. She is a remarkable woman, and I am grateful to be on pilgrimage with her.

NOTES

Prologue

p. 12 "I feel thin": J. R. R. Tolkien, *The Lord of the Rings* (Boston: Houghton Mifflin, 1987), p. 32.

p. 13 "Pilgrimage speaks to a deep need": John Inge, *A Christian Theology of Place* (Burlington, VT: Ashgate, 2003), p. 102.

p. 13 "Pilgrims are stimulated": J. G. Davies, quoted in ibid., p. 102.

p. 15 "how to recapture the sense of endless": Robert D. Kaplan, *Mediterranean Winter: The Pleasures of History and Landscape in Tunisia, Sicily, Dalmatia, and Greece* (New York: Random House, 2004), pp. 8-9.

Chapter 1: Oxford

p. 19 "that sweet city with her dreaming spires": From Matthew Arnold's "Thyrsis," quoted in John Dougill, *Oxford: A Literary Guide* (Oxford: Oxface, 2002), p. 27.

p. 19 "Our most noble Athens": Ibid., p. 1.

p. 20 "marvelous instance of a kindness": Patrick Leigh Fermor, *A Time of Gifts* (New York: Harper & Row, 1977), p. 30.

p. 22 On October 16, 1555, the authorities: For background information on the lives of Cranmer, Ridley and Latimer and their last days in Oxford, see *Thomas Cranmer* by Jasper Ridley (Oxford: Oxford University Press, 1962), pp. 362-41; *Thomas Cranmer: A Life* by Diarmaid MacCulloch (New Haven, CT: Yale University Press, 1996), pp. 554-636; and *The Oxford Martyrs* by D. M. Loades (New York: Stein and Day, 1970), pp. 167-274.

p. 28 "the central goal of life is to be happy": Christian Smith and Melinda Lundquist Denton, *Soul Searching: The Religious and Spiritual Lives of American Teenagers* (Oxford: Oxford University Press, 2005), p. 163.

p. 28 "identity lock box": Clydesdale writes that when students get to college they find that the pull of the world and the surrounding moral popular culture is just too strong to resist. The desire for a lifestyle of materialism, consumerism and sensualism outweighs the desire for what they have been taught in church or at home—a Moralistic Therapeutic Deism. Moreover, they don't want anything to get in the way of success in college, which is their ticket to the good life. Religion would pose a threat to their success. So they set it aside. Growing up, few of these young adults were taught or experienced the faith in such a way that the desire for the kingdom was more powerful than their desire for the consumer market, pornography, binge drinking and hooking up. See Tim Clydesdale, "Abandoned, Pursued, or Safely Stowed?" at religion .ssrc.org/reforum/Clydesdale.pdf.

p. 29   "consequential faith": Kenda Creasy Dean, *Almost Christian: What the Faith of Our Teenagers Is Telling the American Church* (Oxford: Oxford University Press, 2010).

p. 30   "It's a dangerous business . . . going out your door": J. R. R. Tolkien, *The Lord of the Rings* (Boston: Houghton Mifflin, 1987), p. 72.

p. 31   "pilgrimage is symbolic of that larger journey": John Inge, *A Christian Theology of Place* (Burlington, VT: Ashgate, 2003), p. 102.

p. 31   "For Christians, faith means cleaving": Dean, *Almost Christian*, p. 7.

p. 33   he fainted under the strain of it: MacCulloch, *Thomas Cranmer*, p. 589.

p. 34   "spice cakes and bread": Ibid., p. 599.

p. 35   "had hidden in his bosom": Ridley, *Thomas Cranmer*, p. 404.

p. 35   "All such bills which I have written": Ibid., p. 407.

p. 36   "carry memory, power and hope": N. T. Wright, *The Way of the Lord: Christian Pilgrimage Today* (Grand Rapids: Eerdmans, 1999), p. 7.

p. 36   "mumbo-jumbo": Ibid., pp. 2-5.

p. 37   "Tourism is the modern, secular": Ibid., p. 63.

p. 37   "The test of whether pilgrimage": Ibid., p. 64.

p. 37   "was deadly pale": MacCulloch, *Thomas Cranmer*, p. 603.

p. 39   "writing contrary to my heart": Quoted in Andrew Atherstone, *Oxford: City of Saints, Scholars and Dreaming Spires* (Oxford: Day One Publications, 2008), p. 42.

p. 39   "This unworthy right hand": Ibid.

p. 39   "I see Jesus standing": Ridley, *Thomas Cranmer*, p. 408.

p. 40   "fresh steps along the road": Wright, *Way of the Lord*, p. 11.

Chapter 2: Igniting Desire

p. 41   Deep in the night, the call came from the hospital: For re-creating the story of Van and Davy, I relied on Sheldon Vanauken's *A Severe Mercy* (London: Hodder & Stoughton, 1979) and the unpublished manuscript *Sheldon Vanauken: The Man Who Received a "Severe Mercy"* by Will

Vaus (Hamden, CT: Winged Lion Press, 2013).

p. 43   C. S. Lewis, J. R. R. Tolkien and the rest of the Inklings: The Inklings were an informal group of friends centered around Lewis and Tolkien who met twice weekly from the early 1930s to 1949 for conversation and mutual creative encouragement. During term they met each Tuesday morning at an Oxford pub, the most famous being the Eagle and Child, for conversation and camaraderie. On Thursday evenings they met at Lewis's rooms at Magdalen College and sat around the fire sharing and commenting on their literary works in progress. It was here that Lewis's Chronicles of Narnia and Tolkien's *Lord of the Rings* were first read. Along with Lewis and Tolkien, the most famous members were Charles Williams, Owen Barfield and Hugo Dyson, but there were a half dozen or more accomplished professors and writers who attended over the years.

p. 44   Even on my vacations, I still had to work: In *Addiction and Grace* (San Francisco: Harper & Row, 1988), Gerald May writes, "Stress becomes a habit. . . . A severely stress-addicted person can thus be in a completely no win situation, becoming increasingly fatigued but at the same time increasingly uncomfortable with any situation that might offer rest" (p. 87).

p. 44   "We abandon the most important journey": John Eldredge, *The Journey of Desire: Searching for the Life We've Only Dreamed of* (Nashville: Thomas Nelson, 2000), p. 13.

p. 45   "held only on adult authority": Sheldon Vanauken, *Encounter with Light* (1960), available at www.willvaus.com/encounter_with_light.

p. 45   "Such a relief": Ibid.

p. 46   "dedicated, almost religiously, to beauty": Ibid.

p. 46   "If we were caught up in love": Vanauken, *A Severe Mercy,* p. 30.

p. 46   "There was a power—a god—of beauty": Ibid., p. 60.

p. 48   Considered the patron saint of Oxford: As legend has it, after her conversion, the evil King Algar pursued Frideswide for marriage, despite her holy orders. She escaped to Oxford, hiding out in Binsey. Algar marched on Oxford with his army but at the gates of Oxford was mysteriously struck blind. Frideswide had compassion on him, praying that his sight would be restored. As one version of the legend has it, a holy well appeared and she used the water to heal the king's blindness. In appreciation, Algar built a church for Frideswide and her nuns beside the well. She dedicated it to St. Margaret, the daughter of a pagan priest in Rome who after her conversion was martyred for her faith.

p. 48   *Alice in Wonderland*: Lewis Carroll was a tutor at Christ Church, which, in the sixteenth century, took over the priory, moved it into Oxford and changed the name to Christ Church. Carroll was good friends with the vicar of St. Margaret. It was this vicar, Reverend T. J. Prout, who restored the well in the nineteenth century and would have shown it to Carroll who in turn brought the three little girls who first got to hear the story *Alice's Adventures in Wonderland*. Thus the "Treacle Well" in the book.

p. 49   "The whole life of the good Christian": Augustine, Homilies on 1 John 4:6 quoted in James K. A. Smith, *Desiring the Kingdom: Worship, Worldview, and Cultural Formation* (Grand Rapids: Baker Academic, 2009), p. 50.

p. 49   "We are essentially and ultimately": Ibid., pp. 50-51.

p. 49   "ultimate loves": Smith defines "ultimate loves" as "that to which we are fundamentally oriented, which ultimately governs our vision of the good life, what shapes all else, the ultimate desire that shapes and positions and makes sense of all our penultimate desires and actions" (ibid., p. 51).

p. 50   "The Appeal to Love": Vanauken, *A Severe Mercy*, p. 41.

p. 50   "Her sins, she said, had come out": Ibid., p. 68.

p. 50   "classical conviction of sin": Ibid.

p. 52   These secular liturgies teach us: James K. A. Smith writes that these "'secular' liturgies are fundamentally formative, and implicit in them is a vision of the kingdom that needs to be discerned and evaluated" (*Desiring the Kingdom*, p. 88).

p. 52   According to Tim Clydesdale: See Tim Clydesdale, "Abandoned, Pursued, or Safely Stowed?" at religion.ssrc.org/reforum/Clydesdale.pdf.

p. 52   I tried to get them to see that education: Smith writes, "What if education . . . is not primarily about the absorption of ideas and information, but about the formation of hearts and desires? What if we began by appreciating how education not only gets into our head but also (and more fundamentally) grabs us by the gut—what the New Testament refers to as *kardia*, 'the heart.' What if education was primarily concerned with shaping our hopes and passions—our visions of 'the good life'—and not merely about the dissemination of data and information as inputs to our thinking? What if the primary work of education was the transformation of our imagination rather than the saturation of our intellect? . . . What if education wasn't first and foremost about what we know, but about what we love?" (*Desiring the Kingdom*, pp. 17-18).

p. 53   "were to be numbered for ever amongst the lovers of Oxford":

Vanauken, *A Severe Mercy,* p. 75.

p. 53   "had begun to think what we later found to be true": Ibid., p. 76.

p. 54   "The sheer quality": Ibid., p. 77.

p. 54   "there against the darkening grey sky": Ibid., p. 82.

p. 55   "Today, crossing from one side of the room to the other": Ibid., pp. 95-96.

p. 55   "You wish it were true; I strongly hoped it was *not*": Ibid., p. 88, italics in original.

p. 55   "there is nothing in Christianity which is so repugnant to me as humility": Ibid., p. 91.

p. 55   "intellectually stimulating and aesthetically exciting": Ibid., p. 93.

p. 55   "Have you read": Ibid., p. 90.

p. 56   "But I think you are already in the meshes of the net!": Ibid., p. 93.

p. 56   "tarted up": James T. Como, editor, *Remembering C. S. Lewis: Recollections of Those Who Knew Him* (San Francisco: Ignatius, 2005), 334.

p. 58   "Christianity now appeared": Vanauken, *A Severe Mercy,* p. 93.

p. 58   "My prayers are answered": Ibid., p. 102.

p. 58   "for their own sakes": Ibid., p. 139.

p. 58   "schooner under the wind": Ibid.

p. 59   "Go under the Mercy": Ibid., p. 175.

p. 59   "I am here, Davy; I am with you": Ibid., p. 176.

p. 59   "She could not say it to me": Ibid., p. 176.

p. 60   "God could not be as loving as He was supposed to be": Ibid., p. 190.

p. 60   "'All right,' I muttered to myself": Ibid.

p. 60   "One way or another the thing had to die": Ibid., pp. 209-10.

p. 61   "The High, gently curving ancient colleges": Ibid., p. 125.

p. 63   Van continued to struggle: This section relies on Vaus, *Sheldon Vanauken.*

p. 63   "adopted the views of the liberal left": Ibid., p. 218.

p. 63   "If a man diligently followed his desire": Lewis, quoted in ibid., p. 225.

p. 65   "On the last day I met C. S. Lewis at the Eastgate": Ibid., p. 125.

p. 66   "Something in the air smelt very clear and sweet": Ibid., p. 299.

Chapter 3: The Struggle Within

p. 69   According to Smith and Denton, young people are "*incredibly inarticulate*": Christian Smith and Melinda Lundquist Denton, *Soul Searching: The Religious and Spiritual Lives of American Teenagers* (Oxford: Oxford University Press, 2005), p.131, italics original.

p. 69   Part of the problem is that adults: Smith and Denton write, "A major challenge for religious educators of youth, therefore, seems to us to be fostering articulation, helping teens practice talking about their faith, providing practice at using vocabularies, grammars, stories, and key messages of faith" (ibid., p. 268).

p. 71   "a difficult environment to recreate in Oxford": Andrew Atherstone, *Travel Through Oxford: City of Saints, Scholars and Dreaming Spires* (Oxford: Day One Publications, 2008), p. 82.

p. 71   "He lay on his face under the trees": Ibid.

p. 74   "But the strength of Cummy's religious views": Claire Harman, *Robert Louis Stevenson: A Biography* (London: HarperCollins, 2005), p. 21.

p. 75   "Just as in childhood Stevenson had found": Ibid., p. 54.

p. 75   "was often subject to fits of morbid melancholy": Ibid., p. 59.

p. 75   "one of the day, and one of the night": Ibid., pp. 60-61.

p. 75   "I had long been trying": Ibid., p. 300.

p. 78   "I stood already committed": Robert Louis Stevenson, *Dr. Jekyll and Mr. Hyde* (New York: Bantam Classics, 2004), pp. 64-65.

p. 80   "It is indeed a dreadful book": Harman, *Robert Louis Stevenson*, p. 304.

p. 83   "Shame is at root a loss of trust in yourself": Dick Keyes, *Beyond Identity: Finding Your Self in the Image and Character of God* (Ann Arbor, MI: Servant, 1984), p. 58.

p. 83   "Shame strikes directly at our identity": Ibid., p. 59.

p. 84   "My sin is mine, but it's not me": Ibid., p. 96.

p. 84   "He is a sinner who can face his sin because": Ibid., p. 97.

p. 86   "Our destiny is to come fully alive": John Eldredge, *Waking the Dead: The Glory of a Heart Fully Alive* (Nashville: Thomas Nelson, 2003), p. 75, italics in original.

Chapter 4: The Weight of Glory

p. 88   Lewis's sour mood had begun two days earlier: I owe a great deal of thanks to Alan Jacobs, who, during a conversation in April 2012, reminded me of the Lewis-Anscombe debate and the impact it had on Lewis. For more background on the debate see Alan Jacobs, *The Narnian: The Life and Imagination of C. S. Lewis* (San Francisco: HarperSanFrancisco, 2005), pp. 232-36; George Sayer, *Jack: A Life of C. S. Lewis* (Wheaton, IL: Crossway, 2005), pp. 306-9; William Griffin, *Clive Staples Lewis: A Dramatic Life* (San Francisco: Harper & Row, 1986), p. 280.

p. 89   "argument for the existence of God had been demolished": Sayer, *Jack*, p. 307.

p. 89   Lewis biographer A. N. Wilson contended that Lewis was so psychologically damaged: For more on Wilson's critique of Lewis, see "The Green Witch and the Great Debate: Freeing Narnia from the Spell of the Lewis-Anscombe Legend," in Gregory Bassham and Jerry L. Walls, *The Chronicles of Narnia and Philosophy: The Lion, the Witch, and the Worldview* (Chicago: Open Court, 2005), p. 261.

p. 90   "one of the most delightful places": Griffin, *Clive Staples Lewis,* p. 46.

p. 92   "You must picture me alone": C. S. Lewis, *Surprised by Joy: The Shape of My Early Life* (New York: Harcourt, Brace, 1956), pp. 228-29.

p. 92   he would create the character Eustace Scrubb: Jacobs, *The Narnian,* p. 133.

p. 93   "breathed through silver": Lewis, quoted in ibid., p. 143.

p. 94   "the most important [of them all]": Lewis, quoted in ibid., p. 150.

p. 94   "I have just passed on from believing in God": Griffin, *Clive Staples Lewis,* p. 79.

p. 94   "I daresay, for me, personally, it has come in the nick of time": Quoted in Sayer, *Jack,* pp. 266-67.

p. 95   "I remember being at a pub filled with soldiers on one Wednesday evening": Ibid., p. 278; see also Justin Phillips, *C. S. Lewis in a Time of War: The World War II Broadcasts That Riveted a Nation and Became the Classic Mere Christianity* (New York: HarperSanFrancisco, 2002).

p. 95   "a daily cascade of letters from angry": Jacobs, *The Narnian,* p. 223.

p. 97   "I wish I had got a bit further with humility myself": C. S. Lewis, *Mere Christianity: Comprising the Case for Christianity, Christian Behaviour, and Beyond Personality* (New York: Touchstone, 1996), p. 114.

p. 97   "Let's Pretend": Quotes found in ibid., pp. 162-67.

p. 98   "and let Him take us over, the more truly ourselves we become": Ibid., p. 190.

p. 98   "God whispers to us": C. S. Lewis, *The Problem of Pain* (New York: HarperOne, 2001).

p. 98   Like many people outside London: Jacobs, *The Narnian,* pp. 221-47.

p. 99   "main argument is suspect": Sayer, *Jack,* p. 306.

p. 99   "If this is true, Lewis pointed out": Christopher Mitchell, "University Battles: C. S. Lewis and the Oxford University Socratic Club" in Angus J. L. Menuge, *C. S. Lewis, Light-Bearer in the Shadowlands: The Evangelistic Vision of C. S. Lewis* (Wheaton, IL: Crossway, 1997), p. 342.

p. 100   "Lewis had learnt his lesson": Humphrey Carpenter, *The Inklings: C. S. Lewis, J. R. R. Tolkien, Charles Williams and Their Friends* (London: HarperCollins, 1978), pp. 238-39.

p. 100   He also wrote a number of articles defending the faith: See Victor Reppert, *C. S. Lewis's Dangerous Idea: In Defense of the Argument from Reason* (Downers Grove, IL: InterVarsity Press, 2003), pp. 17-21; and Mitchell's "C. S. Lewis and the Oxford University Socratic Club," pp. 343-46.

p. 100 "The debate had been a humiliating experience": Sayer, *Jack,* p. 308.

p. 100 "It seems almost certain": Jacobs, *The Narnian,* p. 238.

p. 101 So he returned to an idea: Alan Jacobs believes that, although the Anscombe debate played a role in the direction of Lewis's writing topics, it was only one factor, and a small one at that. Jacobs contends that from the start of the war Lewis had been contemplating writing children's fiction, and even had written a short outline that looked a great deal like the future *The Lion, the Witch and the Wardrobe.* But when the war started and he was asked to help the war effort, he willingly did his duty, which interrupted his progress toward fairy stories and losing himself in story. By the late forties, humbled by the Anscombe debate and the realization that direct apologetics might not be the best use of his gifts or the best strategy for reaching his generation, he returned to the idea of children's stories.

p. 102 "Fairy land arouses a longing": C. S. Lewis, *On Stories and Other Essays on Literature* (New York: Harcourt Brace, 1982), p. 38.

p. 103 "have confessed that they feel 'clean'": Ralph C. Wood, *The Gospel According to Tolkien: Visions of the Kingdom in Middle Earth* (Louisville: Westminster John Knox Press, 2003), pp. 75-76, cited in Gregory Bassham, "Lewis and Tolkien on the Power of Imagination," in *C. S. Lewis as Philosopher,* ed. David Baggett, Gary R. Habermas and Jerry L. Walls (Downers Grove, IL: InterVarsity Press, 2008), p. 248.

p. 103 "I thought I saw": Lewis, *On Stories,* p. 47.

p. 104 "are not just good stories": Gilbert Meilaender, *The Taste for the Other: The Social and Ethical Thought of C. S. Lewis* (Grand Rapids: Eerdmans, 1978), p. 213.

p. 104 Moral education needs instruction: See Bill David, "Extreme Makeover: Moral Education and the Encounter with Aslan," in Gregory Bassham and Jerry Walls, *The Chronicles of Narnia and Philosophy* (Chicago: Open Court, 2005), pp. 109-13.

p. 105 "engage our moral imagination, provide vivid moral exemplars": See Bassham, "Lewis and Tolkien on the Power of Imagination," p. 250.

p. 107 "my happiest hours are spent with three or four old friends": Armand Nicholi, *The Question of God: C. S. Lewis and Sigmund Freud Debate God, Love, Sex and the Meaning of Life* (New York: Free Press, 2003), p. 115.

p. 108 "This house has a good night atmosphere about it:" Douglas Gilbert and Clyde Kilby, *C. S. Lewis: Images of His World* (Grand Rapids: Eerdmans, 1973), p. 58.

p. 108 "Until you have given up your self to Him you will not have a real self": Lewis, *Mere Christianity,* p. 190.

p. 108 I reached over to the side table: Subsequent quotes found in the chapter
          are from "The Weight of Glory," in C. S. Lewis, *The Weight of Glory*
          (San Francisco: HarperSanFrancisco, 2001), pp. 25-46.

p. 109 "God became man to turn creatures into sons:" Lewis, *Mere Christi-
          anity*, p. 183.

p. 110 "What we have been told is how we": Ibid., p. 172.

Chapter 5: The Call

p. 112 When a well-rested and much-changed William Wilberforce: For his-
          torical background for this chapter, I relied on several books: Kevin
          Belmonte, *Hero for Humanity: A Biography of William Wilberforce* (Colo-
          rado Springs: NavPress, 2002); Kevin Belmonte, *William Wilberforce:
          The Friend of Humanity* (Leominster, UK: Day One Publications, 2006);
          John Pollock, *Abolition: Newton, the Ex–slave Trader, and Wilberforce,
          the Little Liberator* (Leominster, UK: Day One Publications, 2007); Eric
          Metaxas, *Amazing Grace: William Wilberforce and the Heroic Campaign
          to End Slavery* (New York: HarperOne, 2007); Stephen Tomkins,
          William Wilberforce: A Biography (Oxford: Lion Hudson, 2007);
          William Hague, *William Wilberforce: The Life of the Great Anti–slave
          Trade Campaigner* (London: Harper, 2007).

p. 112 "For months I was in a state": Tomkins, *William Wilberforce*, p. 47.

p. 114 "comes to him not from a Burning Bush or a heavenly messenger":
          Pamela Dolan, "What Harry Potter Teaches About Vocation," *St. Louis
          Post-Dispatch*, February 3, 2012, available at www.stltoday.com/life
          styles/faith-and-values/civil-religion/pamela-dolan/what-harry-potter-
          teaches-about-vocation/article_635e20d8-446e-11e1-8474-
          001a4bcf6878.html.

p. 114 "Harry needs to go out into the world": Ibid.

p. 115 "Here at last is the thing I was made for": C. S. Lewis, *The Problem of
          Pain* (New York: HarperOne, 2001).

p. 118 "Yorkshire made Wilberforce a man of power and significance": Pollock,
          Abolition, p. 46.

p. 120 "The first years I was in Parliament I did nothing": Quoted in John
          Piper, *Amazing Grace in the Life of William Wilberforce* (Wheaton, IL:
          Crossway, 2007), p. 38.

p. 120 "Wilberforce, I don't pretend to be a match for you": Belmonte, *Hero for
          Humanity*, p. 79.

p. 120 "in a house separated from the Mediterranean": Ibid., p. 78.

p. 121 "It's one of the best books ever written": Ibid., p. 80.

p. 123 "We went thither by way of Switzerland": Ibid., p. 82.

p. 123   "the same Christianity as Doddridge": Tomkins, *William Wilberforce*, p. 47.

p. 124   "a settled conviction in my mind": Belmonte, *Hero for Humanity*, p. 82.

p. 124   "The deep guilt and black ingratitude": Ibid., p. 83.

p. 124   "My anguish of soul for some months was indescribable": Ibid.

p. 126   "But forgive me if I cannot help expressing my fear": Belmonte, *William Wilberforce*, pp. 44-45.

p. 126   "opened his soul to someone": Tomkins, *William Wilberforce*, p. 48.

p. 126   "If a Christian may act": Belmonte, *William Wilberforce*, p. 45.

p. 129   "Something about going to Newton": Ibid., p. 41.

p. 129   "He told me he always had entertained hopes": Quoted in Jonathan Aitken, *John Newton: From Disgrace to Amazing Grace* (Wheaton, IL: Crossway, 2008), p. 303.

p. 133   "proof that a man can change his times": Ibid., p. 307.

p. 134   "into the bosom of his happy and delighted family": Quoted in Tomkins, *William Wilberforce*, p. 170.

Chapter 6: Broken Beauty

p. 143   The situation was intolerable: For telling van Gogh's story I have relied on the following books: Steven Naifeh and Gregory White Smith's definitive biography, *Van Gogh: The Life* (New York: Random House, 2011); Kathleen Powers Erickson's *At Eternity's Gate: The Spiritual Vision of Vincent van Gogh* (Grand Rapids: Eerdmans, 1998); Anton Wessels, *"A Kind of Bible": Vincent van Gogh as Evangelist* (London: SCM Press, 2000).

p. 143   "There was a time I loved Vincent": Naifeh and Smith, *Van Gogh*, p. 529.

p. 147   "I am a traveler,": Ibid., p. 121.

p. 147   "seeing a journey in every road and a life in every journey": Ibid., p. 123.

p. 147   "if you want to persevere and make spiritual progress": Ibid., p. 124.

p. 147   "Our life is a pilgrim's progress": Ibid., p. 132.

p. 147   "matters more today than any previous period in history": Roger Scruton, *Beauty* (Oxford: Oxford University Press, 2009), p. 188.

p. 147   "addictive pleasures and routine desecration": Ibid., p. 192.

p. 148   "reckless pursuit of pleasure, his heedless surrender to temptation": Naifeh and Smith, *Van Gogh*, p. 563.

p. 149   "Stomach disorders, fevers, and general weakness plagued him": Ibid, p. 570.

p. 150   "foolish and vicious": Ibid., p. 580.

p. 150   "Loneliness, worries, difficulties, the unsatisfied need": Ibid., p. 581.

p. 151 "stimulus addiction": "the hunger to be shocked, gripped, stirred": Scruton, *Beauty,* p. 186.

p. 153 "for delight and good cheer": Nicholas Wolterstorff, *Until Justice and Peace Embrace: The Kuyper Lectures for 1981 Delivered at the Free University of Amsterdam* (Grand Rapids: Eerdmans, 1983), p. 131.

p. 154 "their warmth, their fire, and their enthusiasm": Van Gogh, quoted in Naifeh and Smith, *Van Gogh,* p. 591.

p. 155 "when in a state of excitement": Ibid., p. 647.

p. 155 "I must have a *starry* night": Ibid., p. 649, italics original.

p. 155 When "I have a terrible need of—shall I say the word?—religion": Ibid., p. 651.

p. 155 "Is this all," he asked, "or is there more besides?": Ibid., p. 652.

p. 156 "the hospital looked like a prison, with high stone walls": Ibid., p. 706.

p. 157 "when people prefer the sensuous trappings of belief": Scruton, *Beauty,* p. 190.

p. 157 "emotion is directed away from its proper target towards sugary stereotypes": Ibid., p. 191.

p. 157 "I like to portray the world without the Fall": Kinkade, quoted in Jeremy Begbie, "Beauty, Sentimentality and the Arts," in *The Beauty of God: Theology and the Arts,* ed. Daniel J. Treier, Mark Husbands and Roger Lundin (Downers Grove, IL: IVP Academic, 2007), pp. 57-58.

p. 159 "sought succor for the troubled minds and infirm spirits": Naifeh and Smith, *Van Gogh,* p. 744.

p. 159 "Theo [in a letter] unthinkingly praised a Rembrandt drawing of an angel": Ibid., p. 767.

p. 160 "He identified with the suffering of the dying Christ": Erickson, *At Eternity's Gate,* p. 157.

p. 164 "He had arrived in May holding on by the thinnest thread": Naifeh and Smith, *Van Gogh,* p. 838.

p. 164 "I am far from having reached any kind of tranquility": Ibid.

p. 165 "wild eyes in which there was a crazed expression": Ibid., p. 840.

p. 165 "vast fields of wheat": Ibid., p. 845.

p. 165 "My life is threatened at the very root": Ibid.

p. 166 "[He] was holding his belly": Ibid., p. 850.

p. 167 "The splendor of beauty, its attractiveness, is grounded": William A. Dyrness, *Visual Faith: Art, Theology and Worship in Dialogue* (Grand Rapids: Baker Academic, 2001), pp. 73-74.

p. 168 "Broken beauty is not only true to the human condition": E. John Walford, "The Case for a Broken Beauty," in *The Beauty of God: The-*

ology and the Arts, ed. Daniel J. Treier, Mark Husbands and Roger Lundin (Downers Grove, IL: IVP Academic, 2007), p. 109.

p. 169   "It is an old belief": Vincent van Gogh, *The Complete Letters of Vincent van Gogh,* vol. 1 (New York: Bulfinch Press, 2008), pp. 87, 91.

p. 169   He shot himself, he claimed: In the appendix to *Van Gogh,* Naifeh and Smith make the case that Vincent did not shoot himself, as history has recorded it. Nothing about the popularly accepted account holds up under scrutiny. Rather, they contend that a group of boys, either accidentally or on purpose—we may never know—shot Vincent and that Vincent covered this up to protect the boys, whom he liked even though they often teased him. See pages 869-79.

p. 169   "I want to die like this": Naifeh and Smith, *Van Gogh,* p. 859.

p. 169   "He has found the rest": Ibid.

Chapter 7: Goodness Happened There

p. 172   Now, peering down earnestly on his congregation: All sermon quotes are taken from Patrick Henry, *We Only Know Men: The Rescue of Jews in France During the Holocaust* (Washington, DC: Catholic University of America Press, 2007), pp. xix-xx.

p. 174   We hoped that Le Chambon: By focusing on Le Chambon sur Lignon and Pastor Trocmé and his wife, Magda, I am not discounting the rescue work done by the twelve surrounding villages and the pastors who led them so effectively. As the 1990 colloquium *Le Plateau Vivarais-Lignon: Accueil et Resistance 1939-1944* makes clear, the entire plateau contributed to the rescue movement during the occupation. And according to Patrick Henry, along with the twelve Protestant parishes on the plateau, the Catholics, Swiss Protestants, the Darbyites, American Quakers, some Jewish organizations, *La Cimade,* the Boy Scouts, humanitarians and people from all walks of life participated in the rescue operation. This was a group effort. Henry, *We Only Know Men,* pp. 10-21.

p. 175   "that moral individualism is widespread among emerging adults": Christian Smith, Kari Marie Christoffersen, Hilary Davidson and Patricia Snell Herzog, *Lost in Transition: The Dark Side of Emerging Adulthood* (New York: Oxford University Press, 2011), p. 60.

p. 176   "A large proportion of emerging adults today are lost, confused, or misled": Ibid., pp. 64-65.

p. 176   "They are morally at sea": Ibid., p. 60. Ironically, in some ways, I agree with the young people in the survey. I am not in favor of fundamentalism or intolerance of any kind, whether on the left or the right. It has led to some pretty bad moments in history. But is the only choice

between fundamentalism on the one hand or relativism on the other—
that is, between having an outside authority on which to guide moral
decision making or simply relying on one's own intuition and whatever
the culture says at the time? Or is it possible to possess strong views on
right and wrong, to look to an outside authority and at the same time
be tolerant and loving?

p. 176 — She didn't hear the knock: Story based on Philip Hallie, *Lest Innocent Blood Be Shed: The Story of the Village of Le Chambon, and How Goodness Happened There* (New York: Harper & Row, 1979), pp. 120-22, and Richard P. Unsworth, *A Portrait of Pacifists* (Syracuse, NY: Syracuse University Press, 2012), p. 175.

p. 176 — "May I come in?": Unless otherwise noted, all dialogue used here in this section is directly from or roughly based on Hallie, *Lest Innocent Blood Be Shed*, pp. 119-24.

p. 176 — There were already thirty thousand foreign Jews: Henry, *We Only Know Men*, p. 32.

p. 177 — Later that bitterly cold winter: The following section is based on Unsworth, *Portrait of Pacifists*, pp. 164-69, and Hallie, *Lest Innocent Blood Be Shed*, pp. 129-38.

p. 180 — "The guard laughed at her": Carol Matas, *Greater Than Angels* (New York: Simon & Schuster for Young Readers, 1998), p. 6. This book is a composite based on true accounts.

p. 181 — "You must accommodate": Henry, *We Only Know Men*, p. 34.

p. 181 — Understanding the Old Testament, they also knew about the city of refuge: Bible references taken from ibid.

p. 182 — "For two years we had tried to escape": Hallie, *Lest Innocent Blood Be Shed*, p. 99.

p. 182 — Lamirand arrived around noon: This story is based on Unsworth, *Portrait of Pacifists*, pp. 177-78, 180-84, and Hallie, *Lest Innocent Blood Be Shed*, pp. 98-107.

p. 182 — "We feel obliged to tell you": Hallie, *Lest Innocent Blood Be Shed*, p. 102. Also see Unsworth, *Portrait of Pacifists*, p. 183.

p. 183 — "It cannot be a question of national history": Hallie, *Lest Innocent Blood Be Shed*, p. 103.

p. 183 — "Monsieur Trocmé, you would do well": Ibid.

p. 183 — "Pastor, we know in detail the suspect": Dialogue from Trocmé's "Mémoires" (1953), written years later. Quoted in ibid., p. 107.

p. 184 — Chirac's stated reason for coming: For more background, see the preface to Henry, *We Only Know Men*, p. xx.

p. 184 — I had read an editorial that appeared: The quotes from this event are *p. 187*   taken from "Le Chambon's Challenge Today" by Pierre Sauvage, www .chambon.org/sauvage_lcsl_challenge_en.htm.

p. 187   They had little success though: According to Hallie, they arrested one Jewish man who was later released. They also arrested one elderly Jewish woman whose fate was never conclusively determined (*Lest Innocent Blood Be Shed,* p. 112).

p. 187   "From this time on, Vichy police were closely supervised": Ibid., p. 115.

p. 188   In the summer of 1943: Unsworth, *Portrait of Pacifists,* pp. 4, 201.

p. 188   "You know how these executions happen": From André Trocmé's unpublished memoir (1953), quoted in Unsworth, *Portrait of Pacifists,* p. 5.

p. 191   "Those Gestapo goons looked *perfectly* happy to me": Matas, *Greater Than Angels,* p. 89.

p. 191   "happier than during those years": Henry, *We Only Know Men,* p. 169.

p. 192   "my son, a tall, blond twelve year old boy": This and the other quotes in this section come from André Trocmé's unpublished memoir (1953), quoted in Unsworth, *Portrait of Pacifists,* pp. 13-15.

p. 195   "ordinary to them, for it [is] their normal way of relating to others": Ibid., p. 163. I am indebted to Patrick Henry for making the point that individuals rarely rescue without community support and mentors.

p. 195   "the most persuasive moral teaching we adults do is by example": Quoted in ibid.

Chapter 8: Suffering

p. 199   Corrie heard the buzzer: Unless otherwise noted, the following historical account and all dialogue is adapted and roughly based on Corrie's account in *The Hiding Place* (Corrie ten Boom, John L. Sherrill and Elizabeth Sherrill, *The Hiding Place* [Washington Depot, CT: Chosen, 1971]), and Corrie ten Boom, *A Prisoner and Yet . . .* (London: Christian Literature Crusade, 1954).

p. 212   "We live in a world": Simon Wiesenthal, *The Sunflower: On the Possibilities and Limits of Forgiveness,* Kindle ed. (New York: Schocken, 2008), p. 8.

p. 212   "Very few of us prayed": Ibid., p. 79.

p. 216   She had to see her sister: Between the fever episode and first visit to hospital and her second visit to the hospital, Betsie had spent a number of weeks confined to her barracks. I have collapsed the hospital visits for literary reasons.

p. 217   "She is dead": Ten Boom, *A Prisoner and Yet,* p. 161.

p. 217   "My soul was a battleground": Ibid., pp. 161-62.

p. 218   "He might be either all-powerful but not good": Timothy J. Keller, *The Reason for God: Belief in an Age of Skepticism* (New York: Dutton, 2008), p. 22.

p. 219   On the day of Betsie's death: Ten Boom, *Prisoner and Yet*, p. 162.

p. 225   "The secular view of things": Ibid., p. 32.

Chapter 9: Confident Hope

p. 229   On the morning of July 21, 1944: The following historical account is based on Eberhard Bethge, *Dietrich Bonhoeffer: A Biography* (Minneapolis: Fortress Press, 2000), pp. 780ff. For additional historical background, see Ferdinand Schlingensiepen, *Dietrich Bonhoeffer 1906-1945: Martyr, Thinker, Man of Resistance* (London: T & T Clark, 2010), and Eric Metaxas, *Bonhoeffer: Pastor, Martyr, Prophet, Spy* (Nashville: Thomas Nelson, 2010).

p. 230   "Grim impressions": Quoted in Bethge, *Dietrich Bonhoeffer*, p. 832.

p. 233   "We were approaching the borderline": Eberhard Bethge, *Friendship and Resistance: Essays on Dietrich Bonhoeffer* (Grand Rapids: Eerdmans, 1995), p. 24.

p. 234   "Who stands fast?": Quoted in Metaxas, *Bonhoeffer*, p. 446.

p. 235   Bonhoeffer was taken to the reception area: The following account comes from Eberhard Bethge, *Dietrich Bonhoeffer: A Biography* (Minneapolis: Fortress, 2000), pp. 799ff.

p. 237   "He was beginning to understand": Metaxas, *Bonhoeffer*, p. 210.

p. 237   "The restoration of the church": Ibid., p. 246.

p. 237   "Lord, awake in my soul": Bonhoeffer, "Longing for the Living God," in *A Testament to Freedom: The Essential Writings of Dietrich Bonhoeffer*, ed. Geffrey B. Kelly and F. Burton Nelson (San Francisco: HarperSanFrancisco, 1995), p. 254.

p. 237   "My thoughts turn toward my spiritual homeland": Ibid., p. 256.

p. 238   "Only he who cries out for the Jews": Bethge, *Dietrich Bonhoeffer*, p. 607.

p. 238   "Fallen, fallen is Babylon the great": "Learning to Die," in *A Testament of Freedom: The Essential Writings of Dietrich Bonhoeffer*, ed. Geffrey B. Kelly and F. Burton Nelson (San Francisco: HarperSanFrancisco, 1995), p. 266.

p. 238   "the city which does not cease building": Ibid.

p. 239   "Do not fear the coming day": Ibid., p. 265.

p. 239   "To die in Christ": Ibid., pp. 267-68.

p. 239   "No more are we ready to keep silent": Metaxas, *Bonhoeffer*, p. 293.

p. 240   "Only those who obey can believe": Dietrich Bonhoeffer, *The Cost of*

Discipleship (New York: Touchstone, 1995), p. 70.

p. 242   "both the scene of his greatest achievements": Dietrich Bonhoeffer, *The Way to Freedom*, ed. Edwin H. Robertson (New York: Harper & Row, 1966), p. 16.

p. 242   "the sufferings, which appear so hard and objectionable to us": "The Secret of Suffering," in *A Testament of Freedom: The Essential Writings of Dietrich Bonhoeffer*, ed. Geffrey B. Kelly and F. Burton Nelson (San Francisco: HarperSanFrancisco, 1995), p. 291.

p. 242   "Where there is still hope": Ibid., p. 292.

p. 243   "Death is only dreadful": Quoted in Metaxas, *Bonhoeffer*, p. 531.

p. 245   "moral commitments, decisions, obligations": Christian Smith and Melinda Lundquist Denton, *Soul Searching: The Religious and Spiritual Lives of American Teenagers* (Oxford: Oxford University Press, 2005), p. 156.

p. 245   most young people have no "telos," no "end, goal": Ibid., p. 157.

p. 245   "So much is clear at once": "Learning to Die," p. 264.

p. 246   the importance of destination in our lives: I am grateful to Kenda Creasy Dean for reminding me of this illustration and for helping me think through the importance of eschatology for my family. See *The Theological Turn in Youth Ministry* by Andrew Root and Kenda Creasy Dean (Downers Grove, IL: InterVarsity Press, 2011), p. 204.

p. 247   "Let us go calmly": Metaxas, *Bonhoeffer*, p. 503.

p. 248   "spoke to us in a manner": Ibid., p. 528.

p. 248   "This is the end": Bethge, *Dietrich Bonhoeffer*, p. 927.

p. 250   "all humanity and sweetness": Ibid., p. 920.

p. 250   "[His] soul really shone": Quoted in Metaxas, *Bonhoeffer*, p. 515.

p. 252   "I have not felt lonely or abandoned": Dietrich Bonhoeffer, *Letters and Papers from Prison* (New York: Touchstone, 1997), p. 419.

p. 253   "Come now, O supreme moment": Quoted in *A Testament to Freedom*, pp. 516-17.

p. 253   "It is not a nothing": Bonhoeffer, "Learning to Die," p. 264.

p. 253   "In almost fifty years": Quoted in Metaxas, *Bonhoeffer*, p. 532.

p. 254   "There may be every kind of weakness": Quoted in *A Testament to Freedom*, p. 292.

Chapter 10: Confidence

p. 257   For the past month, with Jordan reading the *Lord of the Rings*: The following discussion has been influenced by Gregory Bassham's "Lewis and Tolkien on the Power of Imagination," in *C. S. Lewis as Philosopher: Truth, Goodness and Beauty*, ed. David Baggett, Gary Habermas and Jerry L. Walls (Downers Grove, IL: InterVarsity Press, 2008).

p. 260	"Why does the captain not look happy with those precious children": All von Trapp dialogue is taken from or roughly based on *The Story of the Trapp Family Singers* by Maria Augusta Trapp (New York: Harper Perennial, 2002).
p. 266	"sensations we never had before": C. S. Lewis, "On Science Fiction," quoted in Bassham, "Lewis and Tolkien on the Power of Imagination," p. 246.
p. 266	"our conception of the range of possible experiences": Ibid.
p. 266	"fresh, childlike wonder": Ibid., p. 247.

Chapter 11: Heidelberg and Normandy

p. 278	The writing of the document was overseen by Zacharias Ursinus: For background on the Heidelberg Catechism see *Body and Soul: Reclaiming the Heidelberg Catechism* by M. Craig Barnes (Grand Rapids: Faith Alive Christian Resources, 2012).
p. 278	"It stands upon a commanding elevation": Mark Twain, *A Tramp Abroad* (London: Chatto & Windus, 1889), p. 526.
p. 279	"Nature knows how to garnish a ruin to get the best": Ibid.
p. 282	"It was built of Pearls and precious Stones": John Bunyan, *The Pilgrim's Progress* (New York: Penguin Classics, 2008), p. 156.
p. 282	"Whose goodly vineyards and Gardens are these?": Ibid, p. 157.
p. 283	"The pilgrim goes on": Vincent van Gogh, *The Complete Letters of Vincent Van Gogh*, vol. 1 (New York: Bulfinch Press, 2008), p. 91.
p. 285	"Solid joys and lasting treasures": From his hymn "Glorious Things of Thee Are Spoken."
p. 285	"seeing beyond the End of the World into Aslan's": All quotes from *Voyage of the Dawn Treader* (New York: Scholastic, 1952), pp. 243-48.
p. 292	"The Road goes ever on": J. R. R. Tolkien, *The Lord of the Rings* (Boston: Houghton Mifflin, 1987), p. 32.

IMAGE CREDITS

Chapter 1

Bocardo prison: Artist unknown; used by permission of Oxfordshire County Council-Oxfordshire History Centre

Portrait of Thomas Cranmer: National Portrait Gallery, London/Wikimedia Commons

Thomas Cranmer's execution: Wikimedia Commons

Chapter 2

Van and Davy: Ariel K. Myers (college archivist), Knight-Capron Library, Lynchburg College, Lynchburg, Virginia. Used by permission.

Chapter 4

Addison's Walk, Magdalen College: Miles Underwood/Wikimedia Commons

Chapter 5

William Wilberforce by Karl Anton Hickel: Wikimedia Commons

St. Mary Woolnoth, Lombard Street, London: Christine Matthews/Wikimedia Commons

Chapter 6

Self-Portrait with Straw Hat: Metropolitan Museum of Art, Bequest of Miss Adelaide Milton de Groot, 1967/Wikimedia Commons

Cafe Terrace at Night: The Yorck Project: *10.000 Meisterwerke der Malerei*, DIRECT-MEDIA Publishing GmbH/Wikimedia Commons

The yellow house: Google Art Project/Wikimedia Commons

Pieta: Wikimedia Commons

Wheatfield with Crows: Wikimedia Commons

Chapter 7

Andre and Magda Trocmé: Photographer unknown; used courtesy of Nelly Trocmé Hewett

Chapter 9

Bonhoeffer in Tegel Prison: Photographer unknown; used by permission of Verlag-scruppe Random House GmbH

Chapter 10

Nonnberg Abbey: Andrew Bossi/Wikimedia Commons

Maria and Captain von Trapp: photographer unknown; used courtesy of Johannes von Trapp

Von Trapp wedding: photographer unknown; used courtesy of Johannes von Trapp

All other photographs are by Jim Belcher.

Subject and Name Index

A NOTE ON THE TYPE

This book was set in two fonts—Bodoni and ITC Berkeley Old Style.

The Bodoni typeface was originally designed by the Italian designer, punchcutter and printer Giambattista Bodoni in 1798, influenced by the older serif fonts of John Baskerville. The Bodoni types of today are a composite, a modern version of the Bodoni style, which have a greater degree of contrast in the thick and thin elements of the letters, producing a luxurious quality that is highly pleasing to the eye.

The ITC Berkeley Old Style typeface was originally created in 1983 by Tony Stan, as a revival of the California Old Style designed by Frederic W. Goudy, a student at the Chicago School of Lettering in Bloomington, Illinois. In the 1950s the University Press at Berkeley sought a new design and commissioned Goudy. When first released in 1956, it was a serif font with elongated descenders and an engaging, light style. Tony Stan's ITC Berkeley Old Style has built on Goudy's inspiration, producing a font with a clear, open and elegant look.

ABOUT THE AUTHOR

Jim Belcher (Ph.D., Georgetown; M.A., Fuller) is associate professor of pastoral studies at Knox Theological Seminary in Fort Lauderdale, Florida. He is best known for his widely acclaimed, award-winning book *Deep Church: A Third Way Beyond Emerging and Traditional* (InterVarsity Press, 2009).

He is the founding and former lead pastor of Redeemer Presbyterian Church (PCA) in Newport Beach, California, where he served from 2000 to 2010 and led a period of steady growth. He is the cofounder of the Restoring Community Conference: Integrating Social Interaction, Sacred Space and Beauty in the 21st Century, a conference for city officials, planners, builders and architects. He and his wife, Michelle, and their four children live in south Florida.

CONTACT JIM

Jim speaks frequently on the topic of this book. He can deliver a keynote, half-day, full-day or sermon version of portions of the book, depending on your needs. He is also available for dramatic readings (with slides) on a number of the chapters in the book. If you are interested in finding out more, please visit his speaking page at

Jimbelcher.net/speaking

You can also connect with Jim here:

facebook.com/jimbelcher65
twitter.com/jimbelcher
info@jimbelcher.net